Correctional Intervention and Research

Correctional Intervention and Research

Current Issues and Future Prospects

Ted Palmer
California Department of
Youth Authority

Lexington Books
D.C. Heath and Company
Lexington, Massachusetts
Toronto

Library of Congress Cataloging in Publication Data

Palmer, Ted.
  Correctional intervention and research.

  Bibliography: p.
  Includes index.
  1. Corrections.   2. Corrections—Research.   3. Corrections—United   States.
I. Title.
HV9275.P34   364.6   77-25777
ISBN 0-669-02166-0

Published simultaneously in Canada.

Printed in the United States of America.

International Standard Book Number: 0-669-02166-0

Library of Congress Catalog Card Number: 77-25777

Contents

Contents   vii

Appendix I   The Public and The Goals of Correctional
                  Treatment   185

Appendix J   Differentiated Analyses and Hypothesis Testing:
                  An Illustration   187

Appendix K   Offender Intervention Scales   189

Appendix L   Psychosocial Development: An Illustration   197

                  Notes   209

                  Bibliography   253

                  Index   257

                  About the Author   275

List of Figures and Tables

Tables

Foreword

This book appears at a time of considerable turmoil in the correctional world. Basic purposes of correctional programming are being challenged. Treatment is portrayed as useless in reducing recidivism of individuals committed to correctional agencies. Correctional administrators are advised to focus their work solely on protecting the community from the offender or, alternately, on protecting the legal rights of offenders. Or, punishment is promoted as the only legitimate purpose of the correctional system.

Correctional treatment is alleged to be not only ineffective but also unethical. Its coercive nature is presented as inevitable. A vision of the reluctant prisoner being forced to knuckle under by participating in group counseling in order to assure a speedy parole is presented to demonstrate that treatment is really punishment. But whether we label correctional programming treatment or punishment, we are led back to the question of the effectiveness of the program in reducing future recidivism. And the most powerful attack on corrections has come in this area because the ineffectiveness of correctional programming has been said by some to be scientifically demonstrated.

Some of us were surprised when the word emerged that "nothing works" in correctional treatment. This was especially true of those of us who, like the author of this book, had spent many years conducting research in correctional intervention, research which clearly showed that for some types of offenders under some conditions, treatment worked very well indeed. Even more astonishing than the news that treatment doesn't work was the eagerness with which some correctional administrators and social scientists received the message.

Palmer's book appears in this atmosphere of turmoil and discouragement, challenging the assumption of the total failure of correctional treatment. In a thorough and uncompromising manner, the author attacks the weak case presented by those who would eliminate correctional intervention because they believe it to be ineffective. Reviewing the position of those who say that nothing works, the author, with detailed and reasoned discourse, shows the positive outcomes to be found in the very research used to demonstrate correction's failures. His critique of the "nothing works" literature is devastating as he points to inaccuracies, contradictions, and the too global "total category" analyses that result in the omission of promising leads regarding treatment outcome.

In this trenchant critique, Palmer saves his biggest guns to abolish the "nothing works" position that for any correctional treatment to be considered effective, it is necessary for a treatment method (viewed as an undifferentiated entity) to receive almost unanimous support from research studies; that is, an absence of contradictory findings among the various studies, all showing effectiveness with all types of offenders and in almost the full range of treatment conditions, both institutional and noninstitutional.

Palmer's basic theme, set forth in the opening chapter and returned to again and again, is that the impact of correctional treatment must be viewed and evaluated with a complexity sufficient to the nature of the task. Outcome may vary with characteristics of the offenders involved in the treatment, with characteristics of the treatment personnel, with the nature of the treatment setting, and with the specifics of the program input. Treatments, to be effective for some, need not be effective for all, and treatments effective in some circumstances need not be effective in all. Effective treatment may best be identified by asking which type of treatment method is most effective with which type of offender, and under what conditions or in what type of setting.

The author has not argued that treatment "works"—except for some offenders under some conditions. He has faced us with the reality that offenders are not all alike in the extent to which treatment may be relevant or helpful, that correctional settings vary in their relevance to correctional outcome, that treatment methods may be matched or mismatched with particular offenders. This theme is buttressed with data from the Community Treatment Project, showing clearly differential outcomes by types of offenders, interacting with a variety of intervention modalities.

The implication of the differential perspective for the correctional adminis-trator is that rehabilitation need not be abandoned as a goal in corrections, since the picture concerning treatment effectiveness is not as bleak as has been painted. Although Palmer clearly acknowledges that we are only beginning to discover what elements or combination of elements in correctional programs are most likely to maximize a desirable outcome, he presents an optimistic view that future collaboration between correctional staff and researchers will permit the conceptualization and implementation of successful rehabilitation programs.

This differential theme should speak as vividly to the correctional researcher as to the correctional administrator. Inadequately complex research (treatment research that ignores differences among offenders, treators, or correctional settings) can result in mixing positive with negative findings so as to conceal more information than is discovered.

In making his plea for a continued focus on rehabilitation in corrections, Palmer reminds us, in case we have forgotten, of the common thread of humanity that exists for offenders and nonoffenders. Individuals brought into the correctional system are people first and offenders second. Palmer calls our attention to the core of common needs that are part of the human condition. Offenders, he believes, are as likely as nonoffenders to take advantage of opportunities that can be offered as a way of improving their lives. Thus, treatment remains a legitimate endeavor in corrections.

The second basic theme in this book is aimed specifically at the correctional researcher. It focuses on the maximizing of the information yield from correctional research. According to Palmer, ". . . corrections is now at a point where it can begin its first systematic analysis of the clues and patterns that have emerged during its own twenty-five or thirty years of scientific investigations." He sees the paths to improved correctional research lying in the direction of increasingly differentiated analyses, and in the direction of sequencing research studies so that knowledge can be organized and integrated, permitting hypotheses for subsequent studies to grow coherently out of the leads of previous studies.

While Palmer is critical of some past attempts to combine information across correctional studies, he clearly supports the concept and feasibility of across-study analyses and integration of findings. He has accepted the challenge inherent in his criticism of previous work by offering alternatives. Perhaps the author's most substantial contribution is in providing an organizing framework for integrating findings from several studies, in offering a language with which to conceptualize such an analysis, and even in suggesting dimensions and specific methods for analysis in a "how-to" format. He illustrates sorting the data of a number of studies in a variety of ways, including grouping for combination and comparative analysis by type of offender, and regrouping for analysis by other types of treatment elements. In careful detail and with instructional quality, Palmer defines paths to increased precision in analysis of correctional data and to potentially increased richness of findings.

This work takes its place in the sequence of documents that focus on the current argument regarding the impact of correctional treatment. It is only a terminal book in the sense that we can hope for the end of simplistic, too global analyses of correctional data. There continues to be room for ongoing dialogue in many areas (such as appropriate success and failure criteria in corrections), as well as comments on new, relevant correctional treatment data. Reactions to the author's proposals for differential analysis, multi-study analyses, and sequential hypothesis-testing research may well lead to a significant increase in information available for this ongoing discussion. Meanwhile, the book's main power is that it raises the level of discussion and enriches the dialogue concerning correctional treatment research.

Marguerite Warren
School of Criminal Justice
State University of New York
at Albany

Acknowledgments

I would like to thank the following individuals for their helpful suggestions in reviewing the original manuscript: John Conrad, Michael Hindelang, Vincent O'Leary, and Marguerite Warren.

Introduction

During the 1970s, correctional intervention or programmed assistance has been seriously challenged. It has been challenged on several grounds.

First, there is the view that it simply does not work—that, according to scientific studies, it fails to reduce illegal behavior among youthful and adult offenders. Next, there is the view that offenders do not need intervention. According to this position, offenders can cope as well as anyone else, but have been caught at activities which, though illegal, are part of normal or at least necessary adjustment within their environment. This position often stresses the idea that offenders can be damaged by the message that there is something wrong with them as individuals, a message which is considered intrinsic to the idea of programmed assistance.

These views are not new. However, during the 1970s, they have emerged with far greater force and impact than ever before. The first view suggests that all offenders respond in essentially the same way to programmed assistance, that differential success or failure does not exist to any substantial degree. The second presupposes that differing needs for assistance do not exist, and that the very idea of assistance communicates a message whose negative impact outweighs all possible gains.

There is, in addition, the much older but also revitalized view that programmed assistance is not a legitimate undertaking, that the justice system should limit its activities to the administration of punishment and, perhaps, the achievement of deterrence by this means alone. In this view, the justice system's "pill" should be bitter, not bittersweet. The system should assume little if any responsibility for the overall future adjustment and interests of offenders, for example, via correctional programs that focus on their needs, abilities, and limitations as individuals. It should focus on the dispensing of evenhanded justice or punishment in response to their *past* adjustment instead—specifically, past misdeeds alone. This position can be, and generally has been, maintained on a priori grounds, independent of (1) scientific findings regarding the effectiveness or ineffectiveness of intervention, (2) specific assumptions or empirical information concerning individual differences among offenders, and (3) the question of normality and deviance. However, since the mid-1970s, it has drawn considerable support from those who assert that intervention does not reduce illegal behavior.

Thus, three current challenges to the use of intervention are that it does not work, that it is not needed, and that it is inappropriate in the first place.

In recent years these challenges have been interwoven with specific issues or options such as the following: voluntary/mandatory participation in correctional programs, right to treatment/right to refuse treatment, determinate/indeterminate sentencing. Viewed as options, each of the preceding represents a condition under which intervention can or should take place, assuming it is used at all. These options can be examined separately from the challenges themselves. For instance, in establishing broad correctional policies through legislative mandates, decisions which relate to each option can be made entirely apart from knowledge of differing needs that may exist among offenders, and independent of offenders' presumed normality or deviance. They can also be made irrespective of information that bears on overall and differential effectiveness. Whether all such decisions should be made entirely apart from the preceding knowledge and beliefs is, in our view, an open question. To some extent the choice may ultimately depend on the quantity and validity of available information. It may also depend on one's concept of justice, and on the role of individualized justice in particular.

On a more philosophical level, some of these issues have been associated with the view that there is something inherently unethical and debasing about correctional intervention, something inconsistent with specific concepts of autonomy, self-responsibility, and dignity. This ethical assessment may be applied not just to programs that focus on an offender's feelings and attitudes toward self and others (e.g., individual or group counseling), but to those which try to alter his behavior, life circumstances, or self-concept in ways that are commonly thought of as down-to-earth and practical (e.g., vocational and educational training). Such an assessment would be considered applicable regardless of any personal gains that may be experienced by an individual as the result of a program—included would be gains that he himself may have desired. Thus, the primary concern of this ethic would not relate to the content, procedures, or goals of given programs; rather, it would focus on the *conditions* under which almost any form of intervention is, and perhaps can be, implemented within any justice system at all. In short, it would relate to the existence of external constraint and, perhaps, to the often harsh realities of compromise or mutual exchange between given individuals and society as a whole.

Even apart from the requirements of this demanding ethic, such issues lead to the question of whether programmed assistance, assuming it is to exist, can best be provided within or outside the justice system. To the practitioner, administrator, and offender, this question may assume increasing importance in upcoming years, especially in view of the numerous social/legal pressures and counterpressures (the deepening clash of values) that are being experienced within this system. This is not to suggest that these challenges and issues would surely disappear if one were to dissociate intervention from the justice system as it exists today, assuming this could be done.

Today's steadily growing pressure to dissociate intervention from the justice system does not mean that offenders, as individuals, are being discouraged from voluntarily seeking assistance within this system, particularly where educational, employment, or other programs do exist. However, this increasing pressure—not just in relation to status offenders, alcohol and drug abusers, etc.—does reflect the challenge that has been directed at the concept of intervening in the life of offenders under almost any conditions. In this connection, it is part of the current shift away from the idea of allocating new or extensive program resources to offenders, collectively. This applies whether these resources are to be offered on a contract basis, a voluntary basis, or otherwise.

No single discussion can thoroughly examine all these challenges, shifts, and complex, interwoven issues. Rather than touch lightly on several such issues, we have chosen to focus on two fundamental areas, those which relate to effectiveness and role. For example, do correctional programs indeed not work, even for specified offenders and in specified settings? Do these programs have any legitimate and useful role in today's world of high crime rates? If they do, what exactly is this role, and what can realistically be expected of it? What are the implications of *not* making programmed assistance available to offenders, within and outside the institutional setting?

These questions can and should be addressed on their own grounds, as independently as possible from issues with which they have been associated (for example, that of right to treatment versus right to refuse treatment). Clarification of these questions may help pave the way for a better focused and less cluttered look at some of the issues, themselves.

To deal with questions of effectiveness and role we will first inspect the view that correctional programming does not reduce recidivism and that it should be largely abandoned or radically altered. This view has had a major impact on policy making in recent years. To examine this position we will focus on two articles by Robert Martinson, the most influential contributor to the idea that nothing or almost nothing works. These articles are perhaps the clearest and most forceful expressions of that view. We will also examine the massive survey, by Lipton et al., which supplied the data that Martinson's articles were thought to represent.

As described in chapter 1, the impact of the view that almost nothing works was not just due to specific studies and conclusions presented by Martinson, in 1974. It was a product of widespread social difficulties, traumatic events within the justice system, and related exposés. These difficulties and events mainly emerged in the later 1960s and early 1970s. They left a deep impression throughout the system.

Since our immediate purpose is to assess the validity of the view that almost nothing works, we will not focus on these difficulties, events, and other external factors that operated to enhance this view's *impact*. (Different circumstances could probably have *reduced* the impact of this view, regardless of its validity.) To assess the almost-nothing-works view itself, to evaluate its intrinsic merit, we will focus on the studies and conclusions themselves; that is, we will examine what has been presented as the scientific basis of, or specific evidence and logic behind, this challenge to correctional intervention. We will, along the way, touch on the remaining factors as well. After that, we will be ready to reassess the role of intervention.

Finally, we will concentrate on a new challenge, one that may become increasingly important in future years. Because of large-scale federal support, the justice system in America has entered an era in which many studies are being produced. More studies have been carried out in the past several years than during the previous thirty. Although their quality is often far from optimal, these studies have produced many valuable results. Given this situation, a new challenge to correctional research is that of tapping into the many findings in ways that can yield a maximum of information regarding the impact and implications of various approaches.

To meet this challenge, one's primary efforts would not center around single investigations as such. They would not, for instance, focus on the development of improved techniques for analyzing the data from each study individually. Instead, they would relate to ways of integrating the findings from groups of studies—methodologically acceptable studies. These efforts would focus on ways of comparing, contrasting, and assessing results from several individual studies, in order to increase the chance of linking up valuable clues that may be contained in each study and to reduce the chance of overlooking important leads and of systematically obscuring positive or negative findings alike. Given this challenge, today's reality of research en masse thus provides a second reason for focusing on Martinson's assessment of correctional intervention.

Martinson's conclusion that almost nothing works was based on a pioneer effort to systematically organize and assess the findings from numerous correctional studies. These studies were first categorized according to *mode of intervention*—for example, individual counseling, group counseling, and milieu therapy. Each category was then evaluated as a unit, independent of all other categories. This effort involved 231 studies and approximately 12 intervention categories. It remains the only evaluation of its type and scope within corrections. (Here we are not distinguishing between Martinson's effort and that of Lipton et al. [27]. In subsequent contexts, this distinction will be made. Bailey's well-known 1961 assessment of 100 correctional treatment studies was mainly organized around type of research design, and the manner in which each study was reported.) Unfortunately, this evaluation contained fundamental flaws and major limitations in terms of the attempts that were made to integrate the results from these studies and categories of studies. These difficulties were reflected in Martinson's conclusions regarding intervention as a whole.

By examining the analytic structure, procedures, and criteria that Martinson used to integrate this mass of studies, we will illustrate some of the difficulties that have emerged within this relatively new area of challenge. This may highlight the critical role that can be played by these and other data-handling approaches with respect to the overall assessment of intervention. Apart from the difficulties and pitfalls that will be illustrated, this examination will suggest alternate approaches to the challenge in question.

Thus, the research component of this book focuses on current and alternate ways of handling large numbers of individual studies. It involves a basic introduction to issues that bear on the integration of empirical findings within an across-studies context.

It is our belief that appropriately chosen data-handling approaches can increase overall research output or efficiency and can lead to a broadly based representation of the findings from any set of investigations. In the long run, such approaches can play a central role in helping to pinpoint increasingly effective and humane ways of interacting with offenders, ways of linking their personal drives, interests, and abilities with the specific opportunities and requirements of society.

How do we regard intervention? In our view, many programs of intervention have substantially reduced recidivism (the recurrence of illegal behavior among convicted offenders), and at least as many have not. Both the former and latter programs have been found within a wide range of categories, e.g., individual counseling, group counseling, and vocational training. Regardless of the category into which they fall, no programs or program models have been successful with every type of offender or in every type of setting. Even the best leave much to be desired.

Still, a cup half empty is also half full. That is, one should not overlook the fact that many programs *have* reduced recidivism and have provided personal assistance to a sizable portion of the offender population. Such programs represent a step in the right direction and provide important clues for future development. This view is supported by an examination of the research studies that were surveyed by Lipton, Martinson, and Wilks, studies which are reviewed in chapters 2, 3, and 7 of this book.

Despite their individual and collective shortcomings, today's intervention programs are the only vehicles that show promise of helping many offenders focus on their needs and life circumstances in concrete, individualized terms and on other than a fleeting or tangential basis. Programs that carefully focus on these areas should receive the support of society and its key decision makers, especially if these programs show promise of meeting such needs (e.g., educational or vocational) and/or reducing recidivism in a humane and relatively efficient way. In addition to supporting and refining such programs, exploration of new and innovative approaches should be encouraged, and programs that show little promise of contributing to these objectives should be abandoned in favor of those which do. Obvious though it may be, this combination—refinement, exploration, and abandonment—is perhaps the only way for corrections to develop a larger number and higher percentage of effective programs across a range of categories.

This does not mean that all offenders must participate in programs of intervention to achieve their personal goals. Nevertheless, some offenders have a greater need for assistance than others, and many are motivated to participate in programs which they believe might be of use. Whenever possible, worthwhile programs (in effect, opportunities or tools) should be made available to these and other individuals.

Society has no humane grounds for abandoning today's more promising programs as long as it has nothing to substitute for them. This view does not derive from practical or strategic considerations, important though they may be.

Nor does it derive from the principle of using the best tools that are available at the time, imperfect though they are. Basically, it springs from long-standing social traditions and values. These values relate not only to the general concept of individual worth and potential, but to the more specific principle that every human being should have as much chance as possible to better his existence, regardless of his past. In or out of prison, he should not be left on a barren island with little to do but pass time.[1]

The view that society has no humane grounds for abandoning today's more promising programs is valid despite recent developments in the area of "deserved punishment" or "deserts" [54]. By itself, the idea of making the punishment fit the crime, and of standardizing dispositions wherever possible, does not address the specifics of an offender's future—his concrete needs and opportunities within an often demanding environment. Nor does it address the often complex task of motivating or realistically helping him come to grips with that environment and, in many cases, with himself.

The preceding view is also valid despite the fact that programs which are successful with convicted offenders are unable, by themselves, to clearly reduce today's high crime rates within society as a whole. Crime rates, after all, are also produced by many individuals other than the convicted offenders on whom correctional programs are focused. As a result, these rates should be clearly distinguished from the recidivism rates of individuals who have participated in given programs.

In short, society—in accordance with its traditions and values—would still be responsible for making at least some assistance available to offenders as human beings, however "just" and uniformly administered *punishment* may become and regardless of whether crime rates continue to be high. This responsibility, which need not fall on the justice system alone, might be easier for society and its decision makers to clearly envision or fully accept during less stressful and in some respects less anger-filled or retribution-oriented times. Finally, this responsibility would still exist despite the fact that what society mostly asks of correctional programs is that they reduce recidivism, not that they specifically embody or necessarily emphasize long-standing ideals.

Despite the controversial (for instance, highly coercive) ways in which correctional intervention has sometimes been used, its goal of providing assistance to offenders need not conflict with the goals of today's reform movements. As a result, intervention need not be viewed as an obstacle to progress within such areas as prisoners' rights, determinate sentencing, and decarceration of status offenders. We believe correctional intervention can dissociate itself from the more questionable or undesirable practices of the past and can be integrated with numerous social concerns and legitimate strivings of the present and future. We believe that correctional intervention can operate within a framework of humane interaction and exchange, despite the inevitable need (outside as well as inside the justice system) for some degree of social control. In short, correctional intervention need not reinforce today's often encountered stereotype: that it is rigid, self-serving, and passé.

Before proceeding to chapter 1, a few points might be noted:

For convenience, we will usually refer to the following documents in abbreviated form. 1. "What Works?–Question and Answers About Prison Reform" will be referred to as "What Works" [31]. Here, Martinson first presented his view that almost nothing works within corrections. 2. *The Effectiveness of Correctional Treatment: A Survey of Treatment Evaluation Studies* will be referred to as *Correctional Effectiveness,* and as Lipton et al. [27]. This massive review by Lipton, Martinson, and Wilks was the source document for "What Works." 3. "California Research at the Crossroads" will be referred to as "Crossroads" [30]. Here, Martinson attempted to defend "What Works" against specific questions which had been raised in a critique by the present author, entitled "Martinson Revisited" [38]. He also took the position that correctional treatment should be largely abandoned or radically altered.

We will use *treatment* and *intervention* synonymously. Each term will refer to what is ordinarily thought of not only as treatment per se, but as external control as well. We will use this approach for two reasons: (1) treatment, when implemented within a justice system, is almost always accompanied by external control; (2) intervention is a concept that can and should reflect both aspects of offender/system interaction, namely, the realities of treatment and control alike.

As will be seen, the view that almost nothing works addresses itself to treatment in particular. To reflect this fact and avoid unnecessary problems of terminology, we will use the word *treatment* much more often than *intervention*. Nevertheless, the former will remain synonymous with the latter, and both terms will be used with the above understanding as regards control.

Notes, usually technical observations and related remarks, have been placed after the appendixes. The text can best be read without stopping to review these notes.

**Part I
The Status of
Correctional Treatment**

1 The Years of Decline

Today, many people believe that correctional treatment cannot justify its existence, that it can make no positive contribution to society. Usually, those who take this position draw heavily on the view that treatment seldom reduces recidivism (the recurrence of illegal behavior). In short, they maintain that correctional programs seldom accomplish the principal job for which they are designed. What is the source of this belief, and why does treatment receive only lukewarm support today?

A Brief Review

The view that correctional programming seldom reduces recidivism virtually exploded onto the correctional scene in early 1974, with the appearance of Robert Martinson's article, "What Works?—Questions and Answers about Prison Reform" [31]. This was a review of numerous experimental studies that had been conducted over a period of 23 years: 1945 through 1967. Its essential conclusion was that virtually no treatment approach had been found to work.

Rarely if ever did a research article have as powerful and immediate an impact on corrections. Almost single-handedly, "What Works" began to change the belief that many practitioners and policy makers had held for several years—namely, that a sizable proportion of correctional programs were at least moderately effective with a sizable proportion of offenders. At the same time, it crystallized many doubts that were felt by other individuals regarding the efficacy and appropriateness of correctional treatment. (The difference between approaches and individual programs will become clear later on.)

Within a year, the view that almost nothing works—reduced recidivism—was widely accepted as having solid scientific backing. This belief was largely based on (1) the conclusion drawn in "What Works," (2) the assumption that this conclusion was fully supported by the extensive but then still unpublished survey of 231 studies that "What Works" was said to represent [27], and (3) the relative lack of formal opposition that this article had received from researchers and academicians alike. Together with factors mentioned below, this view was quickly used to support the scaling down of (or to oppose the expansion of) numerous programs in institutional as well as community settings. The status of treatment had rapidly declined.

The impact of "What Works" was not just the result of the preceding factors or of the specific studies it contained. In part, its impact was due to the fact that it supplied what looked like clear scientific support for feelings and beliefs that had developed over a period of years. These related to crime control, prison environments, and particular methods of rehabilitation; they were a product of unpleasant, often grim realities that had emerged within the United States. These realities and beliefs will now be reviewed.

First and foremost was the occurrence of a marked rise in overall crime rates since the early 1960s, and the related fact that, beginning around 1969, the impact of violent crime had grown acute. By 1971 many people were starting to believe that the latter trend was partly, perhaps largely, caused by offenders who had been given "second (or third) chances" in the community and who had little intention of changing their attitudes or behavior as long as they were not locked up. For these and other offenders, standard and intensive probation began to be thought of as forms of coddling; this was mainly due to the fact that neither approach involved incarceration, especially on a long-term basis. Despite these beliefs, it was widely recognized that incarceration often involved serious problems of its own.

In the midst of these trends and responses there occurred the Attica tragedy of September 1971, with its unmistakable polarization of inmate and "establishment" [59]. Investigations that followed this event soon produced a vivid and even wider awareness of the barren, minimally humane, and sometimes brutal conditions that existed in numerous jails and prisons throughout the United States. Even in the case of violent and repeat offenders, incarceration, under these conditions, could hardly be presented as a satisfactory solution to the problem of crime. In addition, even if one believed that offenders could obtain concrete assistance via institutional *treatment* (a process which could be considered distinct from straight lockup), it was difficult to see how any such process could be adequately implemented under conditions such as existed.[1] Beyond this, the specific institutional treatments that were being focused on in the early 1970s seemed to involve something very different from, or in addition to, assistance, in the usual sense of the word.

Attica, and subsequent exposés, occurred at a period when considerable attention was being paid to techniques that were often described as the brainwashing tools of society. In some settings, these techniques, for instance, specific drug therapies and aversive conditioning, had been used in ways that were regarded by numerous observers as manipulative and dehumanizing. In 1972 such techniques were shown in a markedly negative, generally exaggerated, yet by no means implausible light in the powerful and popular movie, *Clockwork Orange*. These events and descriptions helped to establish, in the minds of many, a close connection between "treatment" and manipulative or dehumanizing experiences.

Clearly, to many observers, institutional treatment was not thought of as assistance. Nor was it considered a form of coddling or a harmless way to pass the time. It was viewed as a repugnant and potentially injurious imposition instead. These and other observers believed that if an offender did have to be incarcerated in the first place (for the benefit of society and/or for punishment), it was not right for him to feel external pressure to participate in any such treatment as well.[2] Lockup itself was difficult enough.

It is hard to estimate the extent to which most people (i.e., the general public) felt that these essentially negative accounts of treatment represented the complete story. Quite possibly they assumed that other, more acceptable approaches were being used as well, or instead, at least in some institutions. Nevertheless, whatever the public may have assumed, the preceding events and descriptions doubtlessly lowered the overall status of treatment to some extent, from an ethical point of view.

During this period, the public's reaction to the idea of brainwashing was compounded by social critics and others who suggested that a sizable percentage of all inmates (student and other demonstrators aside) were political prisoners in a specific, ideological sense of the term. However, this suggestion appeared to be no more than minimally accepted by most people, and the compounding or intensification in question seemed to last no more than a year or two. (This suggestion should be distinguished from the substantially older view that most inmates are victims of social injustice and various forms of discrimination. This view has continued to the present but is rarely linked with the concept of brainwashing.)

On a longer-term basis, and more convincingly, these and other observers helped many people become aware of the connection that sometimes existed between the use of treatment and the presence of overly long or extended prison stays. (This was not taken to mean that the *vast majority* of lengthy stays were a result of treatment. Lengthy stays were correctly understood to be, at base, the product of lengthy sentences.) This relationship was acknowledged by individuals who, collectively, represented the full range of beliefs regarding treatment. For instance, its existence was acknowledged by those who believed, and those who did not believe, that the chief goal of treatment was submission or conformity, and that its primary or even common targets were "political" and assertive, nonconforming offenders.

Even in the early 1970s, many practitioners and policymakers recognized the sharply conflicting values that were reflected in this relationship. On the one hand, they could see the social value of continuing to work with certain offenders (e.g., the highly volatile and bizarre) beyond the termination date of their original sentence. They knew through direct experience that many had become extremely violent or disoriented during their prison stay, partly due to external factors with which they could not cope. On the other hand, these practitioners and policy makers sensed that the idea of extended sentences without additional crimes was inconsistent with specific ideals of justice (e.g., the principle of similar punishments for similar offenses).

At the same time, many individuals recognized the potential for misuse. For instance, if inmates did not "behave," their prison stay could be extended (if determinate) or continued (if indeterminate) on grounds of presumed treatment need and increased safety to the community—that is, treatment could be used as an indirect means of punishment and control. Moreover, the treatment in question might not materialize at all.

Misjudgment and subsequent overuse were also factors. Here, for example, prison stays could be extended or continued for 6 or 12 months by practitioners who genuinely believed that additional treatment would make a decisive difference in an inmate's ability to eventually cope with the realities of community life. Yet, there was no reason to believe that practitioners, however experienced, would be infallible in their assessment of an inmate's potential and in the potential of specific treatment programs. They were bound to make some mistakes, even in relation to programs that would be carried out within a generally supportive or at least nondestructive environment.[3] In addition, given the events and exposés that were still fresh in mind during the early 1970s, it appeared to many observers that institutional environments were seldom supportive or benign in the first place. Instead, it seemed that the impact of long-term lockup would almost certainly be powerful and disruptive enough to counterbalance most gains that would hopefully accrue from additional treatment. Apart from this, it was increasingly believed that work furlough, halfway houses, etc. could provide a more effective transition to the community for most offenders. These approaches were regarded by many as a relatively acceptable form of treatment or intervention.

It seemed clear that these factors—misuse and overuse—could affect many individuals, not just those who were violent, bizarre, or suicidal in the extreme. Largely for this reason it grew increasingly difficult to use the concept of treatment need as the primary basis for extending or continuing an individual's prison stay.[4] Thus, the influence of treatment was being reduced in this domain as well (subsequent to Attica, *Clockwork Orange,* and the like).

During this period, little attention was drawn to the fact that various treatment methods did not just exist within the type of environment that people had come to associate with many jails and prisons. For instance, such methods as group counseling and vocational training could be implemented within environments that were *not* characterized by serious overcrowding, major racial tensions, and frequent use of extreme punishments. They could exist without the use of specific time extensions and the backing of indeterminate sentences as well.

Since treatment was an operation of its own, that is, a process which was not invariably linked with or dependent on any one type of environment, it followed that its contribution to offenders could be thought of separately from the product or impact of any such environment. Yet, even though these contributions could be separated conceptually, it remained a fact that no treatment program existed in a vacuum. In real life, treatment programs operated within a specific correctional setting, whether destructive, divisive, mixed, or benign. As a result, what mattered to offenders was not the impact of treatment alone, but the combined effect of treatment and environment.

Thus, the question remained: might not the contribution of even the most promising programs be outweighed by the negative impact that seemed to be associated with most institutional environments? No one had any scientific data with which to answer this question. However, given the events of the early 1970s, people increasingly felt the answer was yes.

The Emergence of New Priorities

Given these events and feelings, what seemed to be urgently needed was not simply treatment. It was the improvement of specific living conditions and the establishment of less divisive or destructive atmospheres. This belief would undoubtedly have existed even if much more had been said during these years about the potentially constructive aspects of intervention, and if most portrayals of treatment had been less stereotyped and oversimplified than they were.

One example of such portrayals was seen in the frequent suggestion that almost all treatment was based on a "medical model," and that its recipients were generally regarded by treatment personnel as sick and in need of a cure. This stereotyped and oversimplified picture usually had the effect of casting treatment in a negative light, of making it appear not only obsolescent and potentially oppressive but as reflecting a set of narrow or naive assumptions and possibly depreciatory views of human beings.

The need for improved institutions was responded to in a number of ways. One of the most powerful responses was the movement for wards' and prisoners' rights, a movement that had a long history but which swiftly gathered momentum during 1972-1973. The top priorities of this movement were the improvement of everyday life, the establishment of new expectations, and the redistribution of power among inmates and staff. Immediate objectives included the reduction or elimination of (1) minimally humane as well as inhumane living conditions and practices and (2) controversial, unjustified, and possibly unnecessary demands by staff.

These objectives related to broad, institutionwide changes. It was hoped that these changes would be based on a new, formally or informally sanctioned relationship between offenders and the correctional system as a whole. Soon this hope did receive support through major court decisions. This new relationship, in turn, would be based on an increasingly positive view of offenders as human beings.

To effect these changes and establish this new relationship, it seemed necessary to focus much more attention on specified external realities than on programs which dealt with the inner lives of offenders, or on their abilities, interests, and plans as individuals. These external realities usually involved institutional power structures and the political/legal foundations of corrections itself.

Thus, as this movement gathered momentum, many treatment programs and postinstitution objectives acquired a lower standing then before. They were not seen as playing a major or decisive role in the improvement of living conditions and the redistribution of power. Treatment, in fact, was often seen as increasing rather than decreasing the problems of inmate/staff tension and institutional morale. This was due not only to its image as an often-controversial requirement, but to its association with indeterminate and extended sentences. These interacting factors—power, tension, and morale—were reflected in the rapidly increasing importance that was given to the concept of an inmate's right to refuse treatment.

One other movement in which treatment was often seen as more of a problem than a source of help was that of decarceration and decriminalization of status offenders (incorrigibles, runaways, and truants). We need not review the stages through which the decarceration component of this powerful movement progressed, starting around 1965. Suffice it to say that the emotion-laden events of the early 1970s helped crystallize attitudes and promote action within this area. For instance, subsequent to the post-Attica exposés, there was wide and rapidly increasing acceptance of the principle that status offenders should not be locked up for long periods of time—ideally, for any period of time—whether on grounds of punishment or apparent treatment need.[5]

The decriminalization component also surged ahead in the early 1970s. Here, the relevance of treatment was challenged in the context of what might be called original jurisdiction. This challenge centered on the fact that the presumed existence of a treatment need was often used as a legal basis for bringing status offenders into the justice system in the first place. (The original jurisdiction function was distinct from that of later keeping offenders in the system.) Those who challenged the relevance of treatment believed that original jurisdiction should be based exclusively or at least primarily on whether the instant offense was one for which an adult could have been arrested. They felt it should have little or nothing to do with presumed or apparent treatment need, however valuable treatment might conceivably be. In short, they believed that treatment need could not in itself justify such forms of social control as arrest, processing within the justice system, and incarceration in particular.

Another concern related to the possible impact of the official *delinquent* label on the self-concept and social opportunities of these youths. This concern also applied to the implicit *sick* label that many people associated with participation in any of several forms of treatment; it existed whether treatment was looked upon mainly as a form of brainwashing and indirect social control or as out-and-out assistance to the individual. Both the *delinquent* and *sick* labeling issues applied to community and institutional treatment alike.

These concerns were also considered valid relative to another large category of youths: dependency and neglect cases. Here, it seemed extremely difficult to justify not only incarceration (not to mention long-term incarceration), but exposure to *any* negative labels. Thus, by 1972-1973, feelings had grown quite strong that the concept of treatment need should not be used as a basis for bringing these individuals under the formal jurisdiction of the justice system, in the first place. If personal assistance were indeed needed, it should be provided outside the system itself.

Mobilizing for Rapid Change

These events and movements clearly indicated that the justice system was in trouble. Seen en masse (e.g., increase in violence, Attica and other confrontations, numerous exposés, treatment viewed as brainwashing, prisoners' rights movement), they suggested that the system's troubles were widespread and deep. Certainly, they were unprecedented in intensity.

No comprehensive blueprint for change emerged in response to this situation. No detailed or organized plan was adopted by the justice system as a whole, either formally or informally. On the contrary, wide differences became increasingly apparent within the professional community as to exactly what should be done and what the priorities should be. This was despite the appearance in early 1973 of a large-scale National Advisory Commission Report on Criminal Justice Standards and Goals, which had been initiated in 1971 [53]. In many respects, events had overtaken this report by the time it appeared, despite its constructive recommendations. Nevertheless, by 1973, justice system personnel agreed on at least two large and highly visible items: institutional living conditions and inmate/staff relationships were in particular need of change. These appeared to be overriding issues.

Despite the absence of a detailed agenda, there seemed to be a widely shared feeling about *how* to proceed—in effect, a common perception or underlying assumption about how to get moving and keep moving relative to these issues. In part, this feeling may have originated in the sense of urgency that characterized a large section of the professional community, particularly in 1972. That is, it may have derived from the feeling that immediate improvements would probably be needed if one were to avoid a rapid worsening of the situation and a continuing round of confrontations with regard to institutional living conditions and inmate/staff relations.[6] This sense of how to proceed was probably based on an intuitive feeling or further assumption that concerted action would be required as well.

Within the professional community this shared feeling or intuitive strategy appeared to be as follows (this, of course, is the author's reading of the situation; no scientific opinion surveys were conducted at the time, in this regard): to effectively mobilize for change and to then maintain momentum, it would be important to focus on problems for which relief and solutions were widely and intensively sought. This meant a concentration of energies and feelings *against* selected aspects of the justice system, for example, the destructive or divisive conditions previously mentioned. It meant an emphasis on negative aspects of the system far more than progressive or acceptable aspects. In short, one would proceed by focusing attention on high-visibility concerns that people shared, and by demonstrating that the justice system was definitely not making the grade. Since rapid action was a major goal, extended exploration and discussion of alternate views would not be encouraged.

This approach or set of feelings may have contributed greatly to the reduced emphasis that was placed on the more tolerable, generally acceptable, or even potentially helpful aspects of the justice system, beginning around 1973. (These aspects related to institutional milieus that seemed less than deplorable to many inmates, or that even seemed progressive in orientation. They also included community approaches that seemed like promising alternatives to incarceration [3, 24, 26, 29, 46, 48, 56].) For example, many justice system personnel seemed to feel that substantial emphasis on these aspects might weaken the momentum and delay the changes that were needed. Some appeared to feel that, given the tenor of the times, almost any mention of such features might be interpreted as a denial of the negative aspects themselves, and as a naive, dogmatic, or self-serving defense of the justice system as a whole—or of the status quo. This applied in the specific area of treatment as well, especially in the wake of such issues as brainwashing, misuse, and overuse. Still other people (perhaps the majority) simply felt that the most important thing was to highlight the negative features as much as possible—in effect, to strike hard while the iron was hot. This was apart from whether they believed the justice system contained many encouraging or constructive elements in the first place.

Given this reduced emphasis on the potentially helpful aspects of the system and an increased emphasis on other features instead, relatively little energy was in fact diverted from the problems under consideration. In this respect, the preceding approach was strategically correct in terms of facilitating rapid change.

Treatment at Ebb Tide

It was in this context that "What Works" emerged. As indicated, its main conclusion was that virtually no treatment approach had been found to reduce recidivism. Since this conclusion was presumably based on detailed scientific evidence, it seemed apparent that correctional programs were not doing the main job most people expected them to do. This applied whether they were a form of brainwashing or not. At base, this conclusion meant that corrections was not rehabilitating offenders—that its principal claim of effectiveness was unfounded.

Martinson's message was consistent not only with preexisting doubts as to the efficacy and appropriateness of treatment, but with the overall tenor of the times. Partly for this reason and partly because of its intrinsic importance and dramatic nature, this message spread throughout the justice system within a matter of months. Many people accepted it without qualification; others, if they did have serious questions or second thoughts, did not make them known.

As this message reached more and more people, it became clear that something fundamental had occurred: a long-established rationale for particular policies and practices had lost much of its credibility and force. The rationale was that of treatment need (e.g., a need for psychological support and the development of more acceptable and satisfying coping strategies by offenders) and anticipated treatment gain, especially reduced recidivism. For example, if treatment could seldom be expected to reduce recidivism, the concept of treatment need could hardly be used as a principal or even supplementary rationale for the following policies and practices: (1) required participation in almost any program of intervention (counseling, vocational training, etc.); (2) use of indeterminate sentences; and (3) extension of an offender's sentence. If indeterminate sentences, time extensions, etc. were still to occur, they would have to be based on other considerations.

Such policies and practices often related to issues of institutional morale and possible misuse as well as overuse of treatment. These were among the chief concerns of the movement for prison reform and/or that for decarceration/ decriminalization of status offenders. Since these concerns often related to policies and practices that had been partly supported by the concept of treatment gain together with that of treatment need, and since treatment gain now appeared to be an unrealistic expectation, these movements suddenly found themselves faced with less opposition than before. In short, by late 1974 the view that treatment is essentially ineffective had substantially reduced the level of support for certain policies and practices to which these movements were opposed. In so doing, it gave these already powerful movements a definite boost—an enhanced feeling of legitimacy and an added basis for action.

This view also lent support to many individuals who were not directly involved with these or other movements. Many of these individuals were dissatisfied with the justice system as a whole; some were anxious or angry about the high rate of crime, the events of the early 1970s, etc. Others seemed to have found a new sense of direction from the strongly worded views or impassioned pleas that were increasingly expressed in connection with the intuitive strategy previously mentioned. At any rate, "What Works" seemed to provide scientific support for individuals who were not specifically identified with the movements in question, but whose feelings nevertheless related to the idea that the system was in need of major change. Here, as elsewhere, the view that almost nothing works had struck an emotional, not just intellectual or scientific chord.

In sum, starting around mid-1974, the view that treatment is largely ineffective began to increasingly serve as a base from which individuals and specified movements could exert pressure or organize for change. Relative to the former context (that of individuals), this view sometimes helped to focus or channel a number of generalized anxieties, frustrations, and hopes. Relative to the latter context, it often provided additional leverage for efforts that had already made progress along particular lines. In the case of individuals and movements alike, the efforts in question were directed at a wide range of justice system components.

With respect to the treatment component in particular, the view that almost nothing works soon helped accelerate the decline in status that was already apparent by 1972-1973. It did this with assistance from the noticeably strengthened (late 1974) movements themselves. This decline was reflected in a frequent opposition to the expansion or even continuation of given treatment programs in institutional and community settings alike. Such opposition was expressed by administrators, legislators, and academicians alike, in places as widely separated as California and New York.

Shorn of their claim to effectiveness, advocates of treatment were in little position to resist these pressures. Increasingly, treatment was viewed as a process that was in many respects expendable, or of moderate priority only. This was due not only to its apparent inability to reduce recidivism, but to other, more pressing priorities as well. By the end of 1975, the status of treatment had probably reached an all-time low throughout much of the United States, despite the fact that most such programs managed to survive.

Treatment, Recidivism, and the Individual Offender

A few last words before proceeding to chapter 2. There is little reason to believe that correctional treatment can make a decisive contribution to these movements for change, even under the best conditions. Few people, in fact, believe that correctional treatment even *should* be expected to play a direct and significant role in this regard. In any event, it is unlikely that a method which focuses on offenders as individuals can, in itself, play more than a limited role in helping to improve general living conditions or eliminate the use of extreme punishments. For the most part, these objectives must be achieved by other means instead.

Despite this limitation, the following question may be asked. Are there other important objectives to which correctional treatment *can* make a major, possibly even unique contribution? To answer this we must look beyond the turmoil that has surrounded the justice system since the early 1970s.

It has long been accepted that the reduction of recidivism is a legitimate objective, one that is relevant to offenders and society alike. The importance of this goal has been acknowledged by a wide range of observers. This includes individuals who regard reduced recidivism as far less important a goal than those which relate to the institutionwide and systemwide changes mentioned earlier. It has also been generally accepted that reduction of recidivism is the principal objective which most treatment programs are supposed to accomplish, however much they may achieve in other areas as well (for instance, those of attitude change and vocational adjustment). These views have been held in times of turmoil as well as relative calm.

Thus, there is at least one important objective to which correctional treatment may make a major and direct contribution: the reduction of recidivism. Yet, the dominant view today is that treatment does not make this contribution, does not, in effect, do its job.

This view should be closely inspected. To do this, the basic question would obviously be: does treatment make a substantial contribution to the reduction of recidivism? In this sense, does it or doesn't it work? It is in this context, and with the former question in mind, that the effectiveness of treatment will be assessed.

In the chapters that follow, rate of recidivism will serve as the main basis for evaluating correctional treatment. This measure will allow us to focus on the basic job that treatment or intervention is expected to do as far as most people are concerned. Recidivism is the measure that was used in "What Works," as well. Specifically, it was the sole basis on which Martinson evaluated the outcome of all individual research studies that he reported, studies which related to his conclusion that almost nothing works. It was this conclusion which comprised the main scientific input with respect to today's dominant view of treatment effectiveness. It is this conclusion which must be addressed.

For these and related reasons, the present assessment of treatment will not center on the question of how well it can solve, by itself, problems that are faced by today's formal and informal movements. Indeed, few treatment programs have been designed to address most such issues in the first place.[7] Nor will it focus on the content of ongoing discussions and debates concerning the role of coercion in specific social situations, or on the most appropriate setting for working with offenders.[8] Nevertheless, such problems and issues will be touched on at various points.

If this assessment indicates that correctional treatment achieves its main objective to a substantial degree, such a finding would not detract from the importance of the movements for change, for example, that of prison reform. Nor would it diminish the value of their accomplishments to date or imply that today's priorities should be drastically altered. Basically, it would mean the justice system has one more tool at its disposal, one that could be used regardless of its perceived importance and overall priority within the system at any given time. If treatment does *not* achieve its main objective, or hardly "works" at all, the system could then release its energies from this particular tool and direct them to other, more promising areas instead.

Despite the controversial ways in which correctional treatment has sometimes been used, its main objective does not conflict with those of various reform movements. As a result, it need not stand as an obstacle or natural enemy to the resolution of today's overriding issues, for instance, those of prisoners' rights. There are no strong reasons for believing that correctional treatment, if indeed it works, cannot dissociate itself from the more questionable or undesirable policies and practices of the past and cannot be integrated with many of the legitimate needs and valid beliefs of the present and future.

Finally, regardless of the heavy emphasis that must be placed on recidivism in the assessment of treatment, it should be kept in mind that the reduction of illegal behavior is not the only goal of intervention. However critical, in fact paramount, recidivism may be to most people—and, perhaps, quite validly so—this socially centered objective is usually supplemented by one that centers directly on the offender himself, as an individual and human being.

Here, primary emphasis is on providing opportunities and incentives that might help the offender forge concrete, workable links between his personal drives and abilities, on the one hand, and the specific opportunities, limitations, and requirements of society, on the other. In short, primary emphasis is on helping the offender come to grips with his life and obtain, in nondestructive ways, greater satisfaction from his interactions with others. The achievement of this goal may often be reflected in but cannot be directly measured by recidivism alone.

2 Almost Nothing Works: View and Counterview

Almost Nothing Works

The view that correctional programming seldom reduces recidivism was presented by Martinson in 1974, in the article "What Works" [31]. During the subsequent 2 years, Martinson reaffirmed this view, sometimes in stronger terms than were used in the original article and sometimes with important qualification. However, his basic position remained the same. This position, and these developments, will now be reviewed.

The essence of Martinson's position was presented in the opening section of "What Works":

> ... It is possible to give a rather bald summary of our findings: *With few and isolated exceptions, the rehabilitative efforts that have been reported so far have had no appreciable effect on recidivism* [31].

To strengthen this statement, he added:

> Studies that have been done since our survey was completed [December 1967] do not present any major grounds for altering that original conclusion [31].

It was the former statement in particular that numerous individuals used as scientific support for the view that corrections must be largely overhauled.

Toward the close of "What Works," Martinson restated his position in greater detail:

> Do all these studies lead us irrevocably to the conclusion that nothing works, that we haven't the faintest clue about how to rehabilitate offenders and reduce recidivism? ... I am bound to say that these data, involving over 200 studies and hundreds of thousands of individuals as they do, are the best available and give us very little reason to hope that we have in fact found a sure way of reducing recidivism through rehabilitation. This is not to say that we found no instances of success or partial success; it is only to say that these instances have been isolated, producing no clear pattern to indicate the efficacy of *any* particular method of treatment. [31, emphasis added]

The 200 (i.e., 231) studies in question involved a wide range of treatment methods; collectively, they covered institutional and community settings alike. These methods—11 in all—were discussed under such headings as education and vocational training, the effects of individual counseling, group counseling, medical treatment, the effects of sentencing, probation or parole versus prison, psychotherapy in community settings, the effects of community treatment, etc.[1] More specifically, each method was reviewed and evaluated in turn, separate and apart from every other method. Given this extensive review and systematic assessment, Martinson's findings, as reflected in the quoted conclusion, appeared to mean that successful treatment was an infrequent occurrence indeed. At base, this conclusion clearly suggested that no method of treatment had been found to work—not just consistently, but to hardly any degree.

During the next 18 months, Martinson presented his views to interested audiences throughout the United States. His efforts were perhaps climaxed in August 1975, with an appearance on the nationally televised CBS program, "60 Minutes." There, in an interview entitled, "It Doesn't Work," he took the position that no known approach—no method of treatment, no program of rehabilitation—had been found to reduce recidivism, consistently or otherwise. This applied not only to prisons, but to "the system as a whole":

> *Mike Wallace, Interviewer (I):* What you do, say the traditionalists, is train a man while he's in prison. If he has had no job skills, give him some. If he lacks an education, give him some. There's a drawer full of these programs . . . , all aimed at making the convict go straight. But do they work?

> *Martinson (M):* I looked at all the methods that we could find—vocational, educational, and a variety of other methods. These methods simply have no fundamental effect on the recidivism rate of people who go through those prisons, who go through the system as a whole, even—probation, prison and parole, and so forth.

> *I:* No effect at all?

> *M:* No effect, no basic effect. . . .

> *I:* Psychological counseling. A prisoner sits down in a room with a psychologist and talks it out. Does that help to stop prisoners from going back and committing crimes again?

> *M:* No. No. It may be a way to pass the time. It may be even a good way to pass the time, so far as I know. But it has no effect on their—on the crime rate.

> *I:* You're sure of it?

> *M:* Yes, I'm sure of it, sir. . . .

> *I:* The prisoner who has been exposed to no rehabilitation programs— are his chances of going back to crime better, worse, or the same as the prisoner who has had the whole treatment?

M: They're the same. They're the same. I know it sounds astonishing, but they're the same. . . .

M: I did look at an enormous variety of . . . group counseling or group therapy programs.

I: And?

M: They did not seem to reduce recidivism. They did seem to have the effect of making an institution somewhat less tense. . . . But as far as reducing crime, I didn't find any evidence of that [7].

Martinson's message was heard loud and clear:

The impact of Martinson's public utterances . . . has been pervasive and fundamental. . . . Far from the quiet backwaters of academic activity it used to occupy, correctional research has been propelled into popular attention with momentous conclusions drawn from it by policy-makers. [11]

The central thrust of his position was unmistakable, and few people attempted to question it:

. . . The headline of a front page article in the . . . *National Observer* concluded: REFORM IS A FLOP. One of the primary sources quoted by the *Observer* and other publications that have printed articles on the subject is Martinson's study . . . [This study, reported in "What Works,"] landed like an artillery shell on much of the correctional community. What Martinson was saying was that nothing he had studied had worked. . . . [51]

For almost two years Robert Martinson has challenged the ideology of correctional rehabilitation. [Until recently,] the response from correctional thinkers has been surprisingly subdued. [12]

Martinson was aware of this impact, and seemed to regard it as decisive:

[Martinson believes] that his and other research over the last few years has ended what he calls the "age of treatment" and destroyed the "ideology" behind it—that criminal offenders are victims of a social disease that can be diagnosed, treated and cured in correctional programs. "The ideology has been ruptured and broken open at the seams," Martinson said in an interview. The criminal justice system must now be reorganized with other goals in mind, he added. [51]

However, in 1975 correctional thinkers began to question the position that Martinson had taken in "What Works." Palmer, in a review entitled "Martinson Revisited," pointed out that:

Martinson's review strongly suggested that no known methods of treatment contain the "answer" for all offenders. [Yet] it also indicated that some methods are nevertheless of value to at least *some* offenders. However, this latter suggestion did not appear in his oft-quoted concluding remarks ... [which, instead,] focused on the question of whether any methods of treatment are of value, not for particular types of offenders, but for all or nearly all offenders. [38]

Responding to this review, and to various questions that were raised, Martinson pointed out the following:

Our studies ended in December, 1967. How do I know that the next 200 studies won't show tremendous success? [51]

This was a departure from his previous statement (p. 15), that studies which were conducted subsequent to 1967 already *had* been taken into account. Martinson's new position was that they had not been reviewed, or considered, and that their results might lead to a much brighter picture than had been described thus far.

The next development occurred in March 1976, in Martinson's "Crossroads" article. Here, he made pointed reference to certain *positive* research findings (see below), findings which had been described in "What Works" as "isolated exceptions" that made little difference relative to the broader, negative picture. By itself, this seemed like the start of a message which was different, at least in emphasis, from that which had been received for close to 2 years by large numbers of practitioners, researchers, policy makers, and interested citizens.

The Counterview

To determine whether Martinson's new observations did, indeed, reflect a substantive change in position, we must briefly review three points that were raised by Palmer in "Martinson Revisited."

First, Palmer noted that positive findings (i.e., reduced recidivism) were described, in "What Works," in connection with several categories and subcategories of treatment. These were:

1. *Individual counseling*, e.g., in Martinson's words, this study suggests "there is something to be hoped for in treating properly selected amenable subjects"; another study indicates "a favorable outlook for ... individual therapy ... conducted by social workers. ..."
2. *Group counseling*, e.g., "these programs seem to work best when their subjects are amenable to treatment ... and when the counselors are not only trained people but 'good' [skilled] people as well."
3. *Individual psychotherapy in community settings*, e.g., one study, "a pragmatic psychotherapeutic approach which was marked by its small size and

its use of therapists who were personally enthusiastic about the program, [led to] a decline in recidivism rates"; in another, arrest rates declined as a function of "intensity of treatment."

Other categories also contained a sizable proportion of encouraging outcomes or promising leads. These were:

4. *Intensive probation or parole supervision, as versus imprisonment,* e.g., this latter category has "provided . . . encouraging reports on rehabilitative treatment [and indicates] that, by and large, intensive supervision does work—that the specially treated youngsters do much better according to some measure of recidivism."
5. *Milieu therapy,* e.g., "youthful males . . . over 16 appear to benefit more than those under 16" from residential milieu therapy [31].

These and other approaches did, of course, contain several studies with negative findings, that is, with a lack of substantial or statistically significant differences between experimental subjects and their controls. For this reason, these approaches could not, as Martinson suggested in "What Works," be considered a "sure way" of reducing recidivism, that is, a 100 percent assured success under all or nearly all conditions.

(Before proceeding, it should be noted that *categories,* i.e., *methods, of treatment* and *treatment approaches* are synonymous with Martinson's term *independent variable categories.* In the present volume, the term *treatment* is usually substituted for the more inclusive term *intervention.* The latter refers to the combination of treatment and control which is characteristic of most correctional efforts, individual and group counseling included.)

Next, Palmer indicated that, in "What Works," at least 39 individual studies (48 percent of those discussed) were associated with positive or partly positive results, again in relation to recidivism.[2] (Of the remainder, 4 percent were ambiguous and 49 percent were negative, e.g., no reduction in recidivism.) This included studies from a wide range of treatment approaches and settings. In this connection, it was noted that

> a larger number of favorable than unfavorable/ambiguous results were [mentioned, by Martinson] in relation to the use of (a) probation rather than prison and (b) small caseloads and intensive supervision. The numbers were about equal in the case of (c) group counseling within residential settings and (d) psychotherapy within the community. [38]

Finally, Palmer noted three significant patterns that appeared across the numerous studies which were described in "What Works." Specifically, positive and partially positive (mixed) results were reported in connection with the following:

1. *Types of offenders.* Martinson had stated that "the effect of sentence

length seems to vary widely according to type of offender," and that in the case
of probation and parole, various studies suggest that "the personal characteristics
of offenders . . . were more important than the form of treatment in determining
future recidivism." Among the categories and types of offenders that were
specified in "What Works" were individuals prejudged to be "middle risk" on
base expectancy, "treatment amenable," and "prosocial." Those added by
Palmer in "Martinson Revisited" were "higher maturity," "neurotic," and, in the
case of adolescents, "older versus younger."[3]

2. *Setting in which treatment occurs.* This refers to treatment setting in
interaction with specified categories of offenders. For example, Martinson had
observed that "for older youths who were deemed to be good risks for the
future, a minimum security institution produced better results than a maximum
security one," whereas the results were somewhat different for individuals under
16.

3. *Worker characteristics.* In "What Works" several studies were mentioned
in which factors such as therapist skill, level of enthusiasm, or professional
orientation were associated with a reduction in recidivism. In "Martinson
Revisited," a number of other studies were added. These studies cut across
different categories of treatment (e.g., individual counseling and group counseling) and different settings for treatment (institutional and community). They
applied to males and females alike.

Martinson's Reply

In "Crossroads"—a specific reply to the "Revisited" article—Martinson took the
following position. First, he strongly suggested that only *one* category of
treatment, probation, was associated with encouraging and reliable results. (This
category, he indicated, included two subcategories: (1) "the status of probation," in lieu of institutionalization, and (2) "intensive probation supervision for
younger offenders." These, he added, were the "few and isolated exceptions" to
which he had referred in "What Works.") He made no reference to the fact that
positive outcomes were associated not just with probation, but with *several*
categories and subcategories of treatment, e.g., individual counseling, group
counseling, individual psychotherapy in community settings, and milieu therapy.
In chapter 3 we will review the validity of Martinson's rationale for presenting
only one category, probation, as being of substantial value with respect to
recidivism.

Second, Martinson did not directly contest Palmer's observation that 48
percent of all studies had yielded promising results or positive leads. Nor did he
dispute the fact that similar figures were obtained by Adams (59 percent) and
Speer (55 percent) in earlier reviews of comparable quality investigations. (It
might be noted that Bailey, in 1961, also obtained similar figures, even though

the studies he reviewed were not always of comparable quality.[4]) Instead, Martinson suggested that the former percentage is nevertheless misleading and of little value from a qualitative point of view:

> Palmer . . . asks what proportion of the total studies have "positive or partly positive results." (A "partly positive" result is probably akin to a partly pregnant girl friend.) The answer is "48%." With this answer and thirty cents you can buy a cup of coffee in New York. It is meaningless. [30]

Thus, Martinson suggested that the category of partially positive results, like a half pregnant woman, never did exist, and was perhaps conceived by Palmer himself. However, this suggestion was not borne out by Martinson's remarks in "What Works." For instance:

> A study [of milieu therapy] by the State of California also showed partially positive findings; . . . [another, by McCord,] reports mixed results. [Similar results were reported in the Highfields study. Also, in a study of educational and vocational training,] one special subgroup . . . provided an exception to [the overall] pessimistic finding. . . . A third study [of group counseling] does report an overall positive finding as opposed to a partial one. [31]

Specifically, in "What Works" 23 studies were found to have mixed or partially positive results. Such studies had usually shown positive impact for one or more specific offender groups within the total study sample or for a specified portion of the given sample. In other cases, positive results were reported for one index of recidivism or for one followup period, but not another. Partially positive (that is, mixed) findings obviously did exist.

Also with regard to quality, Martinson emphasized that the figure of 48 percent "includes the findings of studies as different as probation placement and castration." He thus suggested, or seemed to imply, that it reflects at least several (possibly numerous) studies of a similarly distasteful or ethically objectionable nature as the latter. As before, Martinson's suggestion was not borne out by the facts. A review of "What Works"—and of the much larger, detailed source document by Lipton et al. (*Correctional Effectiveness*)—clearly indicates that the castration study was an extreme and literally unique example [27]. As such, it represented neither a majority nor even a small minority of studies for which encouraging results had been reported. In most instances, the latter studies were located within the relatively humdrum categories of group counseling, milieu therapy, intensive probation, etc. When the castration study is excluded from investigations that were reported in "What Works," the figure of 48 percent drops to 47 percent.

Finally, Martinson singled out only two of the offender types, or offender characteristics, previously associated with a reduction in recidivism.[5] These were middle-risk offenders, and older as versus younger adolescents. However, he did not point out the positive findings that were reported in "What Works" and "Martinson Revisited" in connection with treatment amenable, prosocial, higher maturity, and neurotic individuals. Nor did he refer to the characteristics of workers, and the different settings in which treatment may take place (in interaction with given offender types), which were also associated with reductions in recidivism.

Thus, the picture which finally emerged in "Crossroads" was as follows. Rehabilitative efforts lead to clearly positive results only in relation to (1) intensive probation supervision, (2) probation status versus incarceration, and (3) middle-risk and youthful offenders.

Martinson regarded this as a scanty product, if not a depressing situation:

> How can it be that all of these intensive . . . activities [studies and efforts] . . . to reform offenders has produced so pitiful an outcome? [30]

However, the product that emerged would have been far from bleak and far less constricted if he had brought to the reader's attention (1) the fact that several categories of treatment, not just one, were associated with a sizable proportion of positive results and encouraging leads; (2) the significance of the 48 percent figure, one which represented scientifically valid studies from nearly all categories of treatment (see chapter 3); and (3) the patterns which emerged across several categories of treatment with respect to offender characteristics, worker characteristics, and the interaction between type of setting and type of offender.

Thus, Martinson's position in "Crossroads" remained essentially the same as that which was reflected in his oft-quoted summary of "What Works," and even more strongly in his televised remarks: if correctional treatment was not already dead, it was probably about to die. This applied despite the fact that a sizable percentage of offenders not only fall within the middle base expectancy category, but are placed on probation, where, theoretically, intensive supervision can improve their level of success.

3

The Defense of "What Works"

Basic Distinctions

To understand and assess Martinson's defense of "What Works" and his overall account of rehabilitation, certain distinctions should be kept in mind. These relate to (1) individual studies versus categories of treatment (i.e., groups of individual studies) and (2) findings from individual studies versus contradictory findings from one study to the *next,* within any category of treatment. For example:

1. In "Martinson Revisited," Palmer noted that negative findings were often obtained in connection with the *individual studies* reported in "What Works." He suggested that some of these results might be due, in part, to the likelihood that the positive performance (reduced recidivism) of some offenders had been counterbalanced or masked by the negative performance of others, and that the net result for individual studies of this type was zero or occasionally minus because *both* (or all) groups of offenders had been lumped together and analyzed as a single group.[1] In addition, he indicated that the conclusion which Martinson had drawn regarding rehabilitation as a whole failed to reflect the positive findings that had been obtained from numerous individual studies within and across several *categories of treatment.*

2. In "What Works," Martinson's rationale for concluding that few if any categories of treatment worked seemed clear. When he inspected all individual studies that comprised any one category of treatment, he invariably found a number of positive studies mixed together with several negative, that is, nonpositive, studies. In light of these contradictory (ambiguous) results, it seemed evident that no single category of treatment could be recommended to policy makers on an across-the-board basis, that is, as a sure way of working with the vast majority of offenders, especially under the widely varying conditions in which the treatment approach was likely to be implemented. (In accounting for the contradictory results from one study to the next within any one treatment category, Palmer noted that the studies in question were often conducted under widely varying conditions.[2] Thus, three independent studies that were each categorized as group counseling may have differed considerably from one another with respect to strategies used by group leader, size of group, number of sessions per week, and overall duration of treatment. Differences of this type were in fact common. In "What Works," Martinson himself placed considerable emphasis on this explanation.)

**Research Quality, Differential Weighting, and
Insignificant Change**

Now then, in "Crossroads" Martinson made no comment about Palmer's account
of the masking effects that were probably operating within the numerous
individual studies, effects which may have made negative outcomes, for individual studies, and contradictory results, from one study to the next, virtually
inevitable from the start. Nor did he indicate that, basically, he (Martinson) had
evaluated the worth of each correctional approach from the standpoint of
whether it could or could not be recommended on an across-the-board basis.[3]
Instead, in order to defend the overall conclusion which he had reached in
"What Works" regarding rehabilitation as a whole, Martinson used the following
approach (this approach was also used to help account for the "pitiful outcome"
described in "Crossroads").

As mentioned previously, Martinson took the position that the only
approach which showed substantial promise of reducing recidivism was that of
probation—probation status and intensive probation supervision in particular.[4]
In essence, each of the 10 remaining approaches, e.g., group counseling or
individual counseling, had to be rejected because it contained many contradictory results from one study to the next and, in any event, was comprised of
numerous individual studies—ex post facto investigations, for instance—which
were not especially strong in terms of basic research design or overall quality.
This explanation implied that most of the positive studies which were judged to
be of good quality (or sufficient overall importance, or both) were those which
had been carried out within the area of probation, and that relatively few had
been found within other areas. At any rate, according to Martinson, in order to
properly assess the actual and potential value of an individual *category* of
treatment or to assess its overall impact on recidivism it was necessary to

> [draw] together often conflicting findings from *individual studies*
> which differ in the degree of reliance that can be placed upon their
> conclusions. [30, emphasis added]

When Martinson completed this task, probation alone seemed to emerge
relatively unscathed. Presumably, the technical adequacy of its studies was
greater than that of other categories—great enough, in any event, to overcome
any conflicting findings from one study to the next.

This explanation by Martinson has a number of defects. First, it is weakened
by the fact that several, not just one or two, contradictory results were observed
within the category of probation from one study to the next. In this respect,
probation was not much different from several other major approaches.[5] For
example, in table 3-1 it can be seen that, counting the Warren study as a single
investigation,[6] 50 percent of all studies that were categorized as probation

Table 3-1
Type of Outcome Obtained for Studies in Eleven Treatment Categories

Treatment Category	No. of Studies[c]	Outcome			
		Positive[a]		Negative[b]	
		No. of Studies	Percent of Studies	No. of Studies	Percent of Studies
Probation	14[d]	7	50	7	50
Imprisonment	16	10	63	6	38
Parole	17	12	71	5	29
Casework and individual counseling	6	4	67	2	33
Skill development	12	7	58	5	42
Individual psychotherapy	9	5	56	4	44
Group methods	16	8	50	8	50
Milieu therapy	17	8	47	9	53
Partial physical custody	4	1	25	3	75
Medical methods	3[e]	2	67	1	33
Leisure time activities	1	1	100	0	0
Total	115	65	57	50	43

[a]Reduction in recidivism.

[b]No reduction in recidivism, i.e., nonpositive.

[c]No one study (finding) is represented in more than one treatment category; i.e., all repeat entries (N = 9) are excluded. Nine additional studies are excluded mainly because information was insufficient or too ambiguous to allow for classification of study as either positive or negative (nonpositive).

[d]The five Warren study entries are counted as a single study.

[e]Excludes the castration study.

efforts in *Correctional Effectiveness* showed essentially no reduction in recidivism. In this respect, half the probation studies were not supported (or were contradicted) by the remaining half.[7] For the categories of imprisonment, skill development, individual psychotherapy, group methods, and milieu therapy, the percentage of studies which showed essentially no reduction in recidivism was 38, 42, 44, 50, and 53, respectively.[8] (See n. 9, on derivation of the sample used in tables 3-1 through 3-5.)

Second, and more basic, Martinson's account is directly contradicted by the following: the technical adequacy of individual studies which made up the category of probation was *not* superior to that of individual studies which comprised several other categories of treatment. For instance, as seen in table

3-2, each of the following treatment approaches had at least as high a percentage of pure experimental designs (rather than ex post facto and simulation designs) among their individual studies, as did probation itself. The figures that follow are straight tabulations of specific statements which appear in *Correctional Effectiveness: (pure experimental design)* casework and individual counseling, 86 percent of all studies; individual psychotherapy, 75 percent; group methods, 68 percent; milieu therapy, 70 percent (probation, 67 percent).

Compared to probation, these approaches had an even higher percentage of top quality ratings (Lipton et al. had given an overall quality rating of A or B to each individual study: A = highest quality, B = acceptable quality; see Appendix A for details.) Thus, the following may be seen in table 3-3: (*A quality rating*) casework and individual counseling, 71 percent of all studies; individual psychotherapy, 67 percent; group methods, 37 percent; milieu therapy, 75 percent (probation, 28 percent). (If the five Warren study entries are treated as a single investigation, the figures for probation would be 57 percent for pure experimental design and 36 percent for A quality ratings.)

Table 3-2
Type of Research Design Used for Studies in Eleven Treatment Categories

| Treatment Category | No. of Studies[a] | Research Design | | | |
| | | Pure Experimental | | Ex Post Facto and Simulation | |
		No. of Studies	Percent of Studies	No. of Studies	Percent of Studies
Probation	18	12	67	6	33
Imprisonment	19	5	26	14	74
Parole	18	9	50	9	50
Casework and individual counseling	7	6	86	1	14
Skill development	15	3	20	12	80
Individual psychotherapy	12	9	75	3	25
Group methods	19	13	68	6	32
Milieu therapy	20	14	70	6	30
Partial physical custody	4	3	75	1	25
Medical methods	5	1	20	4	80
Leisure time activities	1	0	0	1	100
Total	138	75	54	63	46

[a]Includes all recidivism studies listed in *Correctional Effectiveness* within each treatment category.

Table 3-3
Quality Rating Given to Studies in Eleven Treatment Categories

Treatment Category	No. of Studies[a]	A Quality		B Quality	
		No. of Studies	Percent of Studies	No. of Studies	Percent of Studies
Probation	18	5	28	13	72
Imprisonment	19	7	37	12	63
Parole	18	5	28	13	72
Casework and individual counseling	7	5	71	2	29
Skill development	15	5	33	10	67
Individual psychotherapy	12	8	67	4	33
Group methods	19	7	37	12	63
Milieu therapy	20	15	75	5	25
Partial physical custody	4	2	50	2	50
Medical methods	5	4	80	1	20
Leisure time activities	1	0	0	1	100
Total	138	63	46	75	54

[a]Includes all recidivism studies listed in *Correctional Effectiveness* within each treatment category.

In addition, as seen in table 3-4, of all 11 treatment approaches that appeared in *Correctional Effectiveness,* 9 contained a higher percentage of individual studies in which a pure experimental design was *combined* with an overall rating of A, i.e., a higher percentage than probation.

Finally, the existence of quality research in categories and subcategories other than that of probation had been specifically acknowledged by Lipton et al. For example:

> Most of the research concerning the relationship of milieu therapy to recidivism is of high quality. [In the case of individual psychotherapy with institutionalized youths,] the studies used generally sound methodology and report results that are interpretable and stand up under analysis. [27]

Thus, Martinson's research quality explanation does not correspond to the facts. This clear discrepancy between explanation and actual findings is independent of the added fact that, in "What Works," Martinson had carefully described *all* research studies, regardless of treatment category, as being of satisfactory quality and by no means weak.[10]

Table 3-4

Combined Research Design and Quality Rating for Studies in Eleven Treatment Categories

| Treatment Category | No. of Studies[a] | Combination of Design and Rating | | | |
| | | Pure Experimental and A Quality | | All Other Design and Quality Combinations | |
		No. of Studies	Percent of Studies	No. of Studies	Percent of Studies
Probation	18	2	11	16	89
Imprisonment	19	4	21	15	79
Parole	18	3	17	15	83
Casework and individual counseling	7	4	57	3	43
Skill development	15	2	13	13	87
Individual psychotherapy	12	6	50	6	50
Group methods	19	6	32	13	68
Milieu therapy	20	12	60	8	40
Partial physical custody	4	2	50	2	50
Medical methods	5	1	20	4	80
Leisure time activities	1	0	0	1	100
Total	138	42	30	96	70

[a]Includes all recidivism studies listed in *Correctional Effectiveness* within each treatment category.

> We then picked from the [review of] literature all those studies whose findings were interpretable—that is, whose design and execution met the conventional standards of social science research. Our criteria were rigorous.... We excluded studies only for methodological reasons: ... [e.g.,] their results were confounded by extraneous factors, they used unreliable methods.... [31]

All studies had to satisfy at least 9 of 11 specific criteria. On this basis, 231 studies were finally included, whereas some 600 were excluded. Satisfaction of these requirements was also reflected in the fact that studies which involved a pure experimental design were not automatically regarded as being of higher quality than those which involved ex post facto or simulation designs (see n. 10).

In attempting to explain the negative conclusion he had drawn regarding almost all categories of treatment, Martinson, in "Crossroads," supplemented his research quality approach with that of differential weighting: "It is essential to *weigh* the evidence and not merely count the findings as if the studies were peanuts in a sack" [30].

According to this approach, it made little difference if 48 percent or, conceivably, 70 percent of all studies happened to show positive results. What counted, rather than mere positive (or negative) results, was the technical adequacy of each individual study, plus the fact that each study had to be weighted in terms of its overall adequacy. Differential weighting thus made it possible for one especially high quality study, which, say, had produced negative results, to outweigh and thereby cancel out the contribution of several scientifically *acceptable* studies, each of which had produced positive results.

In "Crossroads," Martinson illustrated his differential weighting concept as follows:

> [The treatment category known as group methods] included six weak *ex post facto* studies by Harrison and Mueller and one massive experimental study by Kassebaum, Ward, and Wilner. [Of the former studies, 5 showed modest to sizable reductions in recidivism; in the latter, no reduction was observed.] ... We concluded that group methods are not effective in improving recidivism. [30]

Even if one accepted the differential weighting concept in principle, this approach would hardly have justified such a blanket conclusion with regard to group methods as a whole—certainly not if Martinson had made it a point to round out the picture by adding such information as (1) there were 11 additional studies within the category of group methods; (2) all 11 involved pure experimental as opposed to "weak" designs; (3) of these 11, 6 received a quality rating of A, and at least 5 were associated with a reduction in recidivism. These considerations are independent of the fact that the six Harrison and Mueller studies were as massive as the Kassebaum, Ward, and Wilner study. Collectively, the former involved 4928 subjects (an average of 821 per study); the latter involved 968 subjects. (Martinson did not relate sample size to weighting in "What Works." The role of sample size in *Correctional Effectiveness* is reviewed in Appendix A.)

Quite aside from the blanket conclusion that was present in Martinson's example, several questions can be asked about the differential weighting approach. Most of these questions revolve around a basic issue: how and where do lines get drawn when weighting one scientifically acceptable study over another? For instance, would it indeed make sense for the findings from one unusually high quality study, which, say, yielded negative results, to somehow force us to partially or perhaps completely discount scientific leads that were obtained from two, four, or possibly even six scientifically acceptable studies? Should results from only the former study be regarded as truth? This question would be especially crucial if the former study, and one or more of the latter, involved rather different client populations, different amounts of treatment input, and so on. This situation was in fact quite common among the studies reviewed in "What Works," relative to any one treatment category.

In short, should results from only the former study—one which, regardless of its unusual research quality, focused on particular treatment inputs and involved specific operating conditions—be given more weight, in terms of generalizing about the treatment category as a whole, than several acceptable studies which, collectively, may have covered a wider range of treatment inputs and operating conditions? This question, which focuses on the issue of generalizability (and precisely what is being generalized to what), is relevant even apart from the widely accepted view that one's confidence in research findings is legitimately enhanced when scientifically acceptable studies have been replicated. The importance of scientific replication does not negate that of unusually impressive individual studies. However, the latter value can hardly substitute for the former, even apart from the question of generalizing from one type of investigation (or program) to a treatment category as a whole.

At any rate, neither "What Works" nor *Correctional Effectiveness* contained any weighting formulas or guidelines—specific or otherwise—that bore on the question of how and where to draw such lines.

Despite this, in "Crossroads" Martinson clearly implied that he had relied heavily on the differential weighting approach in his earlier description and evaluation of each category and subcategory of treatment. However, a review of "What Works" indicates that he did not make use of this approach. In fact, in "What Works" he did not refer to it at all.[11] Instead, he presented each study as if it carried essentially the same weight as every other study, within any given category. This equal weighting approach was itself consistent with the fact that every individual study had satisfied the earlier-mentioned, rigorous criteria of scientific validity, criteria which he did regard as very important in legitimizing the studies that were reviewed.

The importance of these criteria was also reflected in the fact that Martinson felt justified in drawing his conclusions about the ineffectiveness of almost all treatment approaches, and rehabilitation as a whole, despite the variations in quality and strength that existed from one study to the next. Of all studies reviewed in "What Works," no less than 52 percent were of B quality (the remaining 48 percent were of A quality). Similarly, no fewer than 42 percent involved ex post facto plus simulation designs (the remaining 58 percent were pure experimental). Finally, no more than 33 percent were of A quality and pure experimental design combined. Apparently, when it came to drawing overall conclusions, other factors or considerations were seen as negating and otherwise compensating for this absence of top quality and maximum strength.[12]

Rather than give differential weight to each study, Martinson placed very heavy emphasis on the factor of interstudy contradictions, i.e., the copresence of positive and negative results, from one study to the next within any one category of treatment. To illustrate the widespread use that was made of this approach, several examples will be given:

[1. In the area of educational and vocational training for] adult inmates as opposed to young ones, the results are [even more] discouraging. There have been six studies of this type; three of them report that their programs . . . produced no significant difference in recidivism rates, and one . . . is almost impossible to interpret because of the risk differentials of the prisoners [who participated]. . . . Two studies . . . *do* report a positive difference from skill development programs. . . . [Despite] the difficulty of interpreting [these studies] *as a whole,* . . . we can be reasonably sure that, so far, educational and vocational programs have not worked. We don't know why they have *failed.* . . . What we do know is that, to date, educational and skill development have not reduced recidivism by rehabilitating criminals.

[2. In the area of (a) individual psychotherapy and (b) individual counseling as well as casework, all within institutional settings,] it's hard to find any more grounds for enthusiasm than we found with skill development and education. . . . [In terms of] individual psychotherapy, we found seven such reported studies. [Three studies found such treatment to be unrelated, or negatively related, to parole success. However,] there were two studies at variance with this pattern [i.e., two studies that showed positive results.[13] . . .In terms of individual counseling and casework, one study seemed] to suggest a favorable outlook for these . . . forms of . . . therapy. [Similar results were found with another study.] But other studies of such therapy have produced ambiguous results. [One study] produced an improvement among some short-term male offenders. . . . On the other hand, [a second study] reported generally non-significant results. . . . One might suspect that the preceding reports reveal not the inadequacy of counseling [i.e., therapy] as a whole but only the *failure* of one type, [namely,] . . . *the individual type.*

[3. In terms of] decarcerating the convict, . . . when one takes the programs that have been administered in institutions and applies them in a non-institutional setting, the results do not grow to encouraging proportions. With *casework and individual counseling in the community,* for instance, there have been three studies. . . . Two of them report that the community-counseled offenders did no better than their institutional controls, while the third notes that although community counseling produced fewer arrests per person, it did not ultimately reduce the offender's chance of returning to a reformatory. . . . [Relative to] *milieu therapy programs* conducted with youthful male probationers not in actual physical custody, [one program] . . . did find that both the Provo boys and those on regular probation did better than those in regular reformatories—*in contradiction,* it may be recalled, to the finding from . . . [another study], in which the direct releases given no special treatment did worse than boys in regular institutions. The third such study of non-residential milieu therapy . . . found not only that there was no significant improvement, but that the longer a boy participated in the treatment, the worse he was likely to do afterwards.

[4.] With regard to more professional group *psychotherapy* [administered in institutions], the reports are also conflicting. . . . One [study of young males] says that this treatment did in fact reduce recidivism. . . . On the other hand, a study by Craft [showed opposite effects]. . . . With regard to young females, the results are just as equivocal. [One study] found that there was no improvement. . . . But [another] study does offer one real, positive finding. . . . As with the question of skill development, it is hard to summarize these results. . . . Such findings . . . are hardly encouraging for a policy planner, who must adopt measures that are generally applicable. . . .

[5.] And with *group* therapy administered in the community, we find yet another set of equivocal results. The results from studies of pragmatic group counseling are . . . mildly optimistic. . . . On the other hand, [other studies show no difference, or negative results].

[6. As to milieu therapy within an institution,] the results of the study of youth are more equivocal. [For example, one study found that milieu therapy] had no significant effect on recidivism; another study . . . found that such a program *did* have a positive effect. . . . In the case of male youths, as opposed to male juveniles, the findings are just as equivocal, and hardly more encouraging. One such study . . . did not produce significant results. . . . [However, another study] shows a partially positive finding. . . .

[7.] The results are similarly ambiguous when one applies . . . intensive supervision to adult offenders.

[8.] The same problems of mixed results . . . have plagued attempts to study the effects of sentence length. [31, emphasis added]

Even if Martinson had used a differential weighting approach in "What Works," the conclusion which he drew would have been plausible only under such conditions as the following: a large majority (75 percent) of all positive findings were produced by investigations which, for whatever reason, happened to be weak, or only barely acceptable, from a scientific point of view. At the same time, an equally large percent of all negative findings would have to have been produced by investigations that happened to be of high quality.

However, positive and negative outcomes were produced by investigations whose average level of quality did not differ by a large amount and did not approach the levels that were required. As seen in table 3-5, of all recidivism studies which showed positive results, 49 percent involved pure experimental designs and 42 percent had a quality rating of A. (Conversely, 51 percent of all studies involved ex post facto plus simulation designs and 58 percent had a rating of B.) Of all studies which showed negative results, 58 percent involved pure experimental designs and 56 percent had a rating of A.

Thus the preceding conditions were not satisfied, or even approximated. As a result, the differential weighting approach—whatever its theoretical value and limits may be—could not justify Martinson's conclusion regarding the ineffectiveness of treatment. This applied not only to his generalized statement regarding almost all categories combined, but to the following individual categories in particular: probation, parole, casework and individual counseling, individual psychotherapy, and milieu therapy. Within these categories, the scientific quality of all studies that produced positive results was almost the same as (or else higher than) that of studies which produced negative results.

Table 3-5
Research Design and Quality Rating of Positive and Negative Outcome Studies in Eleven Treatment Categories

Treatment Category	Design and Rating of Positive Outcome Studies[a]					Design and Rating of Negative Outcome Studies[b]				
	No. of Studies[c]	Pure Experimental		A Quality		No. of Studies[c]	Pure Experimental		A Quality	
		No. of Studies	Percent of Studies	No. of Studies	Percent of Studies		No. of Studies	Percent of Studies	No. of Studies	Percent of Studies
Probation	7	4	57	4	57	7	4	57	1	14
Imprisonment	10	2	20	3	30	6	1	17	3	50
Parole	12	6	50	3	25	5	3	60	1	20
Casework and individual counseling	4	4	100	2	50	2	1	50	2	100
Skill development	7	2	29	2	29	5	1	20	3	60
Individual psychotherapy	5	4	80	4	80	4	3	75	4	100
Group methods	8	4	50	2	25	8	6	75	4	50
Milieu therapy	8	5	63	5	63	9	7	78	7	78
Partial physical custody	1	0	0	0	0	3	3	100	2	67
Medical methods	2	1	50	2	100	1	0	0	1	100
Leisure time activities	1	0	0	0	0	0	0	–	0	–
Total	65	32	49	27	42	50	29	58	28	56

[a]Positive outcome = reduction in recidivism.
[b]Negative outcome = no reduction in recidivism, i.e., nonpositive findings.
[c]See notes c, d and e of Table 3-1. These notes apply to the present table as well.

One last point in this connection. It follows from Martinson's emphasis on quality and design that studies which were classified as pure experimental and given an A rating were those whose findings could be relied on with the highest confidence—they represented the best possible, certainly the best available, investigations. In *Correctional Effectiveness* there were 42 such recidivism studies or entries among the 11 treatment categories combined. We analyzed 38 of these studies relative to the following question:[14] what percent of the pure experimental, A quality investigations yielded positive findings?[15] As seen in table 3-6, the result was 47 percent, a figure almost identical to that obtained in connection with 82 studies described in "What Works."[16] The latter figure—48

Table 3-6
Type of Outcome Obtained for Pure Experimental, A Quality Studies

Treatment Category	No. of Studies[c]	Outcome			
		Positive[a]		Negative[b]	
		No. of Studies	Percent of Studies[d]	No. of Studies	Percent of Studies[d]
Probation	2	1	50	1	50
Imprisonment	3	2	67	1	33
Parole	3	3	100	0	0
Casework and individual counseling	3	2	67	1	33
Skill development	2	1	50	1	50
Individual psychotherapy	6	3	50	3	50
Group methods	6	2	33	4	67
Milieu therapy	10	3	30	7	70
Partial physical custody	2	0	0	2	100
Medical methods	1	1	100	0	0
Leisure time activities	0	0	—	0	—
Total	38	18	47	20	53

[a]Reduction in recidivism.

[b]No reduction in recidivism, i.e., nonpositive.

[c]No one study (finding) is represented in more than one treatment category; i.e., all repeat entries ($N = 1$) are excluded. Three studies are excluded because information was insufficient or too ambiguous to allow for classification of study as either positive or negative (non-positive).

[d]The percentages reported for 10 of the 11 treatment categories cannot be considered reliable or even moderately reliable, given the small number of studies involved in these categories. The percentages for all categories combined *can* be considered reliable.

percent—related to all combinations of research design and level of quality taken together.[17] Thus, whether one focuses on top investigations only or on the full range of scientifically acceptable investigations, more than 45 percent of all recidivism studies are found to yield positive results (see table 3-6).

The "pitiful outcome" that was described in "Crossroads" contained one other important ingredient.

> In "What Works" I was very careful to say that no existing mode of "correctional treatment" has any "appreciable" effect on recidivism rates. I used the term "appreciable" to convey . . . some idea of the range of percentage differences typically found in correctional research. . . . [Even if] research were to uncover an "intervention" which "significantly reduced" recidivism, the public would want to know by how much. Five percentage points? Ten? Fifteen? Or, as Ramsey Clark promised the nation, would it be a 50 per cent reduction? . . . [In sum,] the *addition* of isolated treatment elements to a system (probation, imprisonment, parole) in which a given flow of offenders has generated a gross rate of recidivism has very little effect (and, in most cases, no effect) in making this rate of recidivism better or worse. [30]

In short, this additional ingredient was Martinson's clear suggestion that rehabilitation programs—even those which show positive or statistically significant results—can usually be expected to produce no more than a trivial drop in recidivism. The question that related to Clark's figure was rhetorical only; it was used to emphasize the main point by way of contrast.

Before we present data that bear on this suggestion, it should be noted that whether "percentage differences," "percentage points," or "per cent reductions" were involved, Martinson was emphasizing the same basic idea, that of a very small and inconsequential drop in recidivism. However, as seen in the preceding quote, he began by speaking of percentage differences and went on to present figures that related to percentage points. (*Percentage differences* not *percentage points,* is synonymous with *percent reductions*.) Since this shift has important practical consequences, it is essential that we distinguish between the two.

A reduction in recidivism from 40 to 20 percent represents a percentage difference of 50 percent, even though it involves a percentage drop of 20 points. When most people, statisticians included, think of a 50 percent drop, e.g., a 50 percent reduction in recidivism, what they have in mind is a percentage difference, not a percentage point drop. This is not without good reason. Specifically, it is the percentage difference which must be used in order to compute the *number of offenses* that may be avoided by means of a given treatment program. Thus, a 50 percent drop would mean that half as many offenses would be committed by, say, an experimental group than a control group. (Similarly, percentage difference would be used to compute the number of *offenders* who would not recidivate during a given followup period, as a result of the program.) Martinson did not make this distinction between percentage differences and percentage points in the preceding quote. Thus, a 15 or even 20 percentage point drop is not necessarily trivial. We are now in a position to focus more clearly on his view regarding the extent of reduction in recidivism.

Martinson's position, as expressed in the preceding quote, is not consistent with the facts that are presented in *Correctional Effectiveness.* If one looks at all 48 recidivism studies which showed positive results and which included a behavioral measure of recidivism (e.g., police arrests or incarceration due to a new arrest)—not simply a policy-based measure such as revocation or discharge—the average reduction in recidivism turns out to be 32 percent.[18] This is well above the rate suggested by Martinson.[19] (Probation programs that met the preceding criteria were average in this regard. Their mean reduction was 31 percent.)[20]

By most people's standards, a 32 percent reduction is far from unimportant, however much it leaves to be desired. It means, for instance, that instead of 100 offenses taking place, approximately 68 (100 − 32) could be expected to occur. Similarly, 680 offenses could be expected to occur, rather than a hypothetical 1000. The latter reduction would indeed be significant, or appreciable. This is independent of the fact that, other things being equal, rehabilitation programs which show even a 10 to 15 percent reduction in recidivism would probably be chosen, by most administrators, over those which show no reduction at all.

Three points might be mentioned before concluding this chapter. First, 1000 is 47 percent *greater than* 680; however, the latter number represents a 32 percent *reduction* from the base of 1000. Second, as suggested earlier, the preceding concepts can apply to offenders as well as offenses. Thus, 680 offenders could be expected to recidivate during a given followup period, rather than a hypothetical 1000 offenders. Third, at an estimated $400 per arrest, the cost of 320 police arrests would be $128,000.[21] Projected on a statewide or national scale, this too would be far from insignificant. The $400 figure excludes what Glaser calls "subsequent social costs in monetary terms"—costs associated with "damage done by known and inferred offenses," "court or parole violation hearings," and "production foregone . . . for time locked up or unemployed"[22] [17].

In sum, the factors of research quality, differential weighting, and insignificant change in recidivism did not justify the bleak picture that was painted regarding almost every method of treatment, and regarding rehabilitative efforts as a whole. (As suggested in the preceding pages, Martinson focused on differing factors at different points in time relative to his overall conclusion regarding rehabilitation. See Appendix B for a review of further difficulties (inaccuracies, for instance) that appear in "Crossroads.")

4

Global Portrayal and the Basis of "What Works"

For this discussion, the reader might note the following points regarding subcategories. *Subcategories* are groups of studies that were found in each of the treatment categories discussed thus far. In *Correctional Effectiveness,* most subcategories consisted of four to seven individual studies each. They involved variable combinations such as "younger males in the community," "adult males in the community," younger institutionalized males and females, or "institution- alized male adults." Other subcategories and supplementary analyses focused on such variables and factors as caseload size, quality of supervision, type of offender, and therapeutic emphasis (e.g., pragmatic versus analytic). Their level of abstraction therefore fell between that of individual studies and overall treatment categories, i.e., total categories [27].

The Price of Global Portrayal

To some extent, the picture that Martinson painted regarding treatment was a direct expression of his total category approach, i.e., his assessment of each treatment method not only as a single, undifferentiated entity, but in relation to the offender population as a whole, irrespective of treatment setting. Given this emphasis on global portrayal and generalized evaluation, Martinson was, indeed, logically consistent to have excluded from his summary statements regarding individual treatment categories almost all reference to the promising leads that were observed at the level of major subcategories and supplementary analyses.

Yet, logical or formal appropriateness notwithstanding, the price of these omissions was quite high in terms of information that was not communicated. For instance, the following are subcategory leads as reported in *Correctional Effectiveness,* leads that were not reflected in the blanket conclusions and overall picture presented by Martinson:

1. *Probation.* "Caseloads of 15 are associated with lower rates of recidivism for boys and girls under 18 at a cost usually no greater than that of standard probation."
2. *Parole.* "With juvenile and youthful offenders, adequacy of supervision (independent of the effect of case load size reduction) is strongly related to parole success."
3. *Individual psychotherapy.* "In summary, individual psychotherapy is effec-

tive with [institutionalized young male offenders] when it has a pragmatic orientation and is enthusiastically administered by interested and concerned therapists to older (16-20) amenable offenders."

4. *Casework and individual counseling.* "In general, the evidence indicates that casework providing concrete guidance and help or advice in problems of daily living within the community is more beneficial than casework not oriented in this way (for example, psychodynamically oriented casework)."

5. *Group methods.* "... Six [large scale] studies by Harrison and Mueller indicate, therefore, that group counseling conducted in an adult institution for more than one year with a single leader is more effective than such counseling led by more than one leader. It is also more effective than no treatment at all ... provided that the institution does not emphasize security or the program does not become routinized." Also "when 'community living' became a regular part of the treatment program, ... men receiving this combination-type program were more successful than men who received either the unstable or stable form of group counseling alone."

6. *Milieu therapy.* "In conclusion, these studies indicate that milieu therapy is most effective with youths from 16 to 18 years of age. While *residential* milieu therapy does not seem to increase or decrease recidivism, it has the major advantage of reducing the time youths would have spent in institutions by roughly 5 to 10 months with no measurable increase in harm to the community." Also, "one may reasonably conclude that psychiatrically oriented milieu therapy is probably associated with a reduction in the recidivism rates of disturbed juvenile females whereas routine incarceration in juvenile hall is not."

7. *Skill development.* "There is evidence that vocationally oriented training programs for youthful offenders (over 16) both in institutions and in the community are associated with lower rates of recidivism than standard institutional care or standard parole. These programs appear to be most successful when they provide the offender with a readily marketable skill."

8. *Imprisonment.* "For older offenders ... less restrictive custody and shorter periods of care may be more effective with respect to prevention of recidivism than strict institutional security for longer periods" [27].

Taken together, these and other leads provide something very different from a bleak and constricted picture. Their implications for program planners, practitioners, and administrators are numerous. However, in Martinson's approach they are, in substance, submerged by the generalized evaluations that were made of treatment categories as a whole. As a result, they played essentially no role in his portrayal of corrections.

In sum, Martinson's approach did not bridge the gap between individual studies and subcategories, on the one hand, and total categories on the other. Instead, he shifted from the former to the latter level of analysis; i.e., he switched directly from one frame of reference to the other, in ways that led to contradictory assertions. This was evident in his evaluation of group counseling.

> These programs *seem to work best* when they are new, when their subjects are amenable to treatment in the first place, and when the counselors are not only trained people but "good" people as well. . . . But maybe the reason these counseling programs *don't seem to work* is not that they are ineffective per se, but that the institutional environment outside the program is unwholesome enough to undo any good that the counseling does. [Martinson then rejects this hypothesis.] [31, emphasis added]

In the original text, these inconsistent statements were separated by one sentence and a section heading. The first statement referred to individual studies and to related subcategories. However, the second statement referred to group counseling as a whole. The latter type of statements—total category assessments, in particular ("counseling programs don't seem to work")—*are* reflected in Martinson's basic portrayal of corrections. The former are not. Instead of being subsumed under the total category statement and then integrated (within the totality) in a substantive way, the former statements are, in effect, abstracted out of existence. That is, they are largely eliminated from further consideration. (See n. 1 for related observations).

The Analytic Basis of Martinson's Views

Martinson's portrayal of corrections was a product not only of his total category analysis, but of his independent category approach. Here, each treatment category was evaluated separate from and independent of every other category. For instance, individual psychotherapy was handled entirely separate from casework and individual counseling, from group methods, and from milieu therapy. The latter, in turn, were also evaluated separately from one another.

This approach, which was used earlier in *Correctional Effectiveness,* made sense when evaluating each category as an independent entity. However, in carrying out this evaluation, Martinson utilized each *individual study* on a single category basis alone. That is, he first placed each recidivism study into one of the 11 treatment categories (modalities) under consideration, and he then used the findings, from each such study, in relation to that particular treatment modality alone. (A few studies were placed into more than one category.) Under these conditions, the impact that could be made by any given study on correctional knowledge and practice had to be made in terms of, and through the vehicle of, that specific modality alone. This led to the following situation.

Since each treatment category was assessed independent of every other category, and since each individual study was handled as if it belonged within one treatment category alone, the positive leads that were observed within any one treatment category (for example, milieu therapy) rarely got linked with (in other words, conceptually integrated with) leads that were observed within other categories (for example, group counseling or probation). In this respect, the contribution of each study rarely got extended beyond the confines of the category into which it had originally been placed.

More specifically, studies that contained certain factors in common with one another, but which fell within different categories of treatment from one another, rarely were looked on as having any contribution to make in terms of the factors or positive leads which they shared in common. These factors or leads often related to specific offender characteristics, worker characteristics, offender times treatment-setting combinations, etc. As a result, it was virtually impossible for such studies to make a direct, independent contribution to the assessment of rehabilitation as a whole. Unlike the previously mentioned evaluation, which focused on each treatment category as an independent entity, the latter level of assessment called for an across-categories (not a within-category) approach.[2]

The upshot was that if a particular treatment category, such as milieu therapy, was eventually judged to have "no appreciable effect on recidivism," then any individual study which fell within that category would receive little if any further consideration, at least in the following sense: it would not be called upon to make a possible across-categories contribution. Instead, it would be set aside or handled as if it had nothing more to offer correctional knowledge and practice beyond what it had contributed as a study of milieu therapy. (It might also have been set aside if the treatment category to which it "belonged" was eventually judged to have an appreciable impact on recidivism.) The fact that it may have had certain features in common with other studies, e.g., positive studies of group counseling, would not alter its status in this regard.

Thus, as a direct though not inevitable spinoff of the independent category/single category approach—one that was used to focus on individual treatment modalities as such—Martinson ended up giving very little emphasis to the factors or patterns that were observed *across* differing categories of treatment.

In terms of theory, Martinson seemed to recognize that rehabilitation is a comprehensive, multileveled expression of numerous inputs and expectations, and that these included not broad categories of treatment alone, but relatively specific factors as well. Yet, at the operating level, he largely identified rehabilitation with the set of eleven categories as such. In his analytic and evaluative efforts, he basically approached it as though it were an aggregate or simple sum of these generalized treatment categories alone.[3] In short, he did not actually deal with rehabilitation as though it were an expression of numerous interacting factors—for example, those mentioned above—few of which could be considered unique to any one category.

Martinson's approach involved no major units of analysis other than the eleven treatment categories. Since all but one of these categories appeared to have little "reach" or power in terms of reducing recidivism, and since they were seen, collectively, as being reasonably exhaustive, it seemed to follow that (1) almost no known methods of treatment had any positive influence on recidivism, and (2) there were probably no untapped methods or factors (i.e., no remaining sources of power) that could substantially improve the situation.[4] This, in turn, meant that rehabilitation was itself a relatively powerless tool, since it, in effect, was identified with the eleven categories alone.

Yet, if Martinson's analysis had been organized to deal with factors that cut across a number of these categories, recidivism rates might have seemed more reachable than they did. That is, if a somewhat different conceptual and structural framework had been used to integrate results that were obtained across all individual studies, it would have been easier to separate out, and then focus on, specific conditions (e.g., offender, worker, and treatment-setting characteristics) that were directly related to recidivism.[5] The resulting perspective could have made treatment seem other than weak or ineffective.[6] However, since no such perspective was developed, it was easy for treatment, and therefore rehabilitation as a whole, to sustain an appearance of generalized or, in a sense, unconditional "impotence" [30].

In short, a differently structured analysis, or supplementary analyses, might have provided a basis for reconceptualizing many of the interstudy differences that were difficult for Martinson to integrate, especially within an independent category/single category framework. This problem was reflected in references that he made in "What Works" to the difficult task of summarizing and interpreting the often differing studies and results that were observed within given categories of treatment.

Ways of dealing with the difficulties that have been reviewed are presented in chapters 13 and 14.

A Closing Note

In "Crossroads," Martinson suggested that Palmer's critique of "What Works" was largely based on the latter's misinterpretation of the word *efforts*. More specifically, he suggested that it was based on an erroneous equating of the term *efforts* with *studies*, i.e., individual research studies. According to Martinson, *efforts* should have been taken to mean "independent variable categories"— methods of treatment—milieu therapy or group counseling, for example. (Each treatment method was defined by Martinson as a composite of individual studies.) In addition, he also suggested and implied (1) that given this (presumed) misinterpretation, Palmer did not focus on the central item, independent variable categories,[7] and on the crucial finding, the (supposed) failure of the categories in question; (2) that Palmer limited himself to a review and indiscriminate compilation of individual research studies, instead. In Martinson's view, these (presumed) facts invalidated the critique itself.

Details of this spurious and somewhat confusing issue—largely one of terminology versus concepts—are presented in Appendix C. As will be seen, Martinson's suggestions did not hold up.

5

Offender Classifications and Treatment Modalities

Offender Types: Myth or Practical Reality?

In his assessment of treatment and rehabilitation, Martinson did not follow up on leads relating to a number of major factors. Instead, he increasingly dropped these items from serious consideration. For instance, in "Crossroads," he took the position that offender typologies and classifications are of no practical significance. He also suggested that they correspond to reality no better than classic figments of the imagination.

> Are there really "types" of offenders in any useful sense of this word? In the Christian Middle Ages energy was expended in determining how many angels could dance on the head of a pin. Some bumpkin of that day asked: "But are there angels?" Of course, you can construct as many "types" as you like. . . . You can generate an alphabet soup of maturity-level classifications with scientific-sounding titles. . . . [This, however, only leads to a] search for that demi-semi-demi "type" of offender for which this impotent treatment [all forms of which, collectively, have so pitiful an outcome] is least impotent. [30]

This assessment bears little resemblance to the major summaries and conclusions that appeared in *Correctional Effectiveness,* the source document itself. There, offender types were associated with reduced rates of recidivism in at least four of the eight major treatment categories that were reviewed:[1]

1. *Parole.* "With juvenile and youthful offenders . . . when the type of parole treatment program and supervision is matched to the type of offender, parole success rates are enhanced."
2. *Casework and individual counseling in institutional settings.* "The findings accumulated in this survey indicate that such treatment has different effects on different age groupings and on different offender types; [and, within *community settings,*] if casework is specifically designed for different types of offenders, based on knowledge of deviant subcultures, it is more likely to be successful."
3. *Individual psychotherapy.* "First, studies . . . that fail to take amenability into consideration are more likely to result in findings of no difference since the success of the amenables is likely to be masked by the failure of the nonamenables. Second, since nonamenable subjects are more likely to do

worse than to improve, it is less expensive in personnel and time to concentrate efforts upon amenables alone."

4. *Skill development.* "There is evidence that among both youths and adults, different types of offenders respond differentially to both vocational and educational programs" [27].

(It might be added that the "Crossroads" assessment of typologies did not reflect Martinson's review of one additional category: imprisonment. For example, in "What Works," he stated that, "the effect of sentence length seems to vary widely according to type of offender" [31].) Individually and collectively, these findings were seen in *Correctional Effectiveness* as having a good deal of practical significance; and, some of the methods in question were considered far from impotent.

Classification in a Community Treatment Program

The relevance and predictive validity of certain offender classifications was illustrated in California's Community Treatment Project (CTP), an intensive parole program for adolescent multiple offenders in lieu of institutionalization. Among "conflicted" males, experimentals (E's), namely, CTP youths, were found to have conspicuously fewer law enforcement arrests, per month in the community, than their randomly assigned controls (C's) (see table 5-1).[2] This referred not only to moderate and severe offenses combined,[3] but to violent offenses in particular, e.g., robbery, forcible rape, assault with a deadly weapon, and murder. (Violent offenses were part of the broader category of "severe" offenses, e.g., burglary (first degree) and sale of narcotics. "Moderate" offenses included petty theft, auto theft, possession of a concealed weapon, etc. [41].) It involved not only the period of Youth Authority (YA) jurisdiction (3 year

Table 5-1
Monthly Rates of Arrest for Community Treatment Project Males

Type of Offender	Group	Followup			
		Youth Authority Career		4-Year Postdischarge	
		Moderate and Severe Offenses	Violent Offenses	Moderate and Severe Offenses	Violent Offenses
Conflicted	Experimental	0.034	0.006	0.032	0.005
	Control	0.080	0.013	0.058	0.008
Power Oriented	Experimental	0.055	0.012	0.068	0.013
	Control	0.066	0.016	0.043	0.008

average), but a 4-year postdischarge followup. With few exceptions, these findings also held up relative to court convictions.[4] Yet when it came to "power oriented" males, most E/C rates of arrest and conviction were no longer significantly different; and in some cases, their direction was sharply reversed. (A third group of youths, passive conformists, is omitted in the interests of space [42].)

These and other differential outcomes applied not only to the E versus C comparisons, but to E versus E analyses as well, e.g., conflicted E's versus power oriented E's. They related to *behavior* during and subsequent to the individual's Youth Authority involvement, *not* to rates of parole revocation or YA discharge alone. As a result, they could not be accounted for in terms of "system effects" or policy-based, discretionary decision making on the part of agency personnel.

Thus, this group of Youth Authority wards (E's and C's combined) systematically differed from one another relative to socially unacceptable and interpersonally violent behavior, after they were placed on parole. Had they not been sorted out with respect to "conflicted" or "power oriented" characteristics, these differences might easily have escaped notice, particularly in light of the previously mentioned masking effect [38].

The present findings applied not to a diminutive set of youths, but to a large portion of the 1961-1969 sample: Conflicted youths represented 53 percent of all eligible males;[5] power oriented individuals accounted for 21 percent.[6] Passive conformists comprised an additional 14 percent.[7] Similar if not identical offender types and similar percentages of representation for each type would probably have been found in many of the populations reviewed in *Correctional Effectiveness*.[8]

Thus, CTP findings involved a substantially reduced recidivism rate for more than 50 percent of the sample, and strikingly different outcomes for differing groups of youth. They were by no means the inconsequential products, or end results of futile endeavors, that were envisioned by Martinson with respect to classification research.

> To continue the search for treatment that will reduce the recidivism rate . . . or that will show differential effects [e.g., for the middle base expectancy group] is to become trapped in a dead end. [30]

This also applied to the positive findings that were reported in *Correctional Effectiveness* relative to various typologies. (It might be noted that these and other findings related to programs which were considerably less complex than CTP with respect to the number of treatment components that were used. In addition, most such programs were less intensive in terms of the number of contacts or sessions per month, the total duration of treatment, etc. The approaches used at CTP are outlined in Appendix D.)

Classification and Offense Specialization

A final point concerning Martinson's position relative to offender classifications. In "Crossroads," Martinson took the position that all classification systems or typologies should be judged, principally if not exclusively, on their ability to predict the specific kind of illegal behavior in which offenders are likely to engage. He then implied that offender classifications should be abandoned, since neither they nor any set of independent variables seem able to predict this behavior.

> . . . If there are really "types" of offenders, why did the Wolfgang cohort study find almost no offense specialization? If knowing the last offense committed by a juvenile offender gives you no handle on what he will do next, in what meaningful sense should one persist [in] looking for "types"? [30]

In taking this position, Martinson overlooked a cardinal goal of corrections: the reduction or elimination of future offending. Relative to this goal, a meaningful reason for the existence of any classification system would be the ability of that system to provide information which might contribute to the reduction of illegal behavior. A test which focused on this ability would be very different than the one proposed by Martinson. The latter test would focus on the *way* offenders are likely to offend, i.e., on type of offending alone. In short, typologies can be organized around factors or features other than or in addition to offense specialization.

As seen in *Correctional Effectiveness* and in CTP, specific offender characteristics and classifications do supply information which bears on the above-mentioned goal of corrections. The practical value of this information is in no way diminished by the nonexistence of offense specializations within the offender populations in question.[9] Given this contribution, there would be little if any justification for abandoning offender classifications on grounds that they fail to pass what might be termed the offense-specialization test, or any related test.

Apart from this, it might be noted that many individuals who might be placed within any offense classification (on the basis of their instant arrest) are likely to have accumulated a variety of offenses by the time they are placed on formal probation, or parole. These offenses are not likely to distinguish such individuals from people who fall within a number of other classifications, since the latter individuals are likely to have accumulated a similar assortment of offenses themselves.

Treatment versus Treatments

Given the treatment leads that were noted by Lipton et al. in the areas of casework and individual counseling, skill development, etc., and given the increasingly specific treatment reviews that were provided by CTP during 1967-1971 [39, 40, 45], it would appear that Martinson did not adequately reflect the implications of this information when he referred in "Crossroads" to a presumably

> ... ever more elusive search for a "treatment" which will "reduce the recidivism rate" of that will-o'-the-wisp "middle base expectancy" group or indicate differential effects for that demi-semi-demi maturity-level category. [30]

In effect, Martinson thus predicted that no worthwhile treatment method would, and perhaps could, be found for the two categories of youth in question—categories which he regarded, if taken literally, as unreal, fanciful, or unattainable, and as hybrid or spurious in the first place. (In an earlier-quoted statement (p. 45), he seemed to suggest that a similar "dead end" applied not just to any one modality, but to treatment in general, including, presumably, various combinations of modalities.) Rather than prolong what appeared to be an elusive search, he implied that the case for treatment might just as well be dropped, for these and other categories alike.

In the preceding statement Martinson had focused on the search for *one* treatment modality that would work with youths who fall within the middle base expectancy group or within any one maturity level.[10] Now, evidence certainly suggests that no one modality can reduce recidivism for a high percentage of offenders who comprise these categories. This, however, is partly a reflection of the fact that the base expectancy (BE) and maturity level categories which Martinson singled out are quite broad or heterogeneous, and that individuals who fall within one or both categories represent, collectively, a wide range of personalities and lifestyles. To expect that any one modality will be powerful or flexible enough to deal with the variety of motivations and life circumstances in question does indeed seem unrealistic. This would apply even if one narrowed the range of offenders along such lines as age, sex, IQ, and ethnicity. Very large differences would still be found relative to the specific interests and abilities of these individuals, and the webs of difficulty that surround their lives.

Thus, the inability of any one modality to reduce recidivism for a high percentage of offenders who fall within the categories in question is not a simple function or reflection of the efficacy of particular treatment methods alone. Nor is it a function of the presumed unreal or spurious nature of the categories themselves.

In "Crossroads," Martinson took no position on whether the middle base expectancy and maturity level categories were particularly broad or narrow—assuming they corresponded to reality at all. Nor did he indicate whether the question of category width would be of any significance in the first place, even among categories which might conceivably be considered valid. More specifically, he did not refer to the concept of category width at all, and to the related implications of individual differences among offenders.

These implications will now be reviewed. However, before proceeding, maturity levels should be distinguished from subtypes. As used in CTP, the *maturity levels* referred to the overall degree of self-direction and interpersonal awareness that was attained by given individuals. Subtypes, on the other hand, largely represented specific personality configurations within each level. For example, the higher maturity category—the I_4 level—contained four separate subtypes; the middle maturity category contained three subtypes. Thus, each subtype was much less inclusive and considerably more homogeneous than the level to which it belonged [42, 57].

Now, when dealing with broad offender categories such as middle BE or level of maturity, the task of substantially increasing the percentage of individuals with whom a treatment modality will be effective becomes less than overwhelming only if one first narrows the range of individual differences in question, e.g., personality and lifestyle differences. This can be done, for instance, by subdividing the broad parent group (say, middle BE youths) into smaller, derived groups, e.g., individual subtypes or even subtype groupings. (Conflicted youths are one such grouping; they are a combination of two I_4 subtypes.) The result might be, say, three or four such groups, each of which is built around motivational patterns and personality features that are shared by all individuals within the particular group but which are generally uncharacteristic of those individuals who fall within one or another of the remaining groups. Each derived group, or subtype, would therefore be less heterogeneous than the parent group of middle BE offenders with regard to personality and lifestyle.

Regardless of this strong emphasis on shared characteristics or common features, many important differences would invariably remain *within* each group of offenders. (Apart from this, certain features would also be held in common across any two or more groups.) These differences, while much smaller than in the parent group, would largely center around the concrete needs—for instance, schooling/tutoring or possible out-of-home placement—and personal/social limitations of the individuals in question. Several important differences would also continue to exist in the areas of personality and motivation, again despite the increase in homogeneity just noted.

As a result, even at this more detailed or refined level of classification, exclusive reliance on any single treatment modality for any derived group would continue to be rather limiting. In fact, the specific modality that is used (e.g., individual psychotherapy or skill development) would probably be of minimal relevance to at least some offenders within the derived group, even though it might be of considerable relevance to most. This is apart from the fact that the overall percentage of individuals with whom the modality is likely to be effective will be greater than in the case of the parent group as a whole, since the range of needs, motivations, and life circumstances is likely to be somewhat smaller among the former than among the latter.

Thus, relative to any group of offenders, the search for worthwhile treatment would probably have a greater chance of success if one were to make use of more than a single modality alone, simultaneously or successively. Where feasible, this would involve the use of more than a single pattern as well, i.e., more than one combination of modalities, or differing amounts of emphasis on each modality.

Such an approach would emphasize the integrated utilization of modalities, i.e., treatments. This combined-modalities approach might be one way to achieve that careful fit, and flexibility through time, which could be of relevance to a high percentage of the offenders in question—a flexibility which could make it easier to keep pace with changes that occur within individual offenders and in their environmental situation as well. In any event, the combined-modalities approach would be one way of dealing more directly with the unique combination of motivations, capacities, difficulties, and opportunities that characterizes each offender as an individual.[11] As such, it would be a way of making positive use of scientific classification—a way of using labels not as an end point in one's thinking or a jacket that becomes the chief determiner of an individual's fate, but rather as a starting point, a working hypothesis, and an ongoing guide to planning.

In sum, the strategy of using a combination of modalities rather than one modality alone would apply regardless of the narrowness or breadth of the given offender groups. While this strategy would be of considerable importance in connection with relatively homogeneous groups, it would be of singular importance in relation to those groups or categories which are particularly broad, e.g., the middle base expectancy group. This reflects the wider range of responses that is likely to be provided by the latter individuals to any given stimuli.

In prison settings, a combined-modalities approach could be used within or outside the framework of determinate sentencing. Within community settings it could be applied to "in lieu of institutional" programs, determinate and indeterminate alike. Regardless of setting, it could be of relevance to programs that operate within a framework of voluntary or involuntary participation alike.

Part II
The Role of
Correctional Treatment

6

The Call for Sweeping Reform

In effect, Martinson had asked: What should be done with correctional treatment programs, and with rehabilitation as a whole? (The latter was regarded as a sum total of the former.) In essence, his answer was twofold: (1) sweep them away and forget them; (2) begin this process right now—not only because the programs themselves are useless, if not phony, but because the rehabilitation networks that feed on them are self-serving, increasingly entrenched, and literally helping to increase crime. For example:

[We must recognize] the impotence of treatment to affect the recidivism rate substantially. . . . [Moreover, our] field supervision networks . . . have a stake in recidivism. Business has never been so good in these parts. Agents are hired, "programs" proliferate, new district offices dot the land; the offices become more spacious, the agencies more professional, and the rugs a little deeper each year. . . . I believe [these networks] are now increasing crime. . . . [Let us therefore] leave the "treatment" Philistines to their idle chatter and join in a nationwide campaign to purge our institutions of their "community treatment" bombast. . . . [30]

Martinson's call for sweeping and presumably irrevocable action, beginning as soon as possible, was made despite his suggestion in 1975 that "the next 200 studies" of treatment (those conducted subsequent to the 1945-1967 survey studies) could conceivably "show tremendous success" [51].[1]

In "Crossroads," Martinson related his call for action to three main beliefs and factors regarding programs of rehabilitation. First, scientific studies conducted between 1945-1967 indicated they did not work, i.e., they hardly reduced recidivism. Second, as of 1976, they had not "delivered" on the exaggerated claims that were made regarding their effectiveness, and on hopes that were raised by those claims. Third, they had not alleviated the rising crime rate. These beliefs and factors will be briefly reviewed.

The Almost-Nothing-Works Rationale

As shown in chapters 2 and 3, Martinson's first belief is almost wholly erroneous. To recapitulate, it resulted from his having brushed aside positive findings that were reported in the basic survey by Lipton et al. relative to numerous individual studies. This occurred in relation to each of several categories of treatment, e.g., individual counseling, group counseling, and milieu therapy. Next, at the across-studies level, but still in relation to individual categories of treatment, Martinson overlooked various patterns of findings. Because of his global portrayal of each treatment modality, he automatically eliminated several specific leads as well. Finally, at the across-categories level of analysis, he missed a set of broadly based leads and converging evidence. However, at this third and widest possible level, the omissions in question were also a product of the particular analytic framework he used, namely, the independent category/single category framework. This structure, while valuable in its own right, was intrinsically incapable of tapping the similarities or common factors that existed among studies which, collectively, related to any two or more categories of treatment, but which, individually, had focused on *one* treatment category alone.[2] The upshot was a loss of evidence that would otherwise have converged or overlapped with respect to a variety of treatment categories; in other words, a loss of mutually reinforcing as well as broadly based findings and patterns of findings.[3]

Beyond this, Martinson's appraisal of individual treatment categories (modalities) was almost certain to be negative from the outset. This was a direct result not of the above-mentioned omissions, etc., but of the extremely stringent ground rules he established:[4] to be considered effective, it was necessary for any treatment method (viewed as an undifferentiated entity) to receive almost unanimous support from the research studies that had focused on it. To obtain this support, there had to be a virtual absence of contradictory findings among the studies in question, regardless of their scope, focus, and total number. For this to happen, the treatment method had to be effective with literally all major types of offenders, and with nearly the full range of institutional and/or noninstitutional conditions that were sampled.[5] Anything short of this would result in a substantial percentage of contradictory findings. This was apart from contradictions that would ordinarily be expected to arise in connection with the differing amounts of treatment input, behavioral followup, etc. that were used from one study to the next, i.e., aside from program-implementation and research-related factors alone.

Martinson's unrealistically stringent ground rules appeared to be an expression of his underlying search, in "What Works," for treatment methods that could be recommended to policy makers on an across-the-board basis, i.e., as sure ways of working with almost any set of offenders under almost any set of conditions. Methods that failed to meet this standard were rejected in their entirety. In effect, they were dealt with on an all or none, go or no-go basis as soon as they were brought into the arena of major policy recommendations, and whenever they were treated as undifferentiated entities. Under these conditions, the presence of negative findings or conspicuous shortcomings within any category of treatment went hand in hand with the elimination of any positive findings that had been found as well, relative to that category.

To support his rejection of virtually every treatment method and his resulting, restricted picture of rehabilitation, Martinson, in "Crossroads," presented a series of explanations that shifted attention from the omissions, analytic limitations, and extremely stringent requirements to such factors as "borderline research quality," "negligible reduction in recidivism," etc. However, these explanations fell wide of the mark. For example, research quality was indeed adequate relative to treatment categories that contained many positive results, and substantial reductions in recidivism were in fact observed. As a result, these explanations failed to account for, and justify, the conclusions that were drawn. Thus, Martinson's appeal for sweeping action that would hopefully rid the field of so-called rehabilitation programs was *not* supported by his first and most fundamental belief, namely, that these programs do not work in terms of reducing recidivism.

The Exaggerated-Claims-of-Effectiveness Rationale

Martinson's second factor focuses on the "outlandish" claims that have been made regarding the extent to which recidivism can be reduced. In the following discussion it might be kept in mind that most such claims have been made relative to the offender population as a whole. In this respect, they are overly broad or insufficiently qualified. This problem is somewhat different than, though ultimately related to, the estimated reductions to which Martinson referred.

> Those guilty of making outlandish claims about "treatment" may now feel they've been caught with a bit of egg on the face. . . . [For example,] only five years ago . . . Clark, in his best selling *Crime in America,* confidently claimed that "recidivism can be cut in half." [30]

Martinson suggested that these claims by various message senders amounted to virtual promises, and that these promises falsely raised the hopes of many message receivers. (It might be noted that Clark did qualify his statement in major respects,[6] and that it was not without some foundation in fact.[7])

It is true that many "senders" have made overly optimistic or insufficiently qualified statements regarding the efficacy of treatment. This has indeed misled numerous "receivers." However, it might also be noted that many receivers have disregarded or minimized the accurate and carefully qualified statements that have been made by still other senders.

In any case, Martinson did not point out that certain realities remain the same irrespective of such events. The realities in question—namely, the benefits and accomplishments that are associated with given treatment methods—are in no way altered or negated by overly optimistic predictions, inadequately qualified conclusions, misrepresented findings, underplayed complexities, false hopes, misunderstood messages, wishful thinking, and subsequent disappointment or frustration. Instead, whatever is of value remains of value, no matter how it has been represented by some or understood and responded to by others. Thus, the difficulties that have been created by given senders, and the reactions that have been engendered in numerous receivers, do not constitute valid grounds for rejecting specific methods of treatment or for abandoning rehabilitation as a whole.

The appropriateness of this principle can easily be seen relative to the subject of punishment. One would not, for example, be likely to ask that punishment be swept from the scene if, after careful study, it was found to be incapable of delivering *as much* deterrence for *as many* offenders as some proponents might have suggested it can deliver, or as the man in the street might be led to believe. This would also apply with respect to punishment that was shown to be harmful in a certain proportion of cases. Similarly, one would not be likely to abandon the use of specific vitamins or call off the search for major medical cures if it were found that numerous enthusiasts had overstated or misjudged the actual benefits and rates of progress, or that many people felt stranded and confused because specific predictions were not fulfilled or because the situation was more complex than originally expected.

The Rising-Crime-Rate Rationale

Martinson's third factor stems from his observation that programs of rehabilitation have not reduced our present crime rates. This observation is indeed valid (see below). However, he goes on to imply that if the programs in question had been more than just minimally effective, they quite possibly could have reduced crime, and that the given crime rates are therefore one reflection of the ineffectiveness and lack of worth of the programs.

This inference and implied conclusion is completely incorrect. It springs from Martinson's tacit assumption regarding the existence of a potentially close or substantial relationship between recidivism rates, on the one hand, and crime rates, on the other.[8] For instance:

> The public does not care whether a program will demonstrate that the experimental group shows a lower recidivism rate than a control group; rather, it wants to know whether the program reduced the overall crime rate. [If the program does seem to do so,] ... the public (and those sharp-eyed budget analysts) now tend to ask ... what specific aspects of your "program" accomplished this? Was all this worth it, given the tremendous expense of many of these programs? [30, also see quotations on pp. 61 and 62]

Martinson does not point out that the relationship between recidivism rates and crime rates is, logically and statistically, very distant and weak—by no means close or substantial. Nor does he indicate that the former level of relationship holds true in practically every real-life situation.[9]

Because of its central importance, the relationship between recidivism rates and crime rates will be reviewed.

In the context of rehabilitation, *recidivism* usually refers to new instances of illegal behavior on the part of offenders who either are or have been involved in a given program. (The rate factor enters the picture by means of a time constant.) Crime rates, on the other hand, usually relate to illegal behavior that is produced by all individuals of specified ages who reside within a given geographic area, also during a preestablished span of time; no more than a small fraction of these individuals have ever participated in a treatment program. For this reason, crime rates are usually presented in terms of broad, area statistics alone. When viewed as a sample—not as specific personalities—the individuals who comprise any of the previously mentioned programs are very different from those who comprise the relevant age group within the given geographic area. This applies not only to the specific individuals involved, but to the overall sample sizes as well.

Now, almost every treatment program that was scientifically researched since the 1940s was directed at a specific group of offenders, usually no more than several hundred.[10] Each program was designed to alter the behavior, attitudes, or skills of those particular individuals. It was not, by any stretch of the imagination, designed to focus on or appreciably reduce the rate of illegal behavior on the part of the overall population to which a given crime rate may have applied. The latter population would have included all offenders plus all (thus far) nonoffenders of specified ages who resided within either of the following: (1) any relatively wide geographic area, such as a large city, county, or region or (2) a more limited area, but one that would still be likely to contain many thousands of individuals. Each such area would be likely to contain a large number of nonprogram offenders as well.[11]

Thus, the specific individuals on whom a hypothetical program was focused rarely comprised more than a small fraction of the overall, age-relevant population within the geographic area to which the crime rate applied. As a result, even if the crime rate happened to drop during the time period under consideration, it would be farfetched to attribute that drop to the impact of the treatment program alone—even if the program had been 100 percent successful in eliminating illegal behavior among the individuals on whom it focused. This would apply whether the reduction in crime rate had been slight, moderate, or extreme. It would apply in the case of a rising crime rate as well, again irrespective of whether the program had been a 100 percent success or, for that matter, a 100 percent failure with its particular fraction of the population at risk.

Finally, quite apart from these basic statistical realities, it might be kept in mind that a reported crime rate can be substantially altered via the greater or lesser use of certain approaches and resources whose existence and specific operations are independent of the treatment program in question. These include counsel and release, plea bargaining, and publicly or privately supported youth service bureaus. A crime rate can also be raised or lowered by changes in the physical or technical ability of agencies to detect various types of offense. Approaches, resources, and factors such as these are of relevance to all individuals who come in contact with the justice system, not just those involved in a particular treatment program. In one combination or another, they are likely to have an impact that can easily override and eclipse whatever contribution may be made by the program itself.

In sum, treatment programs have been designed to focus on no more than a small fraction of the population at risk within geographic areas to which crime rates apply. Since the vast majority of known, illegal acts are committed by individuals who have not been involved in these programs, the latter can hardly be given "credit" or "blame" for substantial reductions and increases that may have occurred in the rates of crime.

Related to this, correctional thinkers have increasingly noted that the number of actual offenders within a given geographic area is considerably larger than the number of known offenders (individuals who have been arrested and adjudicated at any point in their life). These observations are largely based on self-report instruments. In short, the population at risk (all individuals of given ages within the geographic area) probably contains many more producers of illegal behavior than is reflected in official statistics alone. In this respect, any crime rate would be generated by a larger number of individuals than is ordinarily thought to be the case. If this is indeed true, the task of any treatment program—dealing as it does with a relatively small number of *known* producers— may be even more formidable than suggested above, with reference to the goal of reducing any specific crime rate.

These considerations are independent of the following. First, the population at risk is seldom even aware of specific treatment programs, and is therefore in no position to be substantially influenced by them, e.g., deterred. Second, the direct impact of any one program on a crime rate may be cancelled by the impact of another. Theoretically, this can occur relative to treatment and deterrent effects alike.[1 2]

Thus, credit or blame would be appropriate only if the program had somehow focused on a large portion of the population at risk (all known offenders included), and if extraneous factors had been controlled. These prerequisites exist independent of the confounding and obscuring effects that are produced by the added resources, approaches, and factors mentioned above. They apply in relation to probation as well, this being the one treatment modality which, according to Martinson, does show substantial promise relative to the reduction of recidivism and, presumably, crime rates as a whole.

To date, these prerequisites have neither been fulfilled nor approached. As a result, Martinson's tacit assumption regarding the existence, in past and recent years, of a potentially close or substantial relationship between recidivism rates and crime rates is clearly erroneous. His related inference and implied conclusion concerning treatment and rehabilitation is therefore without foundation. (This inference and conclusion are as follows: (1) if programs of rehabilitation had been more than just minimally effective, they quite possibly could have reduced crime; (2) observed crimes rates are therefore one reflection of the ineffectiveness and lack of worth of these programs.) In short, although Martinson's third factor did originate in a valid observation, his implied conclusion regarding treatment and rehabilitation is incorrect because it reflects an erroneous underlying assumption and an entirely invalid inference. Thus, his third factor, like those before it, does not constitute valid grounds for rejecting specific methods of treatment or abandoning rehabilitation as a whole.

7 Unrealistic and Realistic Expectations of Treatment

The Interweaving of Recidivism Rates and Crime Rates

Martinson's frequent interweaving of recidivism rates and crime rates is not an academic issue alone. It has played a direct and powerful role in formulating or reinforcing, in the minds of the public, erroneous answers to the following questions: (1) What can and perhaps should be expected, even demanded, of a correctional treatment program? (2) What main criterion should be used to judge the value of such a program? and (3) What support should be given to programs which fail to meet that criterion?

Together with his suggested answer to the first question, the interweaving of recidivism rates and crime rates was seen in Martinson's 1975 appearance on national television:

> [*Interviewer:*] Psychological counseling. A prisoner sits down in a room with a psychologist and talks it out. Does that help to stop prisoners from going back and committing crimes again? [*Martinson:*] No. No. It may be a way to pass the time. It may be even a good way to pass the time, so far as I know. But it has no effect on *their*—on *the crime rate.* [*I:*] You're sure of it? [*M:*] Yes, I'm sure of it, sir. . . . [*I:* What about group counseling programs?] [*M:*] They did not seem to reduce *recidivism.* They did seem to have the effect of making an institution somewhat less tense. . . . But as far as reducing *crime,* I didn't find any evidence of that. [7, emphasis added]

Thus, Martinson implied that it certainly would be possible for a treatment program to reduce the crime rate—at least (or especially) if it was effective in reducing the recidivism of individuals who had participated in it. He did not suggest it was unrealistic to expect that such a program might *not* reduce the crime rate to a substantial degree. In essence, his interweaving of recidivism rates and crime rates implied that correctional programs are simply not doing the job of reducing crime that they theoretically could and should be doing, and quite possibly would be doing if they were more effective in reducing recidivism.

The Primacy of Crime Rates

In "Crossroads," Martinson related this position, as perceived and presumably accepted by the public, to his own somber conclusion regarding the almost total ineffectiveness of correctional treatment. He then drove home its implications in a direct and explicit way:

> The public [now asks:] Has your *"program"* overall reduced the *crime rate?* . . . I believe [these programs] are now increasing crime. . . . I ask [for] a nationwide campaign to purge these institutions of their "community treatment" bombast [and of ineffective programs] and shape them into agencies that can protect the public. [30, emphasis added]

In short, he suggested that answers to the second and third questions are simple and straightforward: no program which fails to substantially reduce the overall crime rate, i.e., which fails to satisfy this overriding criterion, should be supported. This would presumably apply to programs of intensive probation supervision as well, even though these programs might be among the very few which, according to Martinson, have shown substantial promise of reducing recidivism.[1]

Martinson's point regarding the primacy of crime rates was further emphasized in his account of the powerful influence that is exerted, in the mind of the public, by the factor of crime reduction. For example, according to this account, today's public is, and perhaps should be, rudely impatient with any program that does not substantially reduce crime in the streets. Similarly, the public's pointed disinterest in recidivism rates as such is a direct reflection of its intense concern with crime rates instead. Finally, its impatience with the basic strategies and qualitative requirements of scientifically sound research is a byproduct of the desire for either tangible and immediate relief or, ideally, a sweeping and more permanent solution—again, to the problem of crime.

> The public *does not care* whether a "program" . . . shows a lower "recidivism rate." . . . [In reply to those who speak about "research design" and the importance of developing valid and reliable information regarding treatment,] the public would say: "Who gives a damn. We want to go to the moon. . . . Show us a method for reducing crime," [my neighbors] mutter, "or get out of the way." . . . The public now rudely says, "So what?" [if a program's basic accomplishments relate to the lowering of recidivism]. . . . My neighbors in the 20th precinct can no longer afford to be polite; they are too busy avoiding hoodlums and ducking bullets. [30, emphasis added]

In Martinson's view, some of these attitudes are also shared by influential and highly responsible public agencies:

> . . . The public, LEAA and the state planning organizations are no longer very much interested in whether some "program" or other can be shown to "reduce recidivism"; i.e., whether a chi square test will

provide evidence that the experimental group shows a significantly lower rate than the control group. [30]

Thus, even here (when seen in full context), crime reduction was presented as the overriding factor.

In short, Martinson portrayed a besieged public whose paramount concerns relate to its own immediate problems alone, a public which would probably require that all treatment programs make a decided dent in the rate of crime if they are to receive its continued support. If asked to pass judgment on given programs, this public would presumably reject every one that failed to satisfy the preceding requirement, despite the fact that some of these programs, e.g., Program A below, may have made a substantial difference in the attitudes, educational achievement, vocational skills, or recidivism rates of many offenders on whom they focused. Basically, this rejection would reflect the following view. "If Program A does not clearly help us with *our* immediate and primary problem, then we are not really interested in whether it exists at all, and whether 500 or even 5000 offenders participated in it—voluntarily or otherwise—and profited from it as individuals."

(Before proceeding, two points might be kept in mind. First, if the public does not wish to support Program A—and, as portrayed by Martinson, this would almost certainly be the case—at least one of the following conditions would have to be satisfied relative to any intervention that might be offered instead: (a) the substitute would have to be rather different than Program A, and it would have to be acceptable to the public; and (b) the substitute, if similar to Program A, would have to be supported by a source other than the public, e.g., either private enterprise or treatment personnel alone. Martinson neither named an alternate intervention nor suggested that any intervention had demonstrated an ability to satisfy the public's concern with crime reduction.[2] Second, if Program A also failed to receive the support of agencies and organizations that are responsible to the public with regard to corrections, and if these potential sources of support did not make available any alternate programs, opportunities, or approaches—or if they rejected alternate interventions that were proposed—then, from the standpoint of many offenders, in or out of prison, what may already be a rather bleak situation with regard to the availability of opportunities and support, might tomorrow be bleaker still.)

Clearly, the public has every right to reduce its frustrations and fears, and to seek a lasting solution to the problem of crime. In both respects, its motivation is quite high, certainly within the ghetto-like inner-city areas that Martinson heavily underscored. These issues—right, motivation, and demographic focus—stand by themselves, irrespective of specific items with which they happen to be associated. For instance, they remain significant, and timely, regardless of whether Martinson has primarily, and adequately, depicted certain attitudes that are held by the general public, i.e., by broad segments of the overall population rather than one or two important segments alone.

By the same token, these same issues bring to focus timely and significant questions of their own. For example, how can an anxious, strongly motivated, and often impressionable public be helped to proceed along constructive and productive lines? Given the intrinsically weak relationship between recidivism rates and overall crime rates, how valid and useful is it to suggest to this public that an answer to the problem of crime can be found if—and perhaps only if—the vast majority of present-day correctional programs are dismantled? How realistic is it for the public to believe that immediate or sweeping answers can in fact be found, regardless of what is dismantled?

Level 1 and Level 2 Approaches

Martinson's two-pronged approach leaves much to be desired in connection with these questions. For example, at one level (level 1), his focus is on rehabilitation per se, and on its related recidivism rates for offenders who have been exposed to specific programs. Here, rehabilitation is described as a group of programs and networks (1) that work, at best with no more than a small group of offenders and to no more than a trivial degree and (2) which, in major respects, are self-serving and increasingly irrelevant to the needs of their clientele, not to mention the public itself. This portrayal unequivocally suggests to the public that virtually nothing would be lost, certainly from the standpoint of offenders, if most correctional programs were swept from the scene.

At the second level (level 2), Martinson shifts to the question of *crime in general.* Here, he focuses on crime rates for given geographic areas. (Crime rates refer not to the behavior of convicted offenders alone, as in level 1 crime, but to that of nonoffenders, nonconvicted offenders, and an unknown but possibly very large number of undetected offenders.) He then interweaves crime rates with recidivism rates—level 2 with level 1 phenomena—in a way that obscures the marked difference between these two levels of crime and implies that given correctional programs can, in theory, reduce today's crime rates in much the same way that they occasionally reduce recidivism rates.[3] (Martinson does not portray the public as challenging the view that correctional programs can, in theory, reduce today's crime rates; he portrays it as accepting the view that such programs sometimes do reduce recidivism rates.[4])

Given this base, it is easy for the public to take the next step and, by extrapolation, draw the following conclusion: "At least some present-day programs, and perhaps many of tomorrow's hopefully improved programs, can go a long way toward reducing crime-in-general," i.e., level 2 crime. Given the public's present level of motivation—and apart from possible added effects of the specific anxieties described by Martinson—it might be relatively easy for the public to also maintain such a conclusion. This could occur even in the face of seemingly discrepant messages, such as Martinson's stance regarding the current ineffectiveness of virtually every known treatment modality,[5] i.e., ineffectiveness as reflected in recidivism rates on the part of convicted, program-exposed offenders alone (level 1 crime).

In any event, Martinson's interweaving of levels helps the public believe there may be a great deal to gain relative to its own immediate interests by withdrawing support from treatment programs or treatment approaches which show little promise of substantially reducing crime in general and by then applying the level 2 yardstick, namely, reduction of overall crime rates, to those which would be substituted for them.

Regarding the level 1 goal of reducing recidivism among individual offenders, we have seen how erroneous it would be to assume that almost nothing of value would be lost if today's programs were largely eliminated. This is not to say that all correctional tools should be retained. On the contrary, many appear to be of extremely limited value relative to this goal. Nor is it to say that there exists little room for improvement among those which are of value. Nevertheless, it is to say that Martinson's portrayal of rehabilitation offers the public, and its key decision makers, little help in distinguishing between the baby and the bath water of present-day correctional programs. Beyond this, it conveys the message that virtually nothing but bath water exists, and that the baby never was much more than a myth. As such, this message minimizes the destructive component of the purge he has proposed.

The Limitations of Correctional Treatment

Regarding level 2 crime—crime that is not produced by convicted offenders alone—we have seen that it would be equally erroneous to proceed on the assumption that treatment programs can, by themselves, make a significant dent in today's crime rates.[6] However, this does not mean there is no hope anywhere; specifically, it does not mean that a number of complementary or alternate lines of approach cannot be further developed or should not be carefully explored (see below). Nevertheless, it does mean that the problem of crime will neither be resolved nor significantly reduced by having the public, and those responsible to it, make wide-ranging level 2 demands on programs which are designed to focus on convicted offenders alone. Nor would this problem be resolved, or become far more resolvable than in recent years, if the programs in question were simply eliminated, i.e., dismantled rather than modified or radically altered in light of these demands. Finally, the problem of level 2 crime would remain largely unchanged even if one were to retain, without modification, all programs (and only those programs) which had shown themselves to be of value in terms of level 1 objectives, quite apart from possible level 2 demands.

In sum, the growing problem of crime, and the public's understandable frustrations and impatience with it, provides little justification for any large-scale rejection or thoroughgoing modification of today's treatment programs. Neither course of action can by itself provide a way of grappling with this level 2 problem on anything even approaching a sufficiently large scale. Nor can these responses substantially increase the chance of focusing, say, on its strategically critical aspects alone. Finally, neither the former nor the latter response, nor any careful combination of both, would either constitute or pave the way for a quantitatively significant weeding out of actual obstacles to progress within areas that do have to be addressed.

Thus, to deal with today's problem of crime in a productive and telling manner, it must first be recognized that it is futile to place the burden of progress, or even the lion's share, on rehabilitation alone. Once this point is accepted, it becomes clear that the major, possibly decisive contribution to the task of crime reduction has to be made by complementary and alternate approaches instead. More specifically, each separate approach has to add its particular quantum of impact to what would end up as the combined, total contribution of all such approaches. Hopefully, this total would be rather substantial.

For instance, to proceed on a broad front and to concentrate on strategically critical factors, it might be necessary to continue developing, or, in some cases, begin developing, well-integrated programs and procedures within such areas as delinquency prevention (for example, emphasizing preteen and early-teen years), public education, community involvement,[7] expanded social opportunities for disadvantaged groups, earlier apprehension of offenders,[8] and court reform (such as faster processing of defendants, hard-core or career criminals included). Some of these items, e.g., court reform, may help remind us that the justice system includes a good deal more than rehabilitation, and that its impact on crime rates can derive from factors other than that of treatment programs alone.

Nevertheless, given the deep-seated, relatively widespread, and far from quiescent nature of today's crime, progress may have to be made within most of the above-mentioned areas, and during more or less the same period of time, before substantial reductions in crime will firmly take root. This portrayal suggests that a comprehensive and coordinated investment of human resources—justice system and otherwise—may be needed to clearly lower the rate of crime across a wide spectrum of American society. In short, it assumes that today's level 2 task is very large, complex, and difficult. In a much simpler society, or perhaps a future time, the situation might be otherwise.

The Role of Correctional Treatment

Correctional treatment programs should not be rejected if they fail to play a leading or otherwise distinctive and formidable role with regard to this task.

Rather than discard these tools, a more appropriate response would be to continue using them in what might be called their natural or primary context (see below), and to increasingly use them within this context for all they are worth. This does not mean they would no longer play a role in connection with level 2 crime. On the contrary, their influence would go on as before. However, it does mean they would be directed, above all, at the level 1 objectives for which they were designed. It also means that these programs would be focused, wherever possible, on the specific offenders, settings, etc. to which they seem best suited. Finally, this response or policy would call for a clear recognition of their limitations and drawbacks with respect to level 1 objectives, and for a careful accounting of their operational requirements. Together, these objectives and requirements would make it easier for "treatment" to be neither undersold nor oversold relative to level 1 and 2 objectives alike. One would ask and expect neither more nor less of any tools—in any area—including that of "punishment" itself.

To briefly review, aside from the option of rejecting and abandoning today's treatment programs, it would also be futile to somehow reshape them in the hope that this might lead to a sizable reduction in crime rates. To work toward this level 2 reduction, heavy emphasis would have to be placed on complementary and alternate approaches instead, e.g., programs and procedures that might be developed in the areas of delinquency prevention, court reform, etc. For present purposes, these programs and procedures (within each such area) would represent, and may be called, a level 2 approach.[9] Correctional treatment programs (within each modality that was mentioned in chapters 2 and 3) would represent a level 1 approach.

Given this framework, treatment programs (collectively and across modalities) would be looked on as one of several vehicles that can help reduce crime rates. However, despite this level 2 contribution, their main function would relate to level 1 objectives instead, especially that of reducing recidivism. This would apply even if a sizable percentage of all treatment programs (taken individually) were eliminated and only the more promising were retained.[10]

As suggested above, level 1 approaches, by themselves, are likely to play a comparatively small role in the achievement of level 2 objectives. Much the same applies with respect to the impact of level 2 approaches on level 1 objectives: the former are likely to play a relatively modest role in the achievement of the latter.[11] More specifically, level 2 approaches (e.g., public education and court reform) are likely to have much less impact than level 1 approaches (e.g., group counseling and skill development) on the recidivism rates of individuals who are, or have recently been, within the jurisdiction of the formal justice system. This would apply to short-term and, quite probably, longer-term impact as well, relative to any sample of program-exposed offenders. (See n. 12 regarding assumptions that bear on these points.)

For reasons such as these, it would easily be possible, subsequent to the planned and coordinated introduction into a given geographic area of (1) level 2 approaches as such and/or (2) level 1 approaches that have been modified in light of level 2 objectives, for recidivism rates and other aspects of individual adjustment to remain almost entirely unchanged, even though crime rates may have begun to drop.

The significance of this is that any sample of convicted offenders can end up in essentially the same position or "shape" as before, despite the introduction and possible success of these approaches. That is, the behavior and needs of these individuals may be largely unaffected by the approaches in question, even though level 2 progress may indeed have occurred relative to the geographic area as a whole, mainly with regard to individuals other than those participating in treatment programs. This, of course, can also happen if no progress has occurred in connection with level 2 objectives, i.e., if crime rates have continued to rise or perhaps remain unchanged.

It is precisely in this context that the distinctive contributions and dual role of level 1 approaches can be seen. First, it is these approaches which are most likely to reduce recidivism, i.e., reduce illegal behavior that might otherwise remain unchanged despite the possible success or failure of the above-mentioned approaches in terms of level 2 objectives. This contribution is of particular relevance to what might be called the primary or socially centered role of level 1 approaches, a role that focuses mainly on the needs of the general public, not those of offenders as individuals.

Next, it is these same level 1 approaches—actually, specific types of programs[13]—that can help or encourage many individuals to grapple with a range of personal/social needs, problems, and interests, including that of "going straight." Without these programs, most such needs and interests would probably be dealt with in a relatively fleeting or tangential way, e.g., by level 2 approaches. This contribution to the needs and concerns of specific human beings is of relevance to what might be called the secondary or offender-centered role of level 1 approaches. Given this role, the value of correctional treatment programs can be thought of as extending well beyond the reduction of recidivism alone.

The Offender-Centered Role

The offender-centered role is not a theoretical construct only. Findings from the survey by Lipton et al. indicate that many correctional programs already have provided assistance in this regard. This can be seen in the areas of vocational adjustment, educational achievement, and community adjustment. (See Appendix E regarding measures that were used to assess the adjustment or achievement of offenders in each area.)

For instance, as seen in Table 7-1, of the 13 studies that measured

Table 7-1

Type of Outcome Obtained in Studies of Vocational Adjustment, Educational Achievement, and Community Adjustment

Area of Study	No. of Studies[b]	Strong-Positive or Clearcut Gains		Mixed-Positive or Moderate Gains[a]		No Positive Gains	
		No. of Studies	Percent of Studies	No. of Studies	Percent of Studies	No. of Studies	Percent of Studies
Vocational adjustment	13[c]	6	46	3	23	4	31
Educational achievement	10[d,e]	4	40	5	50	1	10
Community adjustment	12[d,f]	5	42	2	17	5	42
Total	35	15	43	10	29	10	29

[a]*Mixed-positive* means positive on some outcome measures but not on others, or positive for some offender categories but not for others.

[b]In the survey by Lipton et al., the number of studies (findings, entries) that appeared under vocational adjustment, educational achievement, and community adjustment was 14, 12, and 16, respectively. In the present tabulations, no study was represented more than once within any one area, e.g., that of vocational adjustment.

[c]One of the originally surveyed entries was omitted from the present tabulations due to difficulties in classifying the outcome as either positive or nonpositive. This difficulty related to the nature of the specific outcome index that was used, not, as in note d below, to difficulties in interpreting the amount of change that had occurred.

[d]One of the originally surveyed entries was omitted from the present tabulations for reasons indicated in note c above.

[e]One entry was omitted because it appeared twice within this area of study.

[f]Three entries were omitted because they appeared more than once within this area of study.

offenders' vocational adjustment, 46 percent showed strong positive results or clearcut gains. An additional 23 percent showed mixed positive results or moderate overall gains. (*Mixed-positive* meant positive on some measures but not on others, or positive for some offender groupings but not for others.) The remaining 31 percent showed no positive results. Of the 10 studies that measured educational achievement, 40 percent showed strong positive results or clearcut gains, and 50 percent showed mixed results or moderate gains. Of the 12 studies that measured community adjustment, 42 percent showed strong positive results or clearcut gains, and 17 percent showed mixed results or moderate gains.

Thus, for the three areas combined, 43 percent of the 35 entries (see below) showed strong positive results or clearcut gains for offenders. Twenty-nine percent showed mixed positive results or moderate gains. The remaining 29 percent showed no positive results. These 35 entries related to 30 separate studies, since five studies appeared in more than one of the three areas. Counting each study ($N = 30$) only once, the results for all areas combined were: strong positive or clearcut gains, 40 percent; mixed positive or moderate gains, 30 percent; and no positive results, 30 percent.[14]

The offender-centered role of level 1 approaches was also observed in relation to personality and attitude change. As seen in table 7-2, of the 57

Table 7-2
Type of Outcome Obtained in Studies of Personality and Attitude Change

		Outcome				
		Strong-Positive or Clearcut Gains		Mixed-Positive or Moderate Gains[a]		No Positive Gains
Context of Study	No. of Studies[b]	No. of Studies	Percent of Studies[c]	No. of Studies	Percent of Studies[c]	No. of Studies	Percent of Studies[c]
Probation	3	3	100	0	0	0	0
Imprisonment	8	2	25	4	50	2	25
Parole	2	2	100	0	0	0	0
Casework and Individual counseling	3	1	33	0	0	2	67
Skill development	3	2	67	1	33	0	0
Individual psychotherapy	5	3	60	0	0	2	40
Group methods	18	6	33	6	33	6	33
Milieu therapy	8	3	38	5	63	0	0
Partial physical custody	0	0	–	0	–	0	–
Medical methods	7	5	71	2	29	0	0
Leisure time activities	0	0	–	0	–	0	–
Total	57	27	47	18	32	12	21

[a]*Mixed-positive* means positive on some outcome measures but not on others, or positive for some offender categories but not for others.

[b]In the survey by Lipton et al., 66 studies (findings, entries) appeared under personality and attitude change, and some of these entries appeared more than once, e.g., once under skill development and once under milieu therapy. In the present tabulations, no study was represented more than once. Three entries were omitted because they were repeats; two were omitted due to the questionable nature of the outcome index (e.g., Should specified change on this index necessarily be considered an improvement?); two were omitted due to difficulties in the original statistical analysis; and, the three Warren-study entries were counted as a single entry.

[c]The percentages reported for most of the 11 treatment categories (e.g., probation) cannot be considered reliable, or even moderately reliable, given the small number of studies involved in these categories. The percentages for all categories combined *can* be considered reliable.

studies that evaluated offenders in this area, 47 percent showed strong positive results or clearcut gains. Thirty-two percent showed mixed results or moderate gains, and 21 percent showed no positive results.[15] (See Appendix E regarding the measures that were used in this area.)

It is difficult to see how most vocational and educational needs or interests of offenders as individuals could be specifically responded to by level 2 approaches—e.g., those which focus on delinquency prevention, public education, earlier apprehension, or court reform. Nevertheless, some aspects of offenders' overall community adjustment doubtlessly could be supported by level 2 approaches that relate to community involvement and expanded social opportunities. In short, the situation need not be conceived as an either/or: level 1 and 2 approaches may both have something to contribute relative to many individuals.

8

Correctional Treatment in Its Own Right

Offenders and Their Destinations

Two analogies will now be used to characterize the roles of level 1 and 2 approaches, and to indicate that the *need* for the former is separate from that of the latter.

First, one may think of level 1 approaches, i.e., treatment programs, as a fleet of airplanes that can help bring individual offenders closer to their personally desired and socially required destinations. To many but not all of these individuals, or passengers, the former goal mainly relates to a less anxiety filled, more rewarding, crime-free existence; as such, it often overlaps with the latter objective. With relatively little fanfare but much effort, this fleet manages to transport many passengers to their specific (local) destinations. It accomplishes this mission year after year, even though its performance leaves much to be desired, both quantitatively and qualitatively.

Next, one may think of level 2 approaches as a group of rockets whose main job is that of helping the general public "go to the moon," to use Martinson's phrase—in other words, to substantially reduce today's crime rates.[1] This mission is yet to be accomplished.

Now, it should be recognized that (1) the "moon" is an important destination; it is certainly no less significant than the down-to-earth, local destinations of convicted offenders; (2) the general public is keenly interested in seeing the results of something other than individual trips to local destinations; and (3) no "local carriers" (airplanes) seem capable of making the distant lunar voyage, regardless of how carefully they are disassembled, reshaped, and refitted; a different and more highly powered vehicle must be sent aloft instead.

These are critical factors, and they are not likely to change or disappear within the near future. Nevertheless, as indicated below, it would be quite unnecessary, and a definite mistake, to ground most planes and cancel many flights because of factors such as these. We have already indicated why such action would be uncalled for, particularly in response to assumptions or situations that are open to serious question, unlike factors (1) through (3) above. The reasons that were suggested need not be repeated here. As to factors (1) through (3), themselves, two reasons will be noted; for present purposes, these should suffice.[2]

1. Physically and otherwise, there is no need for "local air service" to be interrupted, let alone discontinued, in order to launch rockets toward the moon.

Both missions can be operated simultaneously, whether on a coordinated or largely independent basis. This applies despite the logistic complexities and sociopolitical challenges that can conceivably arise.

2. The underlying forces, e.g., personal drives and social requirements, that create and sustain the need for individual trips will not fade away, however well a rocket fleet may carry out its own special task. Instead, they are likely to exert a fairly steady pressure, one that can neither be turned off nor held in check for very long. Relative to any individual, these forces or realities must be dealt with directly, by the offender himself and/or those who may try to assist him. Such forces must somehow be accommodated; they must be responded to and satisfied on their own terms, at least to a large extent.

Pressures from these forces can best be relieved, or directed into acceptable and perhaps rewarding channels, through "individual trips to local destinations." This is largely due to the specific content of the personal drives and social requirements in question.[3] To accommodate these underlying forces, the offender, with or without assistance, must connect and coordinate some of his personal capacities and limitations, on the one hand, with challenges and opportunities that exist in his immediate environment, on the other. He must forge constructive links between his own reality—as an individual with specific characteristics and needs—and the realities that currently exist in that particular environment. Local carriers (airplanes) are vehicles that can help him discover and forge these specific links. Such connections are not likely to be made by means of vehicles (rockets) whose flight plans allow for local deliveries on a tangential or occasional basis only.

Thus, despite today's necessary emphasis on "reaching the moon," it is both possible and important to retain an "air fleet" that is vigorous and relevant enough to help many passengers attain, or at least approach, their personally desired and socially required destinations. In light of its actual contribution to the task of dealing with these forces, or persistent needs, it would therefore be wrong to condemn and largely abandon today's "air fleet" (level 1 programs, collectively) mainly because of a legitimate concern with what it does not accomplish—e.g., on grounds that it neither carries nor delivers far more passengers than it does. More specifically, regardless of today's unquestioned need to "go to the moon," and to improve the local air service itself, it would be wide of the mark to judge today's fleet primarily or solely in terms of the many individuals it is physically incapable of carrying,[4] who are opposed to making any new or different kinds of trip (even if they could be carried), who are very unclear about where they want to go, or whose unusual destinations cannot be reached by the "air service" as it presently exists. The "fleet" should also be judged in relation to individuals it can carry, including those who are in a position to "make the flight" or at least give it a try.

The airfleet and rocket analogy does not mean that level 1 and 2 objectives are entirely independent of each other. However, it means that level 1 objectives are valid in their own right and that movement toward these goals can proceed whether crime rates happen to be high or low. Nor should this analogy suggest that the public and key decision makers, given their overriding concern with crime, would probably remain indifferent toward widespread failure on the part of level 1 approaches with respect to level 1 objectives, socially centered objectives in particular. In this connection, it seems entirely possible that the reaction of these groups to unsuccessful but well-publicized programs can have a very negative influence on the support received by other programs which do seem relatively successful, irrespective of the latters' effect on crime in general.

This suggests that treatment programs, like tools in any field, must achieve or at least approach their objectives in order to receive genuine and fairly reliable support. It also suggests that if level 1 approaches are to play a major rather than insignificant role within the justice system, specific programs that have proven ineffective in terms of level 1 goals must be culled out and actively replaced by those which do show promise. By itself, a culling out will neither achieve nor approach these goals. This evolution in the direction of increasingly effective programs should continue to take place whether the public is indifferent toward, legitimately upset by, or, for that matter, generally supportive of given approaches. It should apply with respect to socially centered and offender-centered goals alike.

The Social Planning Era

Clearly, level 1 and 2 approaches each have something worthwhile to contribute, especially in their areas of principal focus. The public, and its decision makers, should be helped to increasingly recognize these contributions. This, however, is precisely what Martinson does not do. He presents level 1 approaches, i.e., treatment programs, as having essentially nothing to offer relative to their area of primary focus—the reduction of recidivism rates. He proposes that they be largely swept away and replaced by something that will be of value, mainly in relation to a broader and somewhat different area of emphasis—overall crime rates.

In effect, Martinson suggests that any programs which survive this purge should justify their existence not on the basis of their ability to reduce recidivism for specified offenders and to assist these individuals (and the public) in related ways, but mainly in terms of their ability to substantially reduce crime rates as such. (In part, he makes this suggestion via descriptions or interpretations of the presumed feelings and views of specified groups, e.g., the general public, state planning agencies, and LEAA.[5] Aside from this, see n. 6 regarding implications of the requirement in question). In short, he suggests that correctional programs be pressed into a rather different and, in his view, more important type of service, or primary role. There, perhaps, they will have something to contribute.

Martinson thus accomplishes quite the opposite of helping the public and its policy makers increasingly recognize the value of level 1 approaches. Viewed from any angle, his descriptions virtually invite these individuals to conclude that almost nothing of significance would be lost if most correctional programs were eliminated. This paves the way for his own alternate proposal.

Martinson asks that we largely abandon the futile activity known as correctional treatment, and that we move in a different direction instead. (*We* includes the general public, state planning agencies, researchers, etc.) This change, he believes, would open the door to a broader and more meaningful type of activity than presently exists. It would be called the new "social planning epoch," and its overriding objective would be the reduction of crime rates [30].

During this epoch, or era, present-day standards, criterion measures, and issues would be reassessed and realigned in accordance with the objective of lower crime rates. Recidivism rates, in particular, would not be allowed to detract from the paramount issue of crime. In this respect, according to Martinson, we would no longer be "fixated on recidivism," and on the issues or needs that it generally represents [30].

Also during this era, major operations (in other words programs or approaches) would somehow be changed or restructured to implement the shift in objectives and standards. This difficult transformation, and hoped-for advance, would be reflected in our research activities as well.

> [We must] take that painful leap forward from the epoch of "recidivism only" research to the epoch of "social planning" research. [30]

Difficulties notwithstanding, our attention would remain focused on one goal and one goal alone: crime reduction. This would help us achieve a definite break from activities that might otherwise fix our attention on issues relating to recidivism as such, and from the dead hand of the past.[7] For instance:

> The aim of future research will be to create the knowledge needed to reduce crime. . . . The essence of the new epoch is a *change* in the "dependent variable" from recidivism to the crime rate (combined with cost). . . . If the day of "recidivism only" research is about over, the day when small coteries of like-minded professionals can dictate reality is also over. [30, emphasis added]

As described by Martinson, this change would not represent the addition of one objective or type of activity to another; it would involve a complete substitution or fundamental restructuring instead.

This new era or area of activity largely focuses on what we have called level 2 objectives and approaches. We feel this area should be explored as thoroughly as level 1 itself. However, as seen in "Crossroads," Martinson regards it as the only area that should be seriously explored. To complement this view, he believes we should staunchly oppose those activities which do not clearly contribute to the social planning era or which divert substantial attention from its basic goals.

Martinson's belief applies to correctional treatment programs first and foremost; in this connection, his stance is firm and clear. Thus, in "Crossroads," he repeatedly implies, directly and indirectly, that it would be inappropriate to allow recidivism-focused activities (level 1 approaches) to exist side by side with those which focus on crime rates as such (level 2 approaches).[8] More specifically, there neither is nor can be any justification for granting the former activities anything even resembling equal status with the latter, in terms of amount of energy invested. Martinson neither qualifies nor softens this position; he transmits no discernible messages to the contrary, either directly or indirectly.

This insistent, implacable attitude reflects Martinson's genuine concern over today's crime rates. It reflects his belief that correctional treatment programs have become a major obstacle to progress or, at best, a low-yield diversion of energy.[9] Given this concern and belief, he feels we cannot allow ourselves to be barred or deflected from the one path that must be followed, the one direction in which some hope may lie: the social planning epoch. As a result, only level 2 approaches should receive our serious attention; only they should be allowed to flourish. Moreover, we can brook no delay; serious obstacles must be swept aside or quickly neutralized in today's race against crime.

Thus, in words that Martinson ascribes to his neighbors from the 20th precinct of New York, it is now time for level 1 approaches to either reduce crime rates or "get out of the way," i.e., clear the launching pad for today's desired trip "to the moon."

Implications of the Unidirectional Approach

As has been mentioned, it is almost impossible for level 1 approaches to substantially reduce overall crime rates within most large-sized or heavily populated geographic areas, at least by themselves. Thus, if one relied primarily or exclusively on the crime reduction criterion and applied this criterion to most segments of contemporary American society, level 1 approaches would almost certainly fail and would thus be obliged to get out of the way.[10]

However well intentioned and, in some respects, forward looking it may be, Martinson's unidirectional proposal has certain features and harmful implications that must not be overlooked. First, as set forth in "Crossroads," it in effect divides today's range of actual and potential program resources (levels 1 and 2 combined) into two artificially contrasting groups—those which, in Martinson's view, are almost devoid of worth and are obstacles to progress (level 1), and those which are truly worthwhile or progressive (level 2). Without relating all the details, suffice it to say that this amounts to a clearcut polarization of today's resources and a negative stereotyping of treatment programs in particular.

In many situations, factors such as polarization and stereotyping can exert a powerful influence on individuals who seek rapid relief from very real anxieties or pressures and who, under such circumstances, may have little tolerance for complexities, shades of grey, long-term investments, and partial solutions. In the present context, this combination of factors, circumstances, and reactions can substantially increase the chance that various segments of today's public will deny, minimize, or remain only slightly aware of the fundamental need for, and actual value of, level 1 approaches. These responses are especially likely to occur if the public's attention has already been sharply, and understandably, focused on the issue of crime rates instead. Fairly similar responses may be obtained from specific groups, e.g., service agencies, that are particularly sensitive and responsive to the public's immediate concerns and desires.

The second implication is partly independent of the strength and nature of the public's reaction to polarization and stereotyping. If correctional decision makers were to largely implement Martinson's single-purpose policy, this would mean turning a deaf ear to programs that have demonstrated not only some ability to reduce recidivism, but an ability to help many offenders come to grips with a range of basic and often pressing needs, problems, or interests. The former ability relates to the socially centered role of correctional treatment, the latter bears on its offender-centered role. At this point in the history of corrections, there is little reason to believe that socially centered or offender-centered objectives would be focused on by level 2 approaches or by such approaches alone, at least in ways that are likely to help most of these individuals forge concrete, here-and-now links with their immediate environment and thereby direct their energies into more acceptable and perhaps rewarding channels.

In sum, Martinson's unidirectional proposal can increase the chance that large segments of today's public will minimize, disregard, and/or overlook the need for and value of level 1 approaches. It can help key decision makers feel justified in turning a cold shoulder toward such approaches as well. Given these implications, and given today's overriding concern with crime rates, the following might be asked: is it reasonable to think that, from the present day forward, these groups can no longer show much interest in and support for level 1 approaches, i.e., correctional treatment programs? Assuming it were possible to do so, would it be inappropriate to help *increase* their interest in and support for such approaches? These questions, which relate directly to Martinson's rationale for the social planning era, will be dealt with in the next chapter.

9

The Public, Decision Makers, and Treatment

Dominant and Underlying Attitudes

In answering the questions that have been posed, the following distinction should be noted:[1] it is one thing to say that the public and its decision makers are disinterested in level 1 approaches or can be turned against them as a result of specific conditions, expectations, or preferences which these approaches or programs have not satisfied (we will refer to such an attitude or reaction as "conditional opposition," and to the unmet conditions, expectations, or preferences as "specific reasons"); however, it is a different thing to say that these groups are unconditionally or fundamentally set against these programs, e.g., irrevocably opposed to them because of what they are or represent. In our view, these programs can be thought of as an integration of specific content, strategies, and objectives. They represent a philosophy of providing direct and indirect service to individuals and society alike.

Martinson does not suggest that the public and its decision makers are unconditionally opposed to correctional treatment programs. In fact, in "Crossroads" and "What Works," no such concept appears. These groups, he maintains, are disinterested in or opposed to level 1 approaches for what, in our terms, amounts to a "specific reason" (described below). Relative to the questions that were asked on p. 78, and relative to this specific reason, we will now focus on the general public alone, as described in "Crossroads."

According to Martinson, today's public is disinterested in or opposed to correctional treatment programs *not* because it thinks they fail to produce lower recidivism rates, but mainly because it is eager to have something else produced instead. This preference, or specific reason, relates to the question of what exactly should be the principal product or primary role of level 1 approaches.[2] For example:

> The public does not care whether a program will demonstrate that the experimental group shows a lower recidivism rate than a control group; rather, it wants to know whether the program reduced the overall crime rate.[30]

Thus, as long as crime rates fail to drop, the public will presumably remain disinterested in a given program, even though the program may indeed reduce recidivism. In short, its attention will focus on lower crime rates, not on any particular method by which these rates might be produced. This, by our definition, represents a product-centered interest or concern.[3]

In short, Martinson emphasized the idea that today's public has no particular interest in the recidivism rates on which a given program may have focused. This is quite different from suggesting (1) that the public is at odds with the program (the particular method) itself in the unconditional or fundamental sense described above[4] or is adverse to the underlying concepts of treatment and intervention, or (2) that the public disapproves of lower recidivism rates or believes the program is producing something which is harmful in itself, something for which it should be condemned, rejected, or greatly modified.

However, in "Crossroads," Martinson neither qualified nor elaborated on the otherwise adequate concept of the public's disinterest in, or opposition to, treatment programs. This lack of additional specificity or sufficient differentiation made it easy for many readers to overlook the very large extent to which the public's disinterest or opposition may indeed be conditional. It was possible for readers to overlook this despite the fact that Martinson had not actually suggested that the public *is* unconditionally opposed to treatment programs.[5] (See issue 1 below, adequacy of concept.)

Also in "Crossroads," Martinson made no reference to any shortcomings or drawbacks that might possibly exist—or any modifications that might eventually take place—with respect to the public's disinterest or opposition. This left the clear and later reinforced impression that the public's attitude represents a type of insight which is neither open to question nor subject to change, despite its conditional nature in a different sense of the term. (See issue 2, implications of concept.)

Thus, on issue 1—adequacy of concept—Martinson made no reference to distinctions such as those reflected in (1) and (2) above (p. 80). Instead, he offered his assertion that "the public does not care" as a fully developed or settled concept; that is, he offered it as one which required no further refinement or amplification in order to adequately represent—and preclude most misinterpretations of—the public's overall attitude toward correctional treatment programs. (As implied in our earlier comments, "attitude toward . . . treatment programs" can and does include far more than "attitude toward principal products, primary role, etc." This is despite the prominence of these factors.) Similarly, on issue 2, he expressed no reservations or misgivings about the content and implications of the public's presumed or actual attitude. More specifically, he neither questioned, qualified, nor expressed concern about the overall wisdom, foresight, and seeming finality of the disinterest or opposition that he portrayed. Instead, he presented the public's attitude toward treatment programs "as is"—in a sense, as a flawless and immutable reality.

Modifying the Public's View

On the latter issue—issue 2—Martinson's approach differs from our own. We believe that the public's disinterest or opposition should not, in effect, be accepted as (1) an unalterable reality or (2) the expression and possible culmination[6] of a carefully considered, long-range view. Thus, on point (1), large and influential segments of the public have been known to shift position in connection with the type of alternatives under consideration, e.g., little support versus substantial support for level 1 approaches. These shifts have often occurred within a relatively few years. (For present purposes, there is no need to directly focus on point (2). Points (1) and (2) are briefly elaborated upon in Appendix F.)

Even aside from shifts of the past, we see no reason to believe that today's public might lack the basic ability to modify its attitude in the future, or might never feel motivated to do so. We assume that its power to change—in this case, to shift its attitude in the direction of greater interest and support—will remain intact as long as it is not unconditionally opposed to level 1 approaches, and contemptuous of or repelled by concepts of treatment and intervention in general.[7] We also assume that its desire or motivation to change will exist insofar as it recognizes the relevance of level 1 approaches and recidivism rates to its own need for protection. (The factor of desire or motivation is aside from that of power or raw ability. Martinson does not suggest that the public might lack this power.)

Regardless of underlying abilities and potential motivation, where does the public stand today, and what might be reasonable to expect from it in the future? To answer these questions, we will offer what we acknowledge to be speculation—hopefully, reasonable speculation—regarding the public's attitude. These thoughts and hypotheses result from our reading of events on the American scene relative to the past 10 years. They are not a product of scientific investigations designed to tap public opinion concerning the issues in question. As far as we know, no such investigations or surveys have been conducted with regard to these particular issues.

In recent years, the American public—not just the criminal justice community—appears to have been turning away from level 1 approaches to a fairly substantial degree, in the conditional sense described above. This has occurred in response to three main types of stimuli: (1) information inputs, (2) particular expectations or preferences (specific reasons), and (3) current crime rates. It has not occurred in response to any *one* of these factors alone, even though one or the other may have dominated the scene for given periods of time. These factors sometimes differ from one another to a substantial degree, relative to the type and direction of influence they exert.

Despite its turned away appearance—and, at one level, reality—the public's current response to factors (1) through (3) represents neither a settled nor unalterable position. This is in spite of the combined, often simultaneous impact of these factors. More specifically, the public's attitude of disinterest or opposition does not rest inertly in place because of any lack of ability to change or perennial lack of motivation to change. Nor is it held firmly in place by powerful, essentially unchecked, internal and/or external forces instead.[8] The external processes may include the large-scale or long-term forces mentioned in Appendix F.

In part, the unsettled nature of the public's current response and the inherent dynamics of its attitude-formation process in general result from the ongoing, mutual interplay of factors (1) through (3). In this respect, they reflect the relative freedom-to-choose which such an interaction implies. Apart from this, they also result from the relatively steady counterpressure that is exerted by the public's underlying acceptance of level 1 approaches.

Given the potential impact of factors (1) and (2), and given a lack of attitudinal rigidity on the part of the public itself, the following would apply. There are no solid grounds for believing that an alternate or additional set of information inputs and specific reasons would be incapable of helping the public turn toward, or back toward, level 1 approaches—again, in the conditional sense and to a substantial degree. (See n. 9 for further comment.)

The lively history of interactions between the public, on the one hand, and correctional movements or issues, on the other, suggests that a future shift in attitude should come as no surprise. To be sure, in light of the public's justifiable preoccupation with crime rates and in view of the polarized messages and stereotyped portrayals it frequently receives, this change in attitude—or perhaps broadening of perspective—cannot occur at once and without additional input. Nevertheless, under specified conditions, it can occur.[10]

Thus, in answer to the first question under consideration (p. 78), we believe it *is* reasonable to expect that the public would be able—and willing—to show substantial interest in and open support for correctional treatment programs. This interest and support can be expressed despite the public's overriding concern with crime rates and its continued exposure to unidirectional proposals. In addition, it can probably be expressed without the public's having to reject the positive elements in these proposals or minimize the importance of level 2 approaches themselves.

Relative to the second question (p. 78), we believe it would not be inappropriate for policy makers to help increase the public's interest in and support for level 1 approaches. One major way to achieve this goal would be for these individuals to provide information that could help the public more clearly recognize the relevance of treatment programs, not only to offenders but to itself. Information that is communicated regarding the results of level 1 approaches will be called *level 1 inputs.*[11]

As implied earlier, we believe that the public is not as farsighted and error free as possible, in its attitude of disinterest or opposition. In this regard we believe that level 1 inputs should be used to widen its perspective on correctional programs and reduce its misunderstandings as to their actual contribution. This objective and method would be justified whether or not Martinson's portrayal of the public's attitude is basically correct. For example, if his portrayal were essentially correct, this, in our opinion, would mean that today's public probably does need considerable help in recognizing the relevance of level 1 approaches to its need for protection and to many of its traditional ideals. In fact, if his portrayal were correct, the potential value of level 1 inputs would be somewhat greater, relatively speaking, than if our own view were closer to the truth. (We believe the public's opposition, but perhaps not its disinterest, is substantially less than that implied in Martinson's account.) On the other hand, if his portrayal were largely incorrect, level 1 inputs could still be used to make a valuable contribution, though the need for them would no longer be as great.

In either case, we believe it would be reasonable to expect that today's public can, in the long run, show increased interest in and support for correctional treatment programs, provided that level 1 inputs are in fact supplied. However, these inputs should not be used to reflect, indiscriminantly and with equal emphasis, all level 1 programs or program models that happen to be at hand. Instead, they should focus mainly on those which work, or show good prospects of working, relative to specific offenders, specified types of setting, and so on. Nevertheless, they should carefully point up the basic limitations of these programs. They should also bring out the actual failures of remaining programs, but in ways that neither obscure nor minimize the contributions of others which *are* of worth. As we have seen, Martinson's approach falls down at precisely this point.

Finally, it might be kept in mind that the possibility of attitude change ultimately rests on three main assumptions regarding the public: (1) its power to change has neither been undermined nor overwhelmed by internal and/or external forces; (2) its motivation to change can be activated under specifiable conditions; and (3) its current disinterest or opposition is conditional, not unconditional. Given these factors, and given the earlier-mentioned inputs, it would be reasonable to expect that the public's disinterest or opposition need not go on forever, regardless of the major role it may often play today.

Options for Decision Makers

The preceding remarks have focused on attitudes and possible responses of the general public relative to level 1 approaches. A few words will now be added concerning those of correctional decision makers.

The following will illustrate the attitude that Martinson ascribed to major decision makers in relation to level 1 programs and objectives:

... LEAA and the state planning organizations are no longer very much interested in whether some "program" or other can be shown to "reduce recidivism." [Their focus is on crime rates, instead.] [30]

In "Crossroads," Martinson left little doubt that he regarded this disinterest or indifference as an entirely appropriate response, one that would be supportive of and supported by his unidirectional proposal. In essence, this proposal would require that we largely abandon correctional treatment programs and invest the preponderance of our resources in the social planning era instead. To key decision makers, this could easily be interpreted to mean (1) assign low priorities to level 1 approaches, and (2) virtually eliminate these approaches from among our major responsibilities. If Martinson were correct in his portrayal of decision makers, this interpretation would be more likely to occur and be acted upon.

However probable or improbable the preceding interpretation and action may be, we reject the view that it is appropriate for decision makers to adopt an attitude of disinterest in or indifference toward level 1 programs. We do so because of the ongoing need for these approaches, and because of the significant contributions which they make. This need remains legitimate, and these contributions remain valid, regardless of whether level 1 approaches can significantly reduce overall crime rates within contemporary American society. In short, they are important in their own right.

Thus, our position is that decision makers who have broad responsibility for formulating, supporting, or implementing correctional policies *should* remain seriously concerned with programs which focus directly on the personal and social needs, and illegal behavior, of convicted offenders. Despite their already "heavy" mandate to develop strategies and programs for the future, and to reduce overall crime rates, decision makers should neither waive nor be released from their responsibility for shaping the options and opportunities of individuals who must live their lives right now, and must choose from what is available to them in the present. This responsibility would exist even if crime rates were to some day drop, and were to remain at a very low level from that point forward.

(Three brief points before continuing. First, the preceding remarks apply regardless of the accuracy with which Martinson may have portrayed the attitude of key decision makers toward level 1 approaches. In our view, his description reflects only one side of the latter's feelings—and it somewhat exaggerates that side. Second, as suggested earlier, crime rates may drop within given geographic areas even though recidivism rates remain unchanged for program-exposed offenders in those same areas. On the other hand, recidivism rates may clearly rise or fall despite a virtual absence of measurable change in crime rates. Third, the issue of responsibility applies not to decision makers alone, but to the general public as well. However, it applies in a very different and far more diffuse way.)

As suggested earlier, level 2 approaches are not likely to play a large role in helping a sizable portion of today's offenders forge specific links with their immediate environment, links that may help them satisfy personal needs and social requirements. (This does not mean that such approaches can make no important contributions, individually or collectively.) At the present time, level 1 approaches appear to be the only resources that can help forge these links relative to a substantial portion of the offender population. This, in itself, makes it appropriate for major decision makers to support these approaches.

Support does not mean unquestioned acceptance or indiscriminate usage. Clearly, many programs have little positive impact on anyone and merit no support. Nor does it mean that major decision makers should restrict themselves to level 1 approaches, or make few efforts to improve those methods which are of value. What it means is that these decision makers—like those in any field—should utilize, promote, or at least maintain what amount to the best tools and strategies that are available at any given time. (Few people would seriously consider eliminating, say, the vitamins and medicines of today on grounds that they are far from perfect, or in view of the hoped for improvements of tomorrow.) Moreover, decision makers should support these tools and strategies until something equally good, or better, comes along. Finally, it means they should continue to build on the achievements and positive leads that have accumulated to date.

On this latter point, Martinson's virtual polarization of the past, on the one hand, and the present as well as the future on the other, provides an unduly narrow basis on which to proceed.[12] In "Crossroads," the past was presented as bankrupt and as offering virtually nothing positive to build on. In contrast, the present and future appeared to possess a monopoly on positive achievement, or at least hope. More specifically, only the social planning epoch seemed to offer a valid basis on which to proceed. Such a view is incorrect.

As indicated, Martinson believes that key decision makers "are no longer very much interested in whether some 'program' or other can be shown to 'reduce recidivism' " [30]. Even if this belief were mostly correct, it would not, in our view, apply to the full range of decision makers. (Even if *decision maker* were defined to exclude most practitioners, the belief might not apply to the majority either.) For example, reduced recidivism rates are clearly regarded as a fundamental objective by most individuals who offer, require, administer, or implement specific treatment programs. These individuals, whom we will call *front-line decision-makers,* mainly consist of judges, program and department administrators, and a wide range of practitioners (probation officers, etc.). (See Appendix G regarding the standard ad hominem arguments that can be directed against these decision makers relative to their involvement with level 1 approaches. Such arguments do not alter the fact that these individuals are concerned with the achievement of lower recidivism rates.[13])

Generally speaking, the actions and policies of front-line decision makers have a direct, immediate, often irreversible impact on the options, and therefore lives, of specific offenders. Many such decision makers have frequent or personal contact with offenders as individuals. This contact sometimes lasts a number of years, intermittently or otherwise. For these and related reasons, they are often in a good position to observe the personal investments made by numerous offenders in level 1 approaches, and the specific use which these individuals make of such approaches relative to their adjustment. Their observations apply especially, but not exclusively to offenders who are interested in changing their pattern of adjustment or are considering the possibility of doing so. (They also apply over and beyond the stereotype of conning one's way along by playing the treatment game. The fact that some individuals play this game does not mean the majority do so.) Finally, these decision makers are likely to be especially aware of what the unavailability of such resources can mean to offenders, particularly those who wish to change what they may regard as their miserable lot in life. This goes beyond the issue of recidivism rates alone.

Given these investments, responses, and desires on the part of offenders, it is important for decision makers at all levels to keep in mind that the here-and-now needs of these individuals can easily get overlooked or shunted aside. The latter is especially likely to happen if level 1 programs are deemphasized or watered down, for example, as a result of marked changes in priorities or the introduction of unidirectional proposals such as that mentioned above. These considerations apply regardless of the immediate crime reduction value of correctional treatment programs as perceived by the public itself.

Until better programs come along, key decision makers should try to forestall this deemphasis on methods of intervention that are of value to many offenders.

**Part III
Prospects and
Strategies for
Correctional Research**

10 Treatment-Centered Research Today

Focusing in on Leads

As seen in earlier chapters, many leads exist regarding the type of approaches that can reduce recidivism for specified offenders under stated conditions. These leads can supply corrections with a definite direction in which to move and several targets on which to focus. This, of course, does not rule out additional directions and targets.

As seen in "Crossroads," Martinson would have us throw away or ignore most such leads. There, his approach was much the same as that of a hypothetical general who instructs his forces to discontinue their attack precisely when they have started to gather momentum and are ready to zero in on specific targets. Having first halted his armies, he would then send them off in a different direction, hopefully to conquer more formidable objectives and even broader stretches of land. He would do so without allowing them to reach their original objective and without consolidating their position or building on their previous gains.

In terms of long-range strategy, Martinson's position is comparable to that of a scientist or decision maker who might recommend the following: "Let's write off this new area of investigation before going any farther. After all, few studies have produced really interesting leads; and those leads are still miles from giving us the answers that we need." The main shortcoming of such a recommendation centers on the fact that most advances within the exact and applied sciences are preceded by a zeroing in on, and skillful pursuit of, leads which have emerged from the studies and observations in question. The advances themselves take place when one figures out what makes the subject of those leads—for example, relatively successful programs—"tick." (Similarly, break-throughs are almost always preceded by a detailed and often lengthy analysis of specific leads or findings, and by an analysis and integration of the pattern of findings or converging evidence that may only become apparent from one study to the next.)

Thus, if most investigators had followed Martinson's recommendation prior to making a detailed analysis of existing clues and patterns, few advances might have taken place within the long-established sciences during, say, the past 150 years. In terms of conceptual progress (pp. 90-91), corrections is now at a point where it can begin its first systematic analysis of the clues and patterns that have emerged during its own 25 to 30 years of scientific investigation. As a result, this is a time to support correctional treatment as an empirical science, not to write it off.

Two points before proceeding. First, all scientific clues, i.e., new leads, replications, and patterns of findings, are ultimately derived from individual studies or observations. New leads (basic clues) are likely to be obtained from no more than a small group of individual studies.[1] (Like all remaining studies, these are conducted (1) within a general subject area, e.g., that of level 1 programs, and (2) relative to specific categories of analysis, e.g., particular level 1 treatment modalities.) This group of studies—early studies, in point of time—may later be supported by a larger number or higher percentage of studies within and across various categories of analysis. However, without the leads that are supplied by the earlier studies, there would be nothing specific to build on or replicate, and nothing that could eventually become part of a pattern of findings.[2] In this regard, there is no substitute for individual studies and observations, no matter how sophisticated and appropriate one's analytic structure, statistical operations, criterion measures, or simulation models may be.

Second, there is nothing wrong with looking at data from a fresh perspective or exploring new areas and approaches. This is especially true if one has thus far obtained few positive results—basic clues and supportive studies alike. However, as suggested, it is probably unwise to rapidly switch from one framework, area, or approach to another without having thoroughly explored the original area and carefully checked the leads and patterns that already exist. As we have seen, correctional research has produced a substantial number of basic clues and supportive studies with regard to level 1 approaches. To make continued progress in the years ahead—progress at something other than a snail's pace—it would probably be essential to avoid a fragmented, unsystematic exploration of these and other leads. The ideal approach would be to maintain focus and continuity without ruling out fresh perspectives and exploration, i.e., without losing balance and flexibility in the process. This, of course, is easier said than done.

Moving Toward a New Phase

In the early stages of an empirical science, many studies and observations may yield negative findings or even false leads.[3] As a result, the initial sorting-out phase—the search for basic clues from among a large number of observations—may be especially tedious and in some respects unrewarding. The danger of giving up too soon, and of turning to other areas instead, is perhaps greatest at this point. It is probably accurate to say that corrections, as an empirical science, has only recently completed its initial sorting-out phase. If this is indeed correct, it would mean that correctional research is theoretically in a position to now take the next step in its development. As suggested below, this would not mean that its practical problems or conceptual difficulties are over.

Despite its relative youth, correctional research has identified several positive leads and patterns of findings. Ideally, its next phase of development would involve the careful pursuit and integration of these and related leads. However, in science, as elsewhere, development seldom occurs on a straight-line or idealized basis. In the specific case of corrections, there is, for example, no firm reason—certainly no a priori basis—for believing that the initial pursuit/ integration phase will actually get off the ground within the near future, relative to these leads. On the contrary, given the time pressures and range of demands that are increasingly placed on correctional research, there is a good chance it will not. Whatever the exact chances may be—and they will vary somewhat, through time—the following perspective and suggestions would still apply.

Although corrections has been around for centuries, correctional research as a systematic empirical science hardly existed prior to 1950. During these few decades, it has begun to get its bearings and gather momentum, mostly in relation to the complex task of achieving level 1 objectives. At the same time, it has been a science like any other: it has often pursued false leads; it has made naive mistakes; it has proceeded in an inefficient manner; and, today, its ultimate goals seem almost as distant as ever. Yet, despite this, correctional research has developed through its difficult sorting-out phase; it has continued to move forward and gather strength; it has recognized that its main objectives are still of value to offenders and society; and, it has conceptualized the relationship between its capacities and limitations on the one hand and its basic objectives and alternatives on the other.[4]

Knowing these things—knowing its strengths, value, and role—this youthful science should, in effect, refuse to be talked into an inferiority complex by those who would judge it primarily on the basis of its inability to meet their demands for (1) a particular kind of progress, for instance, the achievement of level 2 objectives; (2) more rapid progress; and (3) greater overall achievement than is possible during its initial stages of development. (See n. 5 for further comment.)

Beyond this, correctional researchers should not be turned aside by the fact that many variables or leads which have been sorted out thus far are complex and difficult to control. In this connection, it might be kept in mind that complexity and difficulty did not deter the individuals whose persistence and skill eventually produced a clear picture of the by no means elegant DNA molecule. Here, scientists came directly to grips with the fact that progress, or "quantum leaps forward," usually involve a synthesis of various clues or items of information, an integration of complexity rather than an elimination or avoidance of it. This fact has been recognized and accepted by the long-established sciences, everywhere from the realm of subatomic particles to the unusual soil of Mars. It has been recognized outside the exact sciences as well.[6] Correctional researchers, decision makers, and an often impatient public must, each in their own way, come to terms with the idea that corrections is not exempt from this fact of life.

Research as a Crisis Tool

Finally, correctional researchers should reject the argument that they must undertake, forthwith, a new and very different set of investigations—specifically, that they begin to focus almost exclusively on level 2 objectives because a virtual plague is raging outside. As indicated, today's plague or crisis—intolerably high crime rates—must be responded to by a broad network of efforts. These would include well-integrated programs and procedures in such areas as delinquency prevention, public education, community involvement, expanded social opportunities for disadvantaged groups, earlier apprehension of offenders, court reform—and corrections. Collectively, these efforts or network components might reduce crime rates to a far lower level than they are currently at; in this sense, they could perhaps eliminate today's crisis. However, individually, it is almost certain, in our view, that they could not do so. (On this point, the following assumption might be noted. Compared to the collective or total contribution of the preceding efforts to the level 2 goal of crime reduction, the contributions of individual network components would probably range from very small, in the case of some components, to moderate, in the case of others. The contribution of corrections, as distinct from the justice system in toto, would probably be about average when compared to that of other components.)

Thus, if one compares the rather sizable and still largely irreplaceable contribution that is made by corrections in the area of level 1 objectives (such as reduced recidivism rates), with the much smaller, albiet meaningful, contribution that can probably be made by corrections in the area of level 2 objectives (for example, reduced crime rates), it becomes clear that there would be considerably more to lose than gain by withdrawing support from level 1 objectives in order to redesign today's correctional programs and correctional research centers for primary or exclusive use as level 2 crisis tools. For this and related reasons, the preceding argument (or demand) should be rejected.

Maintaining Continuity and Focus

This rejection would not mean that future research efforts must be a replica of those in the past. As implied earlier, new subject matter, refined methodologies, and more broadly based outcome measures should not, indeed cannot, be excluded from future undertakings. Nevertheless, if one seriously wishes to build on leads and patterns that have emerged thus far, the following approaches and considerations would be essential in terms of maintaining continuity and focus:

1. In upcoming years, correctional researchers would give primary emphasis to the study of offenders, treatment-control personnel (staff), and treatment-control settings. They would focus on offenders and staff separately and in interaction with one another. This would be done largely in the context of

programs that try to take account of the needs, interests, abilities, and limitations of offenders as individuals. Researchers would also study the interaction between offenders and staff, on the one hand, and treatment-control settings, on the other. In all such investigations, rates of arrest and conviction would comprise the main indices of program impact (see item 6). Other outcome measures, e.g., vocational adjustment, community adjustment, and attitudinal change, could provide important supplementary evidence and leads.

2. Although primary emphasis would be on the study of offenders, staff, and setting, other areas of investigation could be included. These might involve "the sociology of the life span . . . the analysis of systems," etc. [30]. However, because of their basic content,[7] these investigations would not provide adequate followup on the majority of leads and patterns that have emerged to date.[8] As a result, they would play a secondary but not necessarily unimportant role with regard to the followup efforts in question, at least within the near and intermediate future. (See Appendix H for further discussion of these areas.) Other major areas of study would be deterrence, incapacitation, and criminal careers.

3. In essence, the investigations mentioned in items 1 and 2 would focus on methods of developing and linking up the personal drives and abilities of offenders, on the one hand, with here-and-now opportunities and requirements of society, on the other. In general terms, they would relate to the following areas: (1) the social psychology of motivational patterns, interpersonal interactions, and environmental challenges; and (2) the analysis of specified resources and settings. The latter area would involve not only the continued refinement and optimal utilization of available programs and settings, but the development of new and better approaches as well. In terms of our air fleet analogy, the overall goal for this as well as the former area would be to help today's and tomorrow's "air fleets" carry a higher proportion of "passengers" to their personal and social destinations, and to complete each journey with a minimum of wear and tear on everyone concerned. Indirectly, this goal encompasses the concepts of effectiveness, appropriateness, and efficiency.

4. Correctional researchers would proceed on the assumption that offenders, collectively, are not an undifferentiated mass of individuals, and that they do not all respond to interpersonal stimuli, program inputs, and environmental challenges in the same way. Thus, whenever possible, future research designs would allow for a separate analysis of program impact in relation to each offender grouping that is likely to be observed within the total sample. (These approaches may be referred to as a form of differentiated analysis.) A classification of treatment-control personnel would allow for similar analyses relative to various offender/staff combinations.

5. Special efforts would be made to test out theoretically and empirically derived hypotheses concerning various categories of offender, staff, setting, program input, and environmental challenge. Here, the primary goal would be to

identify the main factors and interactions associated with success or improvement, i.e., to figure out what makes things "tick." This would mean coming to grips with such questions as: Why does this group of offenders respond positively to this type of program input—or environmental challenge—within this type of setting? In the long-run, answers (even partial answers) to such questions may provide a great deal of mileage with respect to level 1 objectives. This point has been emphasized by Glaser [16].

6. It would be a mistake to downgrade or abandon recidivism as an index of program impact. This applies even apart from the focus and continuity goals in question. The utility of this index has been accepted by Martinson himself. For example, in "What Works," he described recidivism as "the phenomenon which reflects most directly how well our present programs are performing the task of rehabilitation" [31]. He then used this criterion as the sole basis for assessing all 93 studies which were presented in that article. To be sure, this view or position—which related to level 1 objectives—was almost the exact reverse of the markedly rejecting stance that he later presented in "Crossroads" with respect to recidivism. (As seen on p. 62 of this book, the latter position was presented by describing the presumed and/or actual opinions of various groups and agencies, chiefly in relation to level 2 objectives.) However, it was essentially the same as that which had been suggested and implied in *Correctional Effectiveness*, also in relation to level 1 objectives and recidivism:

> Correctional research . . . has spent half a century developing a set of criteria (recidivism) that are both socially legitimate and measurable in relatively reliable and sophisticated ways. . . . [Regarding the assessment of institutional adjustment,] the single most critical issue in this area is the relationship between institutional adjustment and postinstitutional behavior, especially recidivism. . . . [Regarding the assessment of community adjustment,[9]] under no circumstances can it be argued that community adjustment measures are superior to recidivism measures when dealing with offenders. [27]

Nevertheless, a word of caution. To date, *recidivism* has been used in such a variety of ways that it is often difficult to compare the results of differing studies which have employed this measure. For example, recidivism has referred to:

1. Rate of rearrest or reconviction.
2. Percentage of individuals rearrested or reconvicted.
3. Percentage of individuals sentenced to jail or returned to prison for any length of time, not just rearrested and reconvicted, and, entirely apart from total number of rearrests or reconvictions.
4. Rate of or percentage of individuals with 30-day or longer jail/prison sentences, excluding all lesser sentences and other dispositions such as fines or probation.

5. Rate of revocation, a measure which sometimes reflects agency policy as much as (or more than) it reflects offender behavior itself.

Other variations have occurred on top of these. For instance, sometimes only certain kinds or severities of arrest are counted. At other times, the entire range is used, technical violations, minor misdemeanors, and status offenses included. Sometimes all such offenses, minor and major, are given equal weight. Often a fairly short followup is employed, e.g., 3 to 6 months. On other occasions, a much longer followup is used—and even this may vary by 1 or 2 years. Sometimes the followup is started at point of instant arrest or initial exposure to a treatment program. In other cases (not just with respect to jail or prison sentences), it is initiated after a set amount of program exposure or, more often, on completion of the given program. Frequently, all followup information is derived from records maintained by program staff alone. In other cases, it is obtained from official "rap sheets" that are maintained by independent agencies. Finally, researchers often fail to specify the range of offenses, the length of followup, or the source of data which they have used, not to mention the definition of *arrest* itself.

If corrections is to obtain maximum benefit from recidivism as a measure of effectiveness, we believe that it is important for researchers to increasingly use (1) longer-term followups (12 months at least; 18 or 24 months if possible); (2) arrest and, where possible, conviction information, not just specified types of sentence; and (3) records which are maintained by independent agencies, provided, of course, that these records appear to be accurate and relatively complete. It would also be important to separate minor offenses, such as technical violations, from the main analysis itself. Apart from these specific recommendations, we believe that without increased uniformity in the use of recidivism, this index, while potentially valuable as an impact measure for any individual program, may only be of moderate use relative to the continued progress of correctional research as a whole.

11 Challenge and Initial Response

Research en Masse

Today, largely because of substantial federal support, the justice system has entered an era in which numerous research studies are being produced. More studies have probably been conducted since the early 1970s than during the previous twenty-five years. Although the quality of many such investigations has been far from optimal, valuable results have often been produced.

Given this situation, an emerging challenge to correctional research is that of tapping into these results in ways that can yield maximum information regarding the impact and implications of various treatment approaches. This challenge calls for increased emphasis not only on the sorting-out phase, conceived of as an ongoing and fundamental process,[1] but on the pursuit-integration phase in particular. Greater emphasis on the latter phase would have been appropriate even in the late 1960s, irrespective of increased federal support. Given the rapidly accumulating findings that have resulted from several years of such support, this shift in emphasis—and overall increase in emphasis—is even more appropriate today.

To meet today's challenge and implement the called-for changes, correctional research must become familiar with data-handling approaches that make it possible to interrelate the results of individual investigations on an across-studies basis. Toward this end, it must learn to compare, contrast, and assess the findings from different individual studies in ways that (1) increase the chance of linking together clues that may be contained in each study, and (2) reduce the chance of overlooking important leads and systematically obscuring positive as well as negative findings within and across studies.

Increased emphasis on multistudy data-handling approaches would not mean an end to the need for high-quality individual studies. It would mean that the findings from these studies, i.e., the products of sound designs and sophisticated as well as differentiated analyses, could be utilized in a broader context than before. (Data-handling approaches include the strategies, procedures, and criteria that are reviewed on pp. 98-101. They are also discussed in chapters 12 through 14.)

Martinson's conclusion that almost nothing works was based on a pioneer effort to systematically integrate the findings from a large number of individual studies. This integration was to take place via a specific set of data-handling approaches, relative to eleven distinguishable content categories. The approaches he used presented several difficulties with respect to the interrelating and integrating of these findings. These difficulties were largely responsible for his inaccurate yet extremely influential assessment of intervention as a whole.

By reviewing these approaches, we will now illustrate and summarize certain difficulties that can arise relative to today's challenge of multistudy data integration; once specified, these problems may be less likely to recur. This formal and somewhat technical review will suggest certain alternative approaches to today's challenge.

Review of Martinson's Approach

As seen in "What Works" and "Crossroads," a faulty picture of correctional treatment was produced by the following approaches or factors, singly and (for the most part) in combination:

1. A minimizing and/or ignoring of the positive findings from numerous individual studies—studies that related to each of several treatment categories (individual counseling, group counseling, etc.).

2. A framework and orientation ("total-category approach") in which each treatment category was evaluated and primarily described (though not analyzed) as a single, undifferentiated entity. This was done despite the specific, often varied findings that were obtained relative to such dimensions as age, sex, type of offender, type of treatment orientation, and quality of supervision.

3. An analytic structure ("single-category approach") in which the findings from any one research study were used to help evaluate one particular treatment category alone.[2] Such a structure, while appropriate in itself, was especially limiting as a result of the following, joint conditions: (a) it was combined with an analytic framework ("independent-category approach") in which each treatment category was evaluated independently of each remaining category;[3] (b) it was used in the absence of an across-categories approach (see 4 below), e.g., one that might have provided an independent basis for redistributing or extending the potential impact of individual research studies relative to the assessment of rehabilitation as a whole.

4. Lack of an analytic approach that would make it possible to reflect the factors or patterns of findings which cut across differing categories of treatment. Such an approach would represent either a supplement or an alternate to factors 3 and 3a. (Factor 4, of course, is the simple converse of 3b above.)

5. An extremely stringent requirement for determining whether each treatment category "works," i.e., is of sufficient value in relation to a specified objective (see factor 6 below). In "What Works," the following was the

overriding condition that had to be satisfied before a treatment category (e.g., probation) could be said to work. There had to be a virtual absence of contradictions among the findings from all individual studies that comprised the category. More specifically, almost all findings had to be positive, i.e., in the direction of reduced recidivism. This requirement had to be met regardless of (a) the total number of studies that were included within the category, and (b) the scope and focus of those studies, the widely differing operational conditions, amounts of treatment input, amounts of behavioral followup, etc. that existed from one study or treatment program to the next. Moreover, this requirement existed entirely apart from the issue of whether recidivism rates were to be reduced by a minimum, or even an average, of 5, 15, or 30 percent in those programs which did show positive results.

6. An all-or-none acceptance or rejection, recommendation or nonrecom-mendation, of each treatment category, depending on whether the category did or did not work in terms of factor 5. In "What Works," this approach reflected Martinson's search for a "sure" way of handling offenders, i.e., a treatment method which could be applied on an across-the-board basis.

The consequences and implications of these factors were as follows:

Relative to factor 1, the picture that Martinson painted of treatment and rehabilitation would have been far from bleak if it had reflected and specifically illustrated (1) the fact that several treatment categories, not just one, were associated with a sizable proportion of positive results and encouraging leads; (2) the fact that at least 45 percent of all studies had shown positive or mixed-positive results (each study had satisfied the conventional standards of social science research, and almost every study related to such commonly used approaches as probation, group counseling, milieu therapy, etc. rather than such rarely used or literally unique approaches as castration); (3) the patterns that existed across several treatment categories with respect to offender characteris-tics, worker characteristics, and the interaction between type of setting and type of offender. (Item (3) is also a partial reflection of factors 3 and 4 below.)

In accordance with factor 2, Martinson included—in his global assessment of any one treatment category—essentially no reference to the promising leads that were observed at the level of major subcategories and supplementary analyses. Thus, for example, positive findings that related to various groups of individual studies (within an overall treatment category) were subsumed within, and obscured by, his negative assessment of the category as a whole (p. 40). In short, the positive contribution of these groupings or subcategories came to an end as soon as he determined—based essentially on factor 5—that the overall category did not work as a category. (This applied despite relatively rare occasions on which the analytic framework was, in effect, temporarily overridden or ignored.) This elimination or obscuring of impact extended beyond the confines of each treatment category, viewed individually; it applied to Martinson's assessment of rehabilitation as well. More specifically, since rehabilitation, in practice, mainly referred to the 11 treatment categories added together (p. 40), the potentially positive contribution of these groupings or subcategories to his summary assessment of rehabilitation was, in effect, short-circuited or abstracted out of existence by the negative global evaluation that was made of the treatment category itself.

Because of factor 3, each individual study contributed to the assessment of rehabilitation only in the context of the single treatment category into which it was originally classified—and to which it exclusively "belonged" from that point on (see n. 2). Given the addition of factors 3a and 3b, this meant that the positive findings which related to individual studies that belonged to any one treatment category rarely got linked with positive findings from studies that belonged to any other category. Thus, for example, the following applied to any two or more studies, i.e., specific treatment programs, which contained one or more factors in common with one another (e.g., a pragmatic treatment orientation or a high quality of supervision) but which, collectively, had been placed in different treatment categories. Since the findings of these studies could not be linked with one another, they could not make a direct, independent contribution to the assessment of rehabilitation based on the feature(s) which they shared in common. In effect, they each had to remain in their original box or category.

Essentially the same applied to any individual study or program that belonged to a treatment category which was eventually judged not to work (this should be distinguished from the above-mentioned situation, which involved two or more studies from differing treatment categories and which applied regardless of whether those categories worked). The study in question, together with its positive leads, had no further way of contributing to the assessment of rehabilitation, since there was no alternate category into which it could be placed and to which it might offer something of value. In this respect, there was no further path or area of potential impact open to it.

Given factor 4, it was hardly possible for Martinson to move beyond the analytic limitations produced by factors 3 and 3a in combination. Partly for this reason, he ended up giving very little emphasis to the common factors and patterns of findings which, as we have seen, existed across differing categories of treatment and were associated with a substantial reduction in recidivism. However, this lack of emphasis seemed mainly related to factor 2.[4] That is, it largely reflected the fact that the *what* in "What Works" centered not on these leads and patterns, but on the individual treatment categories as such. (As seen on p. 102, it was the individual treatment category, i.e., total category, that comprised Martinson's "unit of analysis" or "legitimate comparison" [30].) In short, Martinson's main emphasis was not on the identification and integration of promising leads, it was on the global assessment of preestablished, individual treatment categories.

Factor 5 made it virtually inevitable that Martinson would end up with a negative assessment of almost every treatment category. This was mainly due to the wide range of strategies, operating conditions, etc. that existed across the several studies or programs which comprised each category. Given these circumstances, and given the fact that each category was to be viewed as an undifferentiated entity, his selection and relatively strict application of the mutual contradictions criterion,[5] in particular, was tantamount to setting up each treatment category for failure.[6] Moreover, since these categories comprised not only the main subject matter (the *what*) of "What Works," but the central analytic units of rehabilitation in particular, it was also the case that essentially nothing, i.e., almost none of the central building blocks, would be found to work within rehabilitation itself.

In conjunction with factors 2 and 5, factor 6 served as the final grounds for rejecting in toto any category that was neither powerful nor flexible enough to work with almost all offenders, under almost all operating conditions. In this connection, these factors or requirements interacted essentially as follows:

1. Strictly speaking, any treatment category (method), viewed as an entity, either would or would not be characterized by internal contradictions—conflicts among the findings of its individual studies.[7]
2. The presence or absence of these contradictions would be the prime determiner of whether the treatment method worked; at least it would indicate whether the given method, e.g., group counseling, could be considered a "sure" way of handling offenders.
3. The outcome of (2) above would determine whether the method in question should or should not be recommended to decision makers. This either/or, go or no-go framework left essentially no room for *degrees* of workability, and for partial or conditional acceptance.

In practical terms and taken at face value, this interaction meant that each treatment method was to be accepted or rejected on an all-or-none, across-the-board basis.[8] In effect, this was like saying that a given vitamin had to be of benefit to almost everyone before it could be recommended for anyone.

Once again, virtually all emphasis remained on the treatment categories themselves, viewed as undifferentiated entities. Almost none was placed on leads and patterns that were associated with positive outcomes within and across those categories. Emphasis on these leads might have paved the way for greater support of such concepts as degrees of workability and partial or conditional acceptance, especially in relation to the previously mentioned subcategories.

Structural Limitations to the Production of Knowledge

In "Crossroads," Martinson reviewed his position regarding (1) the role that is and should be played by individual treatment categories relative to the production of correctional knowledge (*individual treatment categories*—Martinson's independent variable categories—is synonymous with *treatment modalities*, e.g., group counseling); and (2) the formal or structural relationship that exists, and should exist, between individual research studies and individual treatment categories, again with reference to correctional knowledge. He did this by summarizing the basic analytic approach that was used in *Correctional Effectiveness* (in this approach, one that was also used in "What Works," Martinson refers to individual treatment categories as the "legitimate comparison" or "unit of analysis," and to individual studies, i.e., specific treatment projects, as the "individuals in a 'deviant' cell"):

> Individual studies were classified [into a given treatment category] so that the findings of one study could be compared and contrasted with the findings of another [within that same category]. There is a gain in doing this. It leads to a special form of "deviant case analysis" in which the unit of analysis is what might be called the "legitimate comparison" and not the individuals in a "deviant" cell. If the book has any value for our field, it is because it used this method systematically with the aim of accumulating knowledge. [30]

He later added:

> Correctional research is, I hope, growing up and will cease thinking on the project-to-project [study-to-study] level which has characterized so much "evaluation" research in the last few decades. [30]

These statements touch on three points that relate to factors 2 through 4 (pp. 99-100):

1. They clearly suggest that the task of developing correctional knowledge should be organized around the total category, not around individual studies as such. The former, not the latter, should serve as the unit of analysis, i.e., the "legitimate comparison" or focal point in evolving answers to such questions as "What Works?" These quotations, especially the former, also imply that individual studies should, in fact must, remain subordinate to the treatment category into which they have been classified. More specifically, no study should—indeed, within the preceding framework, can—contribute to correctional knowledge outside the context of the given category. Regardless of how powerful or comprehensive the study may be, it neither should nor can be used to make a direct contribution to correctional knowledge,[9] either by itself or in conjunction with studies that belong to any remaining categories. (To make direct contributions, findings from individual studies would have to be handled as integral parts of the information pool that is referred to in n. 9.[10])

2. The analytic structure that is described in the first quotation reflects the fact that the approach which was used by Martinson is not designed to focus on

relationships that exist between treatment categories. The statement includes, for example, neither a mandate nor a reference to any framework for comparing and contrasting various categories in terms of the previously-mentioned dimensions and subcategories.[11] In short, the structure which it reflects allows the treatment categories (individually and in particular combinations) to delimit the number—and, necessarily, the pattern or type—of interrelationships that might otherwise be obtained if one were to utilize the full range, i.e., the across-category pool, of available information sources (individual studies).[12] These considerations are independent of the fact that many studies may not contain given types of information, e.g., information regarding treatment orientation and quality of supervision.

In our view, correctional knowledge, in the sense of valid generalizations, does not inevitably have to be organized around and primarily focused on categories of treatment. It can be developed on the basis of very different units or features, features which can cut across these broad categories (see chapters 13 and 14 for specifics). However, the approach that Martinson has described is not designed to build on these units of information on other than a total category basis. Instead, it is chiefly geared to process information as though correctional knowledge were, and perhaps should be, centered around assertions that relate to individual treatment categories alone. This applies whether the latter are viewed as undifferentiated entities or as composites of specified subcategories.

3. The preceding quotations reflect what might be called a "single-basis, single-opportunity" approach. This refers to any process in which an individual study has only one way, and one chance, of contributing to correctional knowledge. In other words, in this approach there exists no more than a single basis on which its findings can be added to the pool of correctional information, and there is only one opportunity for this contribution to occur. In the case of Martinson's approach, impact or contribution must be made relative to the treatment category within which the study is classified. As indicated, if that category is judged not to work, based on given criteria, this determination can permanently block any contribution the study may be capable of making with respect to correctional knowledge as a whole, i.e., with respect to the accumulation of valid assertions and generalizations which can relate to, or extend beyond, factors and units other than categories of treatment alone.

More specifically, if, say, the positive findings from a study are not supported by the findings from one or more additional studies that fall within the same category of treatment, this, in itself, can virtually ensure the study's lack of impact on correctional knowledge. Thus, given the present structure, the ability of a study to contribute to correctional knowledge is not based on the solidity and scope of its research design and positive findings alone, however impressive they may be. It is heavily dependent on the design and outcome of other studies that fall within the same treatment category. This approach or dependency makes sense relative to the general principle of scientific replication.

However, on further inspection, the particular form of replication that is involved turns out to be rather limited in scope and unidimensional in focus.[13] In addition, the blocking or throttling effect of the latter studies on the potentially positive contribution of the former study can neither be reduced, counterbalanced, nor obviated by the fact that the former may receive clear support—or replication in specified respects—from investigations with which it has one or more characteristics in common, but which are classified within other categories of treatment.[14] Nor can this blocking effect be reduced or eliminated by support that the former study may receive from remaining investigations which fall within the same category of treatment—unless, perhaps, the latter represent a very large majority of studies within that category.

Difficulties which are associated with the single-basis, single-opportunity approach reflect more than the absence of alternate analytic frameworks for processing the results of individual studies, and more than the presence of factor 5 alone. They involve an operational or practical offshoot of the view that these studies should contribute, or can perhaps best contribute, to correctional knowledge in terms of (1) specified features which serve as a basis for comparing the given studies with one another, and in relation to (2) a common reference or method of classification that makes it possible for the research findings from given studies to be brought together and interrelated.[15]

Before we review this offshoot, two points should be kept in mind. First, item (1) immediately above refers essentially to the data-analysis phase of knowledge building; item (2) relates to the data-integration or data-synthesizing phase. Although a study may have been analyzed on a relatively differentiated basis, results of that analysis may nevertheless be grouped or linked (integrated) with those of other studies and analyses on an essentially undifferentiated basis, e.g., in relation to a single, shared characteristic. This lack of differentiation may ultimately be a product of operational, practical, or conceptual restrictions, restrictions which are reflected in the specific information-processing approaches that were established.[16] Second, as used here, data integration necessarily involves a process of comparing the results from any one study with those from any other study or studies in relation to specified dimensions and factors which the studies share in common (see chapter 13). This process can reveal similarities and differences, positive and negative relationships or linkages. The dimensions and factors that are compared may consist of offender characteristics, program features, treatment strategies, etc.—that is, attributes which can cut across various treatment categories. Given these dimensions and factors (treatment processes included), and given their across-categories nature, data integration can take place—links can be established, and findings from individual studies can thus be extended—at various levels and on as broad a scale as possible.[17]

The earlier-mentioned offshoot relates to the fact that in *Correctional Effectiveness* and "What Works," data analysis usually did proceed along the lines of item (1) above; i.e., individual studies often were compared and contrasted on the basis of several distinguishable features.[18] However, in the case of data integration (item (2)), one and only one classification or shared characteristic was used in order to deal with given studies, and results of the given analyses for these studies were linked together or synthesized on this basis alone.[19] (This classification or common reference was the particular treatment modality, e.g., milieu therapy, that allowed these studies to be distinguished from all remaining studies at a readily discernible and easily describable level. This shared characteristic provided the basis for defining the category level itself. Dimensions and factors such as type of offender, type of treatment orientation, and quality of supervision were not utilized as common references at the across-categories level. Thus they could not serve as focal points for integrating the results of these and other studies independent of the original treatment modality.) In short, analyses that were made in connection with item (1) above were utilized on a very limited basis in relation to item (2), the data-integration phase of knowledge building.

The upshot was that information-processing operations associated with item (2) in effect represented an attempt to interrelate the findings of individual studies as if these studies could and perhaps should be regarded as homogeneous or undifferentiated entities. That is, with reference to the integration of findings from any two or more studies, no structural allowance was made for the fact that every study—every treatment program—is a nonhomogeneous, complex entity. As a result, the findings from these studies were utilized in relation to a single, superordinate category or common reference alone.

In reality, any study consists of several structural components and content-related factors, some of which are shared by other studies that may have been placed in different categories, e.g., different categories of treatment.[20] In this connection, the data-integration approach that was used by Martinson did not reflect the following: (1) comparisons which involve these components and factors can be made between the former and latter studies, for instance, between investigations that (collectively) have been placed into two or more treatment categories; and (2) these across-category comparisons can be made just as systematically and with as much statistical sophistication as any others.[21] This approach was used despite the fact that various components and factors had indeed been dealt with at the within-category level relative to the data-analysis phase of knowledge-building.

This lack of across-category comparisons among the basic sources of information, namely, individual studies, constitutes a major omission—in effect, a substantial restriction—relative to the goal of systematically accumulating knowledge. With respect to this goal, across-category comparisons would be no less legitimate than the within-category comparisons referred to by Martinson. Moreover, the leads and patterns that would result from the former comparisons would be no less important than those derived from the latter. This would also apply to the integration of these findings within the context of any overriding framework.

Alternate approaches to the integration of research findings will be outlined in chapters 13 and 14. First, however, we will review a number of general considerations that bear on the tasks, strategies, and tools of correctional research.

12 Tasks, Strategies, and Tools

Background

In one way or another, most correctional treatment programs attempt to help individual offenders come to grips with a range of interests, problems, or needs, including that of "going straight." That is, they attempt to bring offenders closer to their personally desired and/or socially required destinations. This goal extends beyond, yet largely centers around, the lowering of recidivism rates. Its relevance and legitimacy, with respect to offenders and society, would remain unchanged even if crime rates were to dramatically drop.

At this point we will not focus on questions that relate to the relevance, legitimacy, and general acceptability of this goal. We will assume that its validity is already apparent. Instead, we will briefly review the basic questions that have been asked by correctional research in its attempt to identify those methods and conditions which might best achieve this goal. We will then discuss selected issues, strategies, and tools that bear upon the research task itself. (See Appendix I for further thoughts and hypotheses regarding the general acceptability of the above-mentioned goal.)

To date, correctional research has explored many programs and approaches that attempt to develop and link the personal drives and abilities of offenders with specific opportunities and requirements of society. Basically, this research has asked: "Are these programs of value, and if so, in what ways are they of value?" *Ways* refers to recidivism, educational achievement, vocational adjustment, attitude change, etc.

In recent years, additional questions have increasingly been asked: "For *whom* are these programs of value, and under what conditions is this so?" At base, the latter questions are a supplement to and further specification of the former. There is no reason to believe that the latter questions represent an inappropriate narrowing or shifting of research focus. On the contrary, answers to such specific questions can be as valuable within corrections as they have been in other fields. (For an opposing view, see n. 1 regarding Martinson's pointed rejection of these questions.)[2]

Correctional research has made definite progress relative to the preceding questions. In particular, it has identified several leads within and across the treatment modalities that have been explored thus far. In this respect, it has completed its initial sorting-out phase and is ready to focus on the more promising leads.

Efficiency and Rate of Progress

Despite this progress, it is not likely that major breakthroughs are "right around the corner"—not if one judges by past performance. For example, the efficiency with which correctional research has analyzed and integrated its data is fairly low. Related to this, but not to this alone, its overall rate of progress has been slow. This is over and beyond the fact that several of these leads and patterns are not, in themselves, settled realities or thoroughly validated truths.

Nevertheless, various steps can be taken to increase efficiency and speed up progress, at least to some degree. One area in which this can be done is that of data handling. Within this area, two sets of approaches or considerations will be mentioned. The first relates to the handling of individual studies; the second relates to groups of studies. For present purposes, areas other than data handling need not be reviewed.[3]

Individual Studies

Efficiency and rate of progress can be increased via greater use of the differentiated analysis and hypothesis-testing approaches that were mentioned on p. 93. Differentiated analyses can increase efficiency by producing multiple findings within the context of any single study. For instance, they can allow one to answer questions about several groups of offenders within the total study sample rather than one group of offenders alone—namely, the study sample as an undifferentiated whole. By revealing similarities and differences among the former individuals—for instance, similarities in recidivism or vocational adjustment—differentiated analyses can directly speed up the identification of effective treatment approaches and the elimination of unproductive approaches as well.

Efficiency and rate of progress can also be increased via the hypothesis-testing approach. First, this approach can help maintain continuity between past, present, and future—especially, but not exclusively, when combined with the findings from differentiated analyses. (See Appendix J for an example of hypothesis testing by means of differentiated analysis.) More specifically, it can support an empirically grounded evolution or progression with respect to the type of subject matter that is explored and the specific procedures and outcome measures that are used. In this respect, greater utilization of the hypothesis-testing approach can increase efficiency by decreasing the extent to which subject matter is selected in a desultory manner and data are analyzed on a piecemeal or minimally systematic basis. It can influence the rate of progress by increasing the extent to which one pursues emerging leads and, in this sense, maintains one's momentum or presses one's advantage. (See n. 4 regarding the balance between continuity and flexibility, e.g., between an emphasis on old and new subject matter.)

The preceding remarks refer to individual studies, focused on as such. The following will relate to these same studies, focused on collectively; i.e., they will refer to any two or more studies or programs that are compared with one another on the basis of variables or factors which can be applied to each. As such, they involve what might be called approaches to multistudy data analysis and data integration.[5] In this discussion the term *data handling* will refer to data analysis and data integration, taken together. Also, it might be kept in mind that although the individual and collective levels of data handling are related to one another in fundamental ways, the latter can vary independently of the former along substantive as well as formal lines. As a result, it can involve opportunities and problems of its own, the specifics of which will depend on the data-handling approach that is used.

Groups of Studies

When dealing with groups of studies, especially large groups, there is a decided advantage in selecting an approach which involves structures, procedures, and criteria that will facilitate extensive, indepth comparisons among the given studies and will support a broadly based integration of the findings from those comparisons. Basically, the advantage of such an approach or strategy would derive from its role in helping one obtain the most mileage from, or at least get more from, the overall pool of data (studies or programs). This bears directly on issues of efficiency and rate of progress.

Stated differently, the following might be suggested as a way of extracting more from, and moving farther with, the data at hand—or as a way of reducing the possibility that half the treasure will remain untapped and half the story untold. One might increase the extent to which (1) studies are analyzed, collectively, in more than a minimally to moderately differentiated way, and (2) the resulting research findings are integrated on a broadly rather than narrowly defined basis alone.

(A minimally differentiated approach would be one that is characterized by the presence of very few types of comparisons within or between any one or more studies. A narrowly defined integration would be one that reflects the presence of and which includes relatively few variables or factors across specified units of analysis, for instance, specified categories of treatment. In effect, it is based on the delineation or establishment of few substantive dimensions in terms of which the given units can be interrelated or synthesized. It may also involve the establishment of few procedures by means of which this interrelating can be carried out in a systematic way.)

Strategies A and B

The preceding suggestion does not mean that there is no other way to make progress. On the contrary, the data-handling approach which has been used thus far in correctional research involves relatively few differentiations and/or little by way of data integration on an across-studies scale. This type of approach, although used essentially on an informal and impressionistic basis, has produced valuable insights and can undoubtedly continue to do so. Nevertheless, it is quite inefficient; and, by itself, it is not likely to carry the data very far, except over long periods of time.

For present purposes, this data-handling approach may be thought of as somewhat global or simplified, and will be referred to as "strategy A." The approach suggested above may be thought of as relatively specific or differentiated, and will be called "strategy B." (See pp. 111-112 regarding strategy B.)

From a broad time perspective, strategy A can be considered more of an exploratory approach than strategy B, despite its overlap with the latter at a structural and functional level. Nevertheless, strategies A and B may each be used in a sorting-out as well as pursuit-integration context, even though B is likely to reflect somewhat more of an hypothesis-testing orientation than A, irrespective of context.

When strategy A is applied to any pool of data (original data pool), the resulting picture of correctional knowledge is likely to be somewhat simplified or underdeveloped. In principle, this picture can be altered, strengthened, and refined if—and this is usually a large *if*—time and resources are available to carry out supplementary analyses of the original data pool or analyses which relate to new data instead. These modifications can be made without undue technical difficulty, and they can be made via the continued use of strategy A itself.

At any rate, in the case of strategy A, there appear to be no major, built-in barriers to the eventual uncovering and integration of numerous relationships that were simply not focused on in the original analysis of the given data pool.[6] Here, *built-in* means intrinsic or internal to the particular data-handling approach. Thus, built-in barriers consist of structures, procedures, and criteria that can make it difficult to bring about changes and refinements.

Despite this lack of built-in obstacles to eventually increasing the yield from any given data pool, there remains a strong possibility that in actual practice much of the data that are gathered in connection with strategy A will continue to be untapped, and much of the story untold. For example, the attention of researchers may well be directed elsewhere before many supplementary analyses are carried out with regard to the original data pool; this applies to the collection of additional, related information as well. For reasons such as these, strategy B would probably be needed in order to better uncover and integrate very complex relationships. This is apart from its advantage over strategy A with respect to efficiency and rate of progress as such.

In the case of strategies other than A or B—those we will call overly restrictive approaches—built-in barriers do exist. Since many of these barriers are likely to be rather formidable, it can be very difficult to substantially alter the picture of correctional knowledge that may be produced.[7] (This picture may involve a one-sided or otherwise inadequate representation of the full range of findings.[8]) Specifically, given the continued operation of these barriers, the picture that may have emerged from the original data pool can remain essentially unchanged—in effect, resistive to change—despite the subsequent introduction of diverse or even disparate findings which are based on supplementary analyses of the given pool, and on the analysis of previously unavailable data as well. Under these conditions, alternate approaches would have to be introduced to allow for a more balanced picture—a more representative integration—of the full range of findings. These approaches would be used instead of, or at least in addition to, the overly restrictive approach.

Collectively, factors 2 through 6 (pp. 99-101) exemplify the overly restrictive approach.[9] A review of these factors would illustrate some of the difficulties and barriers that can be encountered in connection with such an approach, especially at the level of data integration. In this particular case, it might highlight the fact that one must be careful not to rely heavily or exclusively on any approach whose analytic structure, specific procedures, and assessment criteria (operating jointly, in this instance) are almost certain to:

1. Prevent specified groups of studies from contributing to correctional knowledge in their own right, i.e., apart from the outcome of their relationship to all remaining studies that fall within the given category with which they (the former studies) are associated, and apart from the fate of that category itself.
2. Ensure the failure or virtual failure of each individual category, (or treatment modality) and/or,
3. Make it impossible for leads and patterns to emerge on a broad, across-categories scale, regardless of the apparent success or failure of individual categories.

A few words about strategy B. At this point in the development of correctional research, strategy B represents a promising approach to multistudy data analysis and data integration. This is especially true in terms of its ability to deal with complex relationships in a fairly efficient way. Complexity aside, this approach is in a good position to add depth and breadth to correctional knowledge since it can tap into any given data pool in a relatively differentiated way. This feature or ability gives it a clear head start over strategy A. To take full advantage of this feature and to maintain this early lead, one must make sure that the specific procedures and criteria that accompany strategy B will allow the given results (i.e., the differentiated findings from numerous studies) to be integrated without undue restrictions. This requirement brings the following issue into focus.

Despite its assets, strategy B is not immune to problems and shortcomings that can beset other multistudy data-handling approaches, e.g., the overly restrictive approach. One such difficulty would involve the production of an inadequate portrayal of the numerous findings that are extracted from a given data pool. To prevent this problem from arising, strategy B would have to contain specific structures and criteria which, when operating jointly, would not systematically highlight one type of finding (e.g., positive findings) and unduly restrict the impact of others. A second and somewhat related stumbling block would be that of limited reach, i.e., limited extent of influence on the part of given groups of studies, regardless of the particular type of findings that may be associated with them. To forestall this problem, strategy B would have to contain structures and procedures which (also operating jointly) would not make it inevitable that only certain groups of studies could be compared and contrasted with one another in the first place. Fortunately, these potential stumbling blocks can be avoided without much difficulty in the case of both strategies A and B.

In sum, the data-handling approaches that are used in connection with any strategy can play a critical role in increasing research output or efficiency and in supporting a broadly based representation of the basic data pool. But what exactly is the relationship between these approaches and individual programs or studies (in a sense, the relation between structure and substance)?

Data-Handling Approaches: General Considerations

Data-handling approaches are conceptual tools for processing the variables and factors that are used to describe individual programs and their relationship to other programs. They are used subsequent to the completion of these programs, and they focus on, without actually altering, certain features and products that relate to any such program.[10] For instance, they neither alter its physical conditions and formal characteristics (e.g., setting and caseload size) nor undo the inputs or activities (e.g., treatment processes) that occur during its operation. Similarly, they neither undo the results that are obtained (e.g., recidivism rates) nor modify specific relationships (e.g., shared characteristics or inputs) which exist[11] between the program and other programs. What data-handling approaches do is uncover, organize, and integrate these features and products; i.e., they process these conditions, inputs, results, and relationships, and thereby develop knowledge. In one form or another, similar processing tasks exist within every science—and data-handling approaches are the means by which they are systematically carried out. This applies regardless of how global, differentiated, or restrictive the approaches may be.

Within corrections, and relative to such tasks, data-handling approaches may be thought of as servants of individual programs: 1. Programs comprise the raw material or unorganized content (data sources) from which given variables and factors (data items) are differentiated (singled out). 2. It is by means of data-handling approaches (and in terms of data items) that the conditions, inputs, and results of individual programs are objectively and evenly described, and that relationships among programs are systematically revealed.

Thus, variables or factors that are singled out for processing constitute the points of contact between raw material, on the one hand, and data-handling approaches, on the other. These contact points or data items are the attributes, the "defined content," in terms of which individual programs can be described and on the basis of which they can be compared with others. It is in terms of these attributes, features, and events that data-handling approaches carry out their tasks and knowledge is developed. This series of events is illustrated in figure 12-1.

As indicated on p. 104, although data analysis can proceed on a fairly differentiated basis with respect to any pool of studies, data integration may proceed in an undifferentiated way and with very limited scope, relative to the findings from that analysis. Given the preceding discussion, the source of this difference can be understood as follows. Utilization of several rather than few data items is indeed the key to differentiated rather than global analysis. However, data items play no active role in the integration of findings from any set of analyses. Integration of findings is the province of data-handling approaches instead. Thus, given a set of differentiated findings from a particular group of studies, data-handling approaches, not data items, would be responsible for bringing about (1) differentiated rather than global integrations of those results and (2) broadly based rather than narrowly circumscribed (e.g., within-category) integrations as well.

In this context, *integration* is the end result of a process by means of which the findings from individual studies are added to or otherwise combined with those from other studies. This applies to findings that are associated with data items as well (chapters 13 and 14). By virtue of this process, each study or data item either can or cannot contribute to the pool of correctional knowledge at given levels of integration, e.g., on an across-categories basis. Its ability to contribute at any given level is a direct function of the data-handling approach itself, i.e., the particular structures, procedures, and criteria which are used to

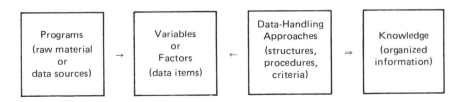

Note: → means "consists of," ← means "operates on," and ⇒ means "leads to."

Figure 12-1. Sources, Elements, and Producers of Knowledge.

bring about the integration. (See pp. 104-105, 120-127, and 140-143 regarding three somewhat different forms of the integration process.) We will now focus on data items in a more detailed and concrete way.

Data Items: Background and Specifics

Data items[12] supply the content base of systematic knowledge, the *what* of "what do we know, in objective terms." Other things being equal, the more items one can work with, the greater the chance of developing a comprehensive picture of any given phenomenon, say, a particular treatment program. By the same token, if only a few data items have been singled out, e.g., few variables that describe the target population or treatment strategies associated with the program, basic limitations will soon appear. First, the program will be difficult if not impossible to describe in a detailed, systematic way. Second, numerous similarities and differences that exist between the program and other programs may be impossible to pin down or scientifically validate. And third, differentiated analyses may be impossible to carry out, depending on which specific items *have* been singled out.[13] These limitations are not without practical and theoretical significance, and as suggested, they probably cannot be fully overcome.

The first limitation, for example, can make it difficult to replicate the given program in other than a fairly general way. This can represent a concrete loss if the findings in question are quite positive in terms of recidivism rates, employment rates, etc. Because they are often one-sided and incomplete, subjective impressions and personal recollections that bear on possible replication of a program cannot provide a reliable substitute for the data items in question—specifically, for the detailed accounts that are usually derived from preestablished, systematically evaluated data items.

The second limitation bears on the identification of reliable leads. Impressionistic reports that focus on the apparent similarities and differences among given programs cannot provide an adequate basis for the identification of such leads. This is because they often involve (1) large amounts of selective recall, "halo effect," and wishful thinking and (2) a possible trend toward overly broad generalizations. Reports that are often subject to such a wide margin of error should not be used as substitutes for systematic observations, those based on preestablished data items and objective rating scales.[14] This applies despite the valuable contributions that are sometimes made by impressionistic reports which draw direct comparisons between small numbers of well-observed programs. In short, whether few or many programs are involved, such reports can provide a supplement to, but not an adequate substitute for, systematic observations. The latter are a necessary ingredient in the development of reliable leads.

The third limitation has already been reviewed.

To avoid these basic limitations and to help advance correctional knowledge, researchers should make special efforts to collect information on a large number of items. They should do so despite the fact that, as individual researchers, they may seldom be able to fully exploit their data, e.g., to systematically compare their findings with those of other researchers relative to particular items. As to researchers and academicians who are in a position to attempt these comparisons or to further analyze single programs, it is almost certain that their efforts will be hampered and quite possibly abandoned if the desired information is not close at hand. In this connection, it is not uncommon for investigators to express the following thoughts when surveying various programs with an eye to possible comparative or supplementary analyses: "If the relevant information (e.g., number of prior arrests) has already been collected, we're in business. If not, it's probably too late to do anything about it now."[15]

Thus, apart from sheer numbers of items, researchers should increasingly attend to a core of standard items, each of which may bear on recidivism or other aspects of adjustment. Collectively, these items would cover a broad range of categories or areas, e.g., offenders, staff, setting, and operations. Within each area and whenever opportunity allows, researchers would gather and analyze information on a large percentage of items such as those presented below. (First, a few words of explanation. In the following list of suggested core items, each area contains two or more subdivisions, e.g., Area I (offenders), subdivisions A and B. There are 10 subdivisions in all, across the four areas in question. In areas I-A, II-A, III-A, and IV-A, all items that appear are mutually exclusive. Within these areas, separate information would therefore be needed on all items. In other areas, e.g., IV-B and the first section of III-B, all items that are listed comprise a single set of alternate choices. Within these areas, information would be recorded only on the particular item(s) that describes the program or setting in question. For details on other areas and subdivisions, see n. 16.)

I. *Offenders*
   A. Background characteristics: age; sex; offense history;[17] base expectancy; IQ; grade level attained; school status at intake; work history; work status at intake; marital status; parental status; residence (urban, semiurban, rural); neighborhood (high, medium, low delinquency); socioeconomic status; ethnicity.
   B. Personal characteristics: developmental level (interpersonal, psychosocial, moral, ego, conceptual, and/or other[18]); classification or personality type (Warren, Quay, Schrag, Megargee, and/or other); trait clusters (communicative-alert, passive-uncertain, defiant-indifferent-alienated, dependent, independent, other); specific factors or generic variables (cognitive complexity, locus of control, internalized standards, affect awareness, impulse control, planfulness/foresight, persistence, rigidity/inflexibility, social consciousness, other) [47,49] .

II. *Staff*

    A. Background characteristics: age; sex; ethnicity; amount of training; type of training; amount of experience; type of experience; work status (professional, paraprofessional, volunteer, other).

    B. Personal characteristics:[19] strength of feelings and opinions; sharpness-alertness; criticalness; past personal difficulties, felt as such; satisfaction with work and accomplishments; socially desired qualities; socially undesirable qualities; aggression-hostility; other.

    C. Treatment orientations: A type versus B type; instrumental versus expressive; relationship/self-expression versus surveillance/self-expression versus surveillance/self-control; I_2 versus Cfm versus Mp-Cfc versus Na versus Nx worker; and/or other classifications; orientation toward change and activity; use of own past experiences as primary basis for working with others.

III. *Setting*

    A. Formal aspects: jurisdiction and sponsorship (justice system; nonjustice system, public; nonjustice system, private; other); size (offender population); physical condition (age, upkeep, space); adequacy of services (food, clothes, medical, other); level of physical security; accessibility to community.

    B. Type: adult prison or youth institution; jail; camp/ranch/farm; day care center; other (specified) community center; halfway house; group home; free community (natural setting, e.g., family, relatives, independent placement); management and decision-making styles; social climate dimensions (Moos); homogeneous offender grouping (e.g., by Quay type) versus nonhomogeneous grouping; coeducational versus noncoeducational.

IV. *Operations*

    A. Formal aspects: basis of assignment (geographic, available case opening or living-unit space, person match, program match, other); offender/staff ratio or caseload size; living-unit size; extent of initial diagnostic workup; direct treatment-centered contacts (frequency, number, total hours, total duration); collateral contacts (frequency, number, total hours); number of treatment modalities; main modality combinations (e.g., individual counseling and remedial education); supervision of staff (type, amount); postprogram or postdischarge contacts.

    B. General features:

        1. Modalities and patterns of intervention: individual psychotherapy; individual counseling; group counseling, noncoeducational; group counseling, coeducational; family therapy or counseling; milieu therapy; education (standard, remedial, other); vocational training; job referral and placement; work release; recreation and cultural enrichment; involvement in community activities; physical chal-

lenge (survival training, Outward Bound); advocacy and legal assistance; crisis intervention; medical approaches (specify); supervised release; standard probation; standard parole; imprisonment or institutionalization; other components or activities (family assistance, referral to other agencies, work assignments, day passes, furloughs).

    2. Orientations and schools: eclectic; analytic (neo-Freudian); behavior modification; Transactional Analysis; Gestalt; other.

C. Specific features:[20]

    1. Goals and areas of focus: reducing delinquent or criminal self-image; modifying attitudes toward adults; increasing internal controls; increasing self-awareness/self-acceptance; countering apathy/indifference; family/parental relationships; peer influence/pressure; everyday practical adjustment; client-worker relationship.

    2. Processes and lines of approach: gaining client's confidence in worker as understanding/capable; expressing personal concern for/acceptance of client; exposure to adult models; preparing client for specific life situations; ego bolstering via success experiences; using positive peer culture; using authority (legitimate power or force); using internal stress as stimulus/motivator; doing the unexpected; client's participation in case planning and decision making; concreteness versus abstractness of verbalizations and interpretations.

    In most investigations, individual researchers would not be able to gather information on the majority of items from all 10 subdivisions that comprise this rather sizable list. However, they might often be able to do so with respect to most subdivisions. This applies even though the present list is not exhaustive, particularly in areas II-B, II-C, and IV-C.

    Whatever information they may gather and analyze, researchers, as individuals, might bear the following in mind. First, the more data items they can study, the faster correctional knowledge can advance. This does not mean that progress is likely to be swift in an absolute sense. It means progress can be accelerated by the exploration of many rather than few items, within and across the areas listed above. Second, studies that involve a sizable number of data items are likely to call for substantial effort on the part of investigators. In this regard, researchers might reflect on a thought that was expressed some 350 years ago. Writing soon after the discoveries of Kepler, Galileo, and Brahe, Francis Bacon remarked that the advancement of knowledge seems to involve a type of investigation which is "laborious to search, ignoble to meditate, harsh to deliver, . . . and minute in subtlety" [4]. Thus, even at the dawn of observational science and at the moment of its early triumphs, the painstaking aspect of progress had already come to light. Bacon's insight into the problems of knowledge building provided a lesson that was eventually accepted by the now-established sciences. It was an insight that applies today, relative to the challenges that face correctional researchers.

It may be asserted that these challenges are of academic interest only. Specifically, it may be said that corrections can no longer wait for those who would "gaze at the stars" and take copious notes, that instead, it must act quickly and decisively, as if at the point of a gun. Relative to this view, it might be mentioned that few people would oppose the idea that corrections must act, and react. Yet, in our view, individuals involved with corrections must ask questions and make careful observations as well. If we (criminal justice personal, academicians, and others) fail to develop our conceptual tools and data base—if all we do is act, and force things through—we will eventually produce not a science, but machinery for waging a form of war. If we grow accustomed to making decisions that are seldom preceded or followed by objective inquiry, we may soon grow accustomed to producing "truth" by fiat or personal conviction alone, that is, to simply proclaiming, as self-evident or intuitively clear, those policies and principles which support the decisions in question. Under such conditions the preceding challenges would indeed be academic. There would be little need for data items, labor, and subtlety, since new information is superfluous when knowledge deemed infallible exists.

Before proceeding to chapter 13, two technical yet fundamental points might be mentioned. First, to help corrections obtain maximum payoff from any given item, researchers, collectively, would utilize identical or virtually identical categories when describing that item. For instance, on age of offender, they could better compare their respective findings if each researcher were to subdivide the item into standard groupings, say, 0-12, 13-15, 16-18, etc., than if some were to use those groupings while others were to use 0-11, 12-14, 15-17, 18-21, and still others were to use 0-13, 14-16, 17-20, etc. To be sure, in many investigations or for specific reporting purposes, some categories would be more appropriate than proposed standard categories and would naturally be used. This, however, would not preclude the use of standard categories in connection with additional analyses and reporting, either by the original investigators or by others with whom raw data are shared.

Second, the concept of standardized categories bears on the broader need to develop uniform definitions of data items, and uniform methods—specific rating scales, for example—for assessing those items. In the case of most items, this need can probably be met without great difficulty. In cases where complete uniformity does not seem possible, any movement in this direction would still constitute a gain. Standardization, together with uniformity or at least similarity of definitions, is a prerequisite for meaningful communication and efficient knowledge building within every science.

13 The Next Steps

We will now review three steps that can be taken to help develop effective intervention based on findings from large numbers of studies. Each step or approach involves an analytic structure or reflects a framework for integrating data which differs from that used in "What Works." For example, each approach deals directly with individual data items and individual studies. None are organized around treatment modalities viewed, or integrated, as undifferentiated entities.[1] And each approach makes it possible for individual studies to contribute to correctional knowledge independently of the treatment modality to which they belong, and regardless of whether the modality itself would be judged effective on the basis of such factors as 5 and 6 (p. 101), singly or in combination.

Before reviewing these methods, we will briefly suggest two ways in which the overly restrictive approach can itself be improved. First, modify the independent category approach (p. 39) by eliminating the boundaries that presently exist within each of the following, proposed modality sets: parole and partial physical custody; group methods and milieu therapy; casework/individual counseling and individual psychotherapy. Thus, by combining the individual modalities that presently comprise each of these three sets, individual studies that now belong to one modality or the other (within the given set) would have more opportunity to contribute their findings to the total pool of correctional information. Specifically, the findings from each study, within any one modality, would be given an opportunity to link up with those from other studies that presently fall within the second modality. While this structural modification would eliminate the distinctions that presently exist between these modalities, it would open the door to the identification of leads on an across-modalities basis. This would apply to any set of modalities, old or new.

Second, use the present subcategories and combinations of individual variables as a basis for integrating the findings of individual studies on an across-modalities level. That is, conduct a series of supplementary analyses which are organized around individual subcategories (e.g., therapeutic emphasis) and combinations of individual variables (e.g., young, noninstitutionalized males), and which cut across the present treatment modalities.

By following the first suggestion, we would no longer be asking whether each of the present treatment modalities work. We would be focusing on broader aspects of treatment instead (for example, postinstitutional, multiple client, and one to one). By following the second suggestion, we would be moving in an opposite direction and focusing on more specific questions: Which program components show promise? Under what conditions do positive results occur? For whom do these components work?[2] These opposite yet complementary approaches could represent a productive modification of the modality-centered, total-category framework that was used in "What Works"—provided the issue of realistic assessment criteria is dealt with:

If an across-modalities approach were used, a greater number of studies would be compared with one another than is presently the case, and a greater number of contradictory findings would undoubtedly be observed within almost any set of studies. If factor 5 were retained, these findings would make it virtually impossible for any combined modality to be seen as working. As a result, it would negate the potential gains associated with the first and second suggestions alike.

For this reason, and because it represents an unrealistically stringent criterion in any event, factor 5 should be dropped as a primary basis for assessing the worth of any treatment modality. Nor should it be used to determine the presence or absence of subcategory leads, and those which relate to combinations of individual variables. Increased emphasis should be given to the differential-weighting approach, instead (Appendix A). However, even this approach should be used with considerable caution in view of the major content differences, e.g., differences in specific techniques of counseling or skill development, that exist among many if not most programs that fall within any treatment modality, expanded or otherwise. This point is of particular relevance to situations in which the end product will be a global or undifferentiated assessment of given modalities, subcategories, or variables.

Whatever approach may be used, at our present stage of knowledge building it is less important to focus on global assessments than to identify and pursue leads that relate to specific data items and combinations of items. Toward this end, the differential-weighting approach might best be used in combination with the type of statistical techniques described later.

We will now outline three approaches to the analysis and integration of findings from large numbers of studies. These will be called the *preselected targets, model programs,* and *systematic scanning* approaches. Their main purpose is to identify the above leads and to help integrate them in ways that can result in more effective intervention. At this point, these approaches are theoretical only; they are being outlined for perhaps the first time and are yet to be applied to any actual mass of studies. To be used effectively—certainly to their maximum potential—they require a more systematic recording of research information than has occurred to date, within and especially across studies.

Preselected Targets

In this approach we try to determine which data items are associated with successful outcome for preselected combinations of offenders, settings, staff, and/or operations. The preselected combinations will be called *targets* or *target variables*. The data items which are associated with successful outcome for these targets will be called *identified positive factors* or *link variables*.

In implementing this approach, the first step is to decide which targets to focus on, e.g., which combination of offenders and setting to analyze. Once this is decided (say we focus on males in prison), we are ready to consider the following question: What operations, staff, and additional characteristics of offenders as well as settings are associated with successful outcome for this particular target? For analytic purposes, we would ask this question in a more focused way: What specific operations, characteristics of staff, types of setting, etc. are associated with successful outcome for males in prison? Or we might ask: What general operations, orientations of staff, formal aspects of settings, etc. are associated with successful outcome for males in prison? Such terms as *specific operations, types of setting,* and *orientations of staff,* refer to major subdivisions of the item list in chapter 12.

Once we have analyzed the data and answered this question, we can select a new target (say, females on probation) and repeat the question or series of questions. This process can also be repeated for various combinations of targets and for increasing portions of the total offender population.

The decision about which targets to select can be made largely on practical or theoretical grounds, or by a combination of both. In the account which follows, we will first look at targets that reflect the more practical or immediate concerns.

Selections Based on Practical Need

For purposes of institutional management, standard caseload handling, large-scale budgeting, reports to governing bodies or regulatory agencies, etc., most correctional personnel would probably want to focus on particular combinations of offenders and setting. These, at least, would probably be the first areas about which they would seek information and in terms of which they would want that information organized. With respect to offenders, their primary sphere of interest might relate to sex and age; in terms of setting, it would probably relate to type. By combining sex, age, and type of setting, and by utilizing various distinctions within these items, researchers could initiate their response to these interests or concerns by establishing potential targets such as the following:

1. Males, ages 0-12, in day care and other community centers
2. Males, ages 16-18, in camps, ranches, and farms
3. Males, ages 22-29, in prisons and jails
4. Females, ages 16-18, on standard probation

Other potential targets could be added or substituted, depending on the interests of correctional personnel. (See n. 3 regarding standard categories that might be used for age and type of setting.)

As indicated, once we have established a target—say, 22- to 29-year-old males in prisons and jails—we can begin the search for data items that are associated with positive outcome in studies which relate to that target (target studies). In conducting this search for link variables, we would analyze—time and resources permitting—all items on which there is sufficient information for meaningful statistical handling, across all target studies that have been selected. We would not limit the analysis to those items in which a practical interest had been expressed.[4]

To answer "What items are associated with successful outcome?" we would first divide all target studies into two criterion groups, successful and unsuccessful. For any given study, we would define success as a reduction in recidivism of 15 percent or greater, as compared with a control group. For all successful programs, we would then analyze every item, i.e., each potential link variable, on which there is sufficient information. More specifically, we would find out if successful programs were more likely to receive one type of score or rating than some other type of score or rating, on each given item. This procedure could also be applied to combinations of items. (See chapter 3, n. 8 regarding the 15 percent criterion of success.)

To illustrate this process, let us assume there exists a complete set of scores or ratings on all items in each of 40 target studies, half of which are successful. (Collectively, these studies may involve a wide range of treatment modalities: vocational training, milieu therapy, etc.[5] In the present procedure, all 40 studies would be analyzed together, regardless of their particular treatment modality. In this respect, the analysis would proceed on an across-modalities basis.) Now, let us focus on the following data item: *physical condition of setting* (dichotomized at above average versus average and below average. The higher the score, the better the conditions. This potential link variable is from area III-A of the suggested item list; in an actual analysis it would be defined specifically.) To determine if there is a significant relationship between program success and scores on this item, the following procedure would be used.

First, we would ask if successful programs are just as likely to have an above average score as an average or below average score. If we hypothesize that such programs are just as likely to be associated with better than average conditions as with average or below average conditions, we would expect to find an above average score in approximately 10 of the 20 successful programs and an average or below average score in the remaining 10. This would represent a 50/50, or chance, distribution of scores. However, if we hypothesize that such programs are more likely to be associated with better than average conditions than with average or below average conditions, we would expect to find a score distribution that is significantly different than chance. Say we choose the latter hypothesis.

Next, we would tabulate the results from all 20 successful studies in order to see how the scores are actually distributed. Say that our tabulations reveal the following: 15 of the 20 programs are found to have an above average score and the remaining 5 are found to have an average or below average score. Since chance alone would have produced a score distribution of approximately 10 versus 10, the finding of 15 versus 5 represents a statistically significant (nonchance) difference ($p < .05$). This difference would indicate that successful programs are indeed more likely to be associated with better than average physical conditions than with average or below average conditions, in the case of 22- to 29-year-old males in prisons and jails [2].

Several points might be noted before continuing. First, the procedure just described can also be used with the 20 unsuccessful programs. Here, the question would be: What data items are associated with unsuccessful outcome? Second, in the present procedure, all studies are given equal weight, mainly because each one would have satisfied the qualitative requirements of social science research in order to be part of the analysis. However, if one wished to distinguish between acceptable and excellent investigations and give greater weight to the latter, it would be possible to develop a scoring system that combined the present technique with the differential-weighting approach referred to in Appendix A. Third, as more and better data become available, there would be increasing opportunity to use statistical techniques that are not centered around simple dichotomies. This applies to criterion groups (e.g., successful versus unsuccessful) as well as scores or ratings on potential link variables. Fourth, by comparing the results for any one target with those for other targets, we can assess the generalizability of our findings. For example, if the results on 16- to 18-year-old and 19- to 21-year-old males, in prisons and jails, are similar to those obtained for 22- to 29-year-olds, this would indicate that above average physical conditions are of rather widespread importance with respect to these settings. Fifth, supplementary analyses may sometimes provide important information about the target itself. For instance, by analyzing the interpersonal dimension on the present target offenders, we might find that the 15 versus 5 result breaks down as follows: lower- and middle maturity individuals, 10 versus 0; and higher maturity individuals, 5 versus 5. In short, the overall finding may be largely accounted for by the former offenders, and better than average physical conditions may not be a significant component of success in the case of higher maturity offenders.

To supplement the information that is provided by the preceding approach, the following might be asked: Is there a significant difference between the scores obtained in successful programs and those obtained in unsuccessful programs? Here, we would no longer focus on successful programs alone. Instead, we would ask whether a particular score on a data item is more likely to be found in successful than unsuccessful programs? If the answer is the same as that obtained for successful programs alone (e.g., yes, as to above average physical conditions), this would broaden the importance of the data item under consideration.

To illustrate the technique used in answering this question, a set of hypothetical findings is shown in table 13-1. First, for physical condition of setting, we observe that 15 of the successful programs are above average and 5 are not; this is a simple carryover of our earlier results. However, we also observe that 8 of the unsuccessful programs are above average, while 12 are not. Using a Chi-square test, we find that this difference in scores between the two groups of programs cannot be accounted for by chance ($p < .05$).[6] Specifically, it suggests that above average physical conditions are more likely to be found in successful than unsuccessful programs. As indicated, this conclusion would broaden the significance of our earlier finding regarding successful programs themselves. Yet, findings do not always fit together so neatly, and the implications of this fact may sometimes be complex.

As we have seen, scores on some items—say, an above average score on adequacy of services—may be associated with successful programs. Yet, conceivably, they may be associated with unsuccessful programs as well. For instance, say we observe with respect to the 40 target studies under consideration that (1) 15 successful programs are operating in settings that are above average in adequacy of services, and the remaining 5 are not; and (2) 15 unsuccessful programs are operating in settings that are above average in adequacy of services, and the remaining 5 are not. These findings indicate that above average service does not exist in successful programs alone. Clearly, it is just as likely to exist in unsuccessful programs. Since adequacy of service does not distinguish successful from unsuccessful programs, does this mean it is not an important factor?

In answering this question, two points might be kept in mind.

First, findings that are obtained in connection with successful programs can retain a basic meaning or importance that does not depend on those which relate to unsuccessful programs. Thus, in the present example, it remains the case that average and below average scores on adequacy of services are not associated with successful programs, whereas above average scores are. These results have

Table 13-1
Number of Successful and Unsuccessful Programs with Specified Scores on Physical Condition of Setting

| | Program and Scores | | | |
| | Successful Programs[a] | | Unsuccessful Programs[b] | |
Variable	Above Average	Average or Below Average	Above Average	Average or Below Average
Physical condition of setting	15	5	8	12

[a]$N = 20.$
[b]$N = 20.$

practical implications independent of the fact that above average scores are quite likely to be found in successful and unsuccessful programs alike. Specifically, if one wishes to increase the chance of building a successful program, one would try to establish above average services irrespective of the findings on unsuccessful programs. If average or below average services were associated with unsuccessful programs, one would have reason to try even harder.

Second, although an item may not in itself distinguish successful from unsuccessful programs, it may do so when combined with other items. Thus, for example, a combination of above average adequacy of services and smaller than average living-unit size might be more likely to be found in successful than unsuccessful programs. This hypothetical relationship would have to be uncovered through a direct assessment of the two items in combination (see table 13-2). It would receive independent, albeit partial and indirect, support if smaller than average living-unit size were associated with successful but not unsuccessful programs, when taken by itself (see table 13-3).

Combinations and patterns are always difficult to deal with, especially when many items are involved simultaneously. In every science and at all stages of knowledge building, it is extremely difficult to determine with certainty which combination of items is making the decisive difference between positive and negative results. This remains a problem even when detailed analyses have helped identify numerous combinations that are associated with positive results and that account for a sizable portion of those results, i.e., of the "total variance."

Despite this limitation, the preselected-targets approach can eventually produce the following:

1. A list of individual data items that are associated with successful programs for particular targets, and a separate list of items that are associated with unsuccessful programs, for those same targets.
2. A list of individual items that are more often associated with successful than unsuccessful programs, for particular targets.
3. A list of items which, when combined with each other, are (a) associated with successful programs and/or (b) more often associated with successful than unsuccessful programs, for particular targets.

Through a careful exploration of targets and potential link variables, each of these item lists could be modified or developed, via deletions and additions as needed.

For instance, within the offender area, any given list might be modified in order to include new targets, such as females or certain age groups (e.g., 16-18 and 19-21). As to setting, it might be modified to include camps plus ranches plus farms, and perhaps day care or other community centers.

Similarly, for any given target (expanded or otherwise), the list in question could be broadened to include new link variables. In relation to staff, it might

Table 13-2
Number of Successful and Unsuccessful Programs with Specified Scores and Ratings on a Combination of Variables

	Program and Scores/Ratings			
	Successful Programs[a]		Unsuccessful Programs[b]	
Combination of Variables	Above Average AOS, Smaller than Average LUS	All Other Combinations of AOS and LUS	Above Average AOS, Smaller than Average LUS	All Other Combinations of AOS and LUS
Adequacy of Services (AOS) and Living-unit size (LUS)	13	7	6	14

[a]$N = 20.$
[b]$N = 20.$

Table 13-3
Number of Successful and Unsuccessful Programs with Specified Scores or Ratings on Selected Variables

Variable	Program and Scores or Ratings			
	Successful Programs[a]		Unsuccessful Programs[b]	
	Above Average	Average or Below Average	Above Average	Average or Below Average
Adequacy of services	15	5	15	5
	Smaller than Average	Average or Larger	Smaller than Average	Average or Larger
Living-unit size	16	4	8	12

[a]$N = 20.$
[b]$N = 20.$

come to include treatment personnel with an instrumental rather than expressive orientation. In connection with operations, it might include such areas of focus as "family/parental relationships" or "everyday practical adjustment." In addition, it might include such lines of approach as "exposure to adult models" or "use of positive peer culture."

This process of modification and expansion would represent a direct approach to the integration of findings that have been obtained with respect to individual targets, for selected link variables and combinations thereof. Lists that result from this process could be used as a blueprint for the development of effective intervention programs with targets or combinations of targets that have been established largely on a practical basis. Similar lists could be produced in connection with the theory-guided approach that is described in subsequent pages.

Thus far we have reviewed two procedures for determining which data items are associated with specified outcomes, for preselected target groups. Both procedures have focused on potential link variables which were drawn from among the many features, i.e., data items or variables, that can be used to characterize given studies. A third procedure will now be outlined, one which focuses on those particular items (also potential link variables) which were used as independent variables in the classical sense of the term. This procedure—operationally, a simple variant of those already described—involves direct comparisons between the independent variables that are associated with successful target studies and those associated with unsuccessful target studies. (Each study contributes one such variable to any given analysis.[7]) Here the question is, "Were any such variables, for example, work furlough, associated with successful programs more often than with unsuccessful programs?" From a global perspective it may be said that work furlough *is* the program, at least the experimental program.

To answer this question, we would first construct a list of independent variables, separate for successful and unsuccessful programs. For each variable that is listed with sufficient frequency to allow for meaningful exploratory analysis, we would then apply the statistical technique that was described on pp. 122-125. Thus, in the hypothetical example shown in table 13-4, we observe that work furlough was used as an independent variable in 8 of the 40 programs listed. If chance alone were operating, this variable would be associated with approximately 4 successful and 4 unsuccessful programs. However, its appearance in 7 successful programs as compared with only 1 unsuccessful program suggests that work furlough is more likely to be associated with the former programs than with the latter, in the case of 22- to 29-year-old males in prisons and jails ($p < .05$). No significant differences ($p < .05$) or statistical tendencies ($p < .10 > .05$) are observed relative to each of the remaining independent variables that are listed.[8] (Actually, only a few of these variables are listed often enough to allow for a meaningful exploratory analysis relative to the target in question. If several targets were combined, a larger number of meaningful exploratory analyses could be conducted.)

Table 13-4
Independent Variables in 40 Hypothetical Programs

Successful Programs[a]	Unsuccessful Programs[b]
1. Individual counseling	21. Individual counseling
2. Individual counseling	22. Individual counseling
3. Group counseling	23. Group counseling
4. Milieu therapy	24. Group counseling
5. Milieu therapy	25. Group counseling
6. Milieu therapy	26. Milieu therapy
7. Small living-unit size	27. Milieu therapy
8. Small living-unit size	28. Milieu therapy
9. Homogeneous offender grouping	29. Milieu therapy
10. Homogeneous offender grouping	30. Small living-unit size
11. Postprogram contacts	31. Small living-unit size
12. Postprogram contacts	32. Homogeneous offender grouping
13. Halfway house	33. Homogeneous offender grouping
14. Work furlough	34. Homogeneous offender grouping
15. Work furlough	35. Postprogram contacts
16. Work furlough	36. Postprogram contacts
17. Work furlough	37. Halfway house
18. Work furlough	38. Halfway house
19. Work furlough	39. Halfway house
20. Work furlough	40. Work furlough

[a]$N = 20$.
[b]$N = 20$.

Selections Based on Theory

Thus far we have focused on targets whose selection was most likely to be guided by practical considerations. We will now turn to a somewhat different set of items: targets and potential link variables whose selection would most likely be guided by theories of causation and change.

Selections that are likely to result from theories of causation and change would be a direct reflection of the latters' specific focus and scope. Usually, these theories focus on one or more offender samples. They postulate and describe a set of conditions that engender or support illegal behavior on the part of these offenders. Finally, they suggest various ways of altering the behavior or attitudes of these individuals, or of others who are considered central to their adjustment. These suggestions may be explicit or implicit [1,9,10,14,22,32, 33,34,36,52,55].

Theories that deal with broad, social preconditions and concomitants of illegal behavior usually emphasize such factors as offenders' residence (e.g., urban or nonurban), neighborhood, socioeconomic status, and ethnicity. On the other hand, theories that deal with "the inner man" usually emphasize the role of specific factors (such as impulse control), personality group, or developmental level. Factors such as school status, work status, age, and sex may be given moderate to considerable weight in both types of theory. However, they are not likely to be seen as primary or decisive. Finally, these or other theories may involve complex combinations of sociological and psychological factors.

Rather than pointing to targets that involve various combinations of age, sex, and type of setting, these theories are likely to suggest such groups as the following (sociological theories would emphasize the first two groups; social-psychological theories, the latter groups):

Lower socioeconomic status, black or Hispanic, urban males

Unemployed, below average in grade level males, from high delinquency neighborhoods

Middle level of interpersonal development, immature conformists, from high delinquency neighborhoods

Indifferent or alienated, higher maturity, middle-class Caucasians.

As to behavior and attitude change, they may direct attention to combinations of staff, setting, and operations which, theoretically, are of maximum relevance to the offenders in question. For example, the following combinations of potential link variables might be seen as optimal with respect to the first two target groups: minority staff, paraprofessionals or volunteers who use their past experiences as the primary basis for working with others, nonjustice system sponsorship, job referral and placement, advocacy and legal assistance, and emphasis on countering apathy and indifference. On the other hand, the following might be considered important in connection with the third target group: professionally trained staff, community-center setting, matched assignment, group counseling (noncoeducational), increasing internal controls, ego-bolstering via success experiences, using positive peer culture, and concreteness of verbalizations.

Thus, the theory-guided approach can help focus attention on targets that might receive little emphasis based on various practical concerns alone, e.g., those which relate largely to system maintenance. It can also direct attention to potential link variables that would receive little if any emphasis based on practical considerations alone. This especially applies to combinations of variables that are theoretically related to one another in terms of the target group they would be designed to serve.

By connecting given targets with potential link variables, the theory-guided approach suggests relationships that might not have been considered before, at least not explicitly. In effect, it sets up hypotheses for testing. The statistical techniques for evaluating these hypotheses would be the same as those described in earlier pages, for any target and potential link variable. However, the challenge of handling combinations of variables, as combinations, would be even greater in connection with the present approach.

Finally, when using a given theory as the basis for selecting data items, one must recognize the danger of overlooking numerous variables that fall outside the theory's specific focus and scope. This inevitable shortcoming—one of theory-limited content—can be greatly reduced by utilizing a range of theories, a very broad theory, or a combination of the theoretical and practical approaches. It can be avoided entirely by using the systematic-scanning approach described in chapter 14.

Before turning to the second method of data handling, we might note that the preselected-targets approach allows us to test both theoretically and *empirically* derived hypotheses concerning the role of, and interactions among, offender, staff, setting, and operations variables. In testing these hypotheses, especially the latter, continuity with the past is maintained by pursuit of leads that have emerged from observations and conceptual integrations to date. In both cases, these hypotheses are tested by assessment of the relationship between selected data items (potential link variables) and selected targets. Through use of this hypothesis-testing strategy, the fragmented, unsystematic type of exploration mentioned in chapter 10 can be minimized. At the same time, by interrelating still other data items and targets—largely on theoretical grounds—new areas and new levels of analysis can be explored.

Model Programs

Basically, the preselected-targets approach is designed to identify individual items and combinations of items that are associated with positive outcome relative to large numbers of programs. While this seems like a promising and fundamental approach, it may not provide certain information that is needed to develop an actual operating program. Two main reasons for this are as follows:

1. Link variables that have been identified by the preselected-targets approach may have to be supplemented by other items. The latter items, assuming they were analyzed, may not have emerged clearly with regard to the given target. For example, they may have approached but not attained statistical significance, or they may not have been combined with other items that would have helped them emerge more clearly.[9] Alternately, these "unidentified" items may not have been analyzed in the first place. In either event, the originally mentioned items—link variables or identified positive factors—may therefore represent important (perhaps even necessary) but still not sufficient conditions for a successful program operation, with respect to particular offenders and settings.

2. Some identified positive factors can perhaps operate effectively only in the absence of certain items that have not been identified as potentially detrimental, relative to the given target. For instance, unidentified negative factors may prevent a set of identified positive factors from even getting off the ground in connection with the early phase of a program. Alternately, they may undo many positive influences which these link variables have in fact exerted during the early, middle, or later phases of a program. Even though we may have identified several negative factors in an earlier analysis of unsuccessful target studies, we may not have isolated several others that operate negatively, especially when interacting with the particular set of factors that have been identified as positive for the offenders and setting under consideration.[10]

To deal with these complexities and potential shortcomings, some assistance may be obtained by focusing on programs that have shown unusual promise—those which have clearly worked, (1) given their particular combination of positive factors and (2) despite the possible presence of negative factors. These programs would be drawn from the total set of studies already analyzed, or available for analysis, in connection with the preselected-targets approach. Under most conditions, they would comprise a small to moderate portion of all target studies. Analysis of these unusual studies and integration of their findings with those of other studies will be called the *model-programs approach.* (For present purposes we will assume that the preselected-targets approach has already been applied to a group of target studies that include a number of these unusually promising programs.)

In this approach we would single out all programs that were particularly successful with respect to the given target, e.g., 22- to 29-year-old males in prisons and jails. We might define, as models, those programs which reduced recidivism by at least 40 percent for the offender sample on which they focused.[11] Relative to such programs (positive models), our basic questions would be: What elements, if any, do these programs share in common? Which of these elements or data items are new, i.e., not included among the group we have already identified as positive for the target sample as a whole?[12]

Answers to these questions may help us obtain the information that is needed to develop actual operating programs. This is despite the fact that an emphasis on positive models would not, in itself, allow us to single out the possible negative factors mentioned above. To help us isolate particularly detrimental elements, we might have to focus on negative models as well, e.g., programs that have increased recidivism by 20 percent or more. Here, the goal would be to identify any elements that these programs share in common, especially those which are not among the negative factors already identified as such. However, even if this goal were achieved, the findings would have to be used with caution.[13]

In the positive model approach we would be focusing on a collection of data items or factors that have in all likelihood (or, one could say, by definition) interacted positively with respect to actual program operations. This direct, whole-program approach is quite different from the preselected-targets approach. The latter is designed to isolate individual factors and groups of factors which are statistically associated with success relative to a large number of programs, but which, collectively, may or may not have interacted positively with respect to actual program operations. At this point in our knowledge-building efforts, there is no way of solidly estimating the absolute and relative strength of these alternate yet complementary approaches, i.e., strength with reference to the goal of developing effective intervention.

As to the complementary relationship itself, this can probably exist with respect to a range of situations. For example, on logical grounds it seems likely that the model-programs approach could add useful information to the preselected-targets approach even if the latter turned out to be quite powerful in terms of developing real-life programs. At the same time, if the power of the preselected-targets approach simply remained uncertain or rather variable, the model-programs approach could probably make a valuable contribution, even if it supplied no information about *new* data items: if positive models were found to contain several factors that had already been identified as link variables via the preselected-targets approach, this would substantially strengthen the operational implications of the latter findings.[14] This interpretation would be reasonable on grounds that if any programs can be said to have worked in real life, it would be the positive models.

The following issues might be kept in mind relative to model programs, regardless of the latters' potential contributions to the preselected-targets approach. First, any such program may be difficult to reproduce in its entirety, and to operate under a wide range of conditions. If this is true, it is possible that the individual elements of success which are most readily exportable (elements that model programs may share in common) are those most likely to be singled out in connection with the preselected-targets approach itself, i.e., singled out on the basis of a larger number, and probably much broader range, of programs. While this may be possible, or even plausible, there is no way of presently estimating its level of probability. At any rate, we should not a priori rely heavily on any one model program if our goal is the development of correctional programs that are successful under a wide range of conditions.

Second, any model program may contain several superfluous elements—components that are neither helpful nor harmful in terms of recidivism but which may reduce efficiency and exportability, or increase overall cost. By focusing on elements which are shared by any two or more model programs, it may be possible to substantially reduce this "excess baggage." (This suggestion assumes that one such program is not a planned copy of the other.) Excess baggage may exist in any single program, model, or otherwise. In this respect, the preselected-targets approach (which involves a relatively large number of programs) may automatically result in an elimination of many or most such elements. At any rate, link variables that result from the latter approach are much more likely to be significant contributors than superfluous ingredients.

Third, since few model programs may be found in relation to any one target, replication of findings, as distinguished from reproducibility and transferability of many or all program operations, can be a significant concern. Given the present stage and state of corrections as both a practice and science, replication of findings may have to occur mainly on a partial, indirect basis in the case of many model programs. This form of replication exists when one observes similar findings in operationally similar programs that focus on adjacent targets, e.g., 19- to 21- or 30- to 39-year-old males rather than the 22- to 29-year-old males under consideration. (Supportive findings of this nature would also bear on generalizability.) As to replication in the ordinary sense, the preselected-targets approach would be in a stronger position than the model-programs approach since it is likely to involve a larger number of studies that bear on the specific target in question. This would apply at any point in time.

Finally, there is the question of generalizing one's findings, either to a target or from that same (basic) target. In the first case, a problem would arise if we could not locate a model program in connection with the basic target but could locate such a program with respect to a nearby target, for instance, an adjacent age group or similar setting. If we wished to apply our findings from the latter program to the basic target, we would face the uncertainties of generalizing from one area to another.[15] In the second case, a problem would arise if we found a model program for the basic target but did not find such a program for similar or adjacent targets. In both cases, the problem of generalizability would have been triggered by the absence of model programs, either in the basic target area or in nearby areas.

To broaden the basis for valid generalizations and to continue dealing with the potential shortcomings mentioned on pp. 130-131, we might use a variation of the model-programs approach: the *targeted, prominent-programs approach.* Here, we would focus on the more successful or notable, but not necessarily topmost or model, programs that exist relative to the specific targets in which we are interested. (In the basic model-programs approach, the programs that are available may or may not relate to targets of greatest concern.) We might include, as prominent, the upper one-third of all successful programs for any given target (upper, in terms of reduced recidivism). Since prominent programs will not always reduce recidivism by at least 40 percent, we can think of these studies as falling somewhere between the average successful program and most model programs. For any given target, we would expect to find substantially more prominent programs than model programs, even though the former can include any number of the latter. Finally, we would ask the same questions of these programs that we asked of model programs: Do they contain common elements? Are some of these elements new, i.e., over and beyond those already observed for target studies as a whole?

In sum, as compared with the basic model-programs approach, the modified approach would allow us to construct samples of studies that relate to basic and adjacent targets of particular concern. Equally important, it would supply a larger number of programs with which to work. As a result, it could be of use in addressing the question of generalizability, and it would increase the amount of information that is available for dealing with the potential shortcomings of the preselected approach itself.

Forces that Underlie Change

The model-programs approach can furnish valuable, often specific clues as to what works. However, it does not tell us *why* given methods work, or why they work better than others. Certainly, it does not tell us this in a comprehensive, systematic way. In order to develop effective programs, it is essential that we continue to isolate the *what* of "what works," and to do so in relation to general as well as specific factors. However, to efficiently improve these programs, what we may need is an increasingly systematic understanding of why they influence the lives of individuals. To isolate the *whys*—the interrelated factors and forces that can lead to change—we must return to the theory-based approach.

One group of forces we might wish to isolate, for example, are those which help individuals link their abilities and interests to the opportunities and requirements of their environment. To conceptualize these forces, we might draw on a type of theory that focuses on individual motivation and development within a broad social context. Such a theory would postulate one or more overriding motivations and would outline the major stages or developments in the establishment of person/society links. It would, in particular, postulate specific forces that help promote and maintain those links. The forces in question, e.g., particular skills, motives, and external supports, might then be added to the list of data items that would be explored in relation to ongoing or completed correctional programs. Additional programs might be established to further test these postulates and to support, refine, or refute the theory as a whole. (This postulate-and-test approach could be used with more than one theory at a time, and in relation to other groups of forces as well. There are many possible ways to describe the motivations and psychosocial developments under consideration. One example is shown in Appendix L.)

The type of theory in question could supply a framework for understanding why individuals invest in certain goals, activities, and roles at particular points in their lives. It could provide a framework for evaluating the potential significance of given programs, and above all, for understanding why individuals either perceive or do not perceive those programs as being of relevance to their lives. By learning more about the motives and investments of offenders as individuals, we may be able to place increasing weight on methods than can help them want to establish more satisfying and acceptable links with their environment, and want to develop the personal and social skills that can help establish those links. We might also be able to minimize or eliminate those elements which are superfluous or counterproductive relative to these goals.

Programs that tap individual motivation and increase personal involvement in the process of change might not only be more effective, they would doubtlessly be more humane. By reducing the individual's resistance to external input (by increasing receptivity and genuine motivation instead), such programs might increase efficiency and decrease overall wear and tear as well.

If we could isolate the main factors and forces (essential ingredients) that promote constructive change, we might eventually design a range of programs that would all contain these ingredients but which could still be quite different from one another on the surface. By building on these and closely related ingredients (assuming they exist and are exportable), it might be possible to adapt given programs to the opportunities as well as practical requirements of local justice systems and social settings without significant loss in terms of effectiveness, humane treatment, or efficiency.

In effect, by retaining and emphasizing the essential ingredients, and by varying their specific expression as needed, we might establish an increasingly acceptable and operable link between correctional programs, on the one hand, and local justice systems as well as specific social settings, on the other. In the long run, such a link would be of service to offenders and society alike. By helping us focus on essential ingredients, the theory-based approach may be the best way to achieve this end. Used together with the model-programs approach, its contribution might be even greater in this regard.

The third method of developing effective intervention based on findings from large numbers of studies will be described in chapter 14. Operationally, this is perhaps the most taxing method of all.

14 Systematic Scanning and Related Techniques

We will now describe the third major approach to working with data from large numbers of studies: systematic scanning. Here, the relationship between all potential link variables and all possible targets is systematically assessed. We do this to ensure that no variables and major combinations of variables are overlooked in terms of their potential contribution to correctional knowledge. All data items that comprise the variables and targets which enter into these analyses are drawn from item lists such as that shown in chapter 12.

For present purposes, potential link variables that consist of any single data item (e.g., adequacy of services) will be called *test items,* i.e., individual items which are tested for statistical significance. Potential link variables that are combined with one another to form a composite item (e.g., adequacy of services and living-unit size) will be called *composite test items.* As seen in earlier pages, test items and composite test items can each be analyzed in essentially the same way relative to any target.

Systematic scanning involves a large number of analyses. For instance, in this approach we might statistically relate each of 75 or more test items to each of 75 or more individual targets.[1] We might also relate twice that number of composite test items to twice that number of individual and composite targets, again, one by one.

Analysis of this many items cannot be seriously considered without the aid of high-speed computers. This would apply even if no more than: (1) 30 or 40 single data items were analyzed rather than 75 or more, and all composite test items were excluded; (2) 15 or 20 single data items were analyzed but composite test items were included; (3) 30 or 40 data items were analyzed and each composite test item, and composite target item, was allowed to contain a maximum of five or six individual data items. Given the scope and taxing nature of this analysis, it might be helpful to remember that the potential contribution of the present approach springs from the very detail it involves.[2]

Systematic scanning can be carried out within a preselected-targets framework. That is, it can be applied to findings from studies that relate to already established targets, e.g., 22- to 29-year-old males. In addition, it can be implemented with regard to all studies—therefore, all targets—taken together. This approach will first be reviewed in relation to preselected targets.

Scanning with Preselected Targets

Here, the main goal is identical to that of the preselected-targets approach: the discovery of link variables for specified targets. This goal is achieved by statistically assessing the relationship between test items and targets. Procedures for assessing this relationship, and for integrating the results, are also identical to those used in the preselected-targets approach. Additional goals and procedures are reviewed on pp. 140-143.

To assess the relationship between test items and targets, the first task would be the establishment of the targets themselves. For purposes of systematic scanning, we would establish the broadest possible range of targets. The following might be a useful way of conceptualizing this total range.

First, there are targets that relate to single data items, items such as age, sex, or base expectancy. Each data item that is found within any content area (offender, staff, setting, operations) can produce one or more targets. For instance, items such as age can produce several potential targets: 13- to 15-year-old offenders, 16- to 18-year-old offenders, etc. Items such as day care centers or milieu therapy produce only one target: themselves. Targets that relate to a single data item will be called *single-item targets*. Thus, if our target were 13- to 15-year-old offenders, the data item to which it relates would be age.[3]

Next are targets that derive from combinations of single data items. These targets (say, two-item targets) may be derived from any one of the four content areas mentioned above, as in the case of age and sex. Alternately, they may come from two different content areas, as in age and living-unit size. Regardless of their source and content, targets that involve a combination of single data items will be called *composite targets*. These targets can, and often would, consist of three or more items from within or across any one, two, three, or more content areas. Thus, one such composite target might be 22- to 29-year-old males who reside in halfway houses and are directly supervised by paraprofessional staff.[4]

The next task would be the establishment of test items, i.e., potential link variables. Here, the total range could be conceptualized exactly as it was in the case of targets. Thus, there would be single test items and composite test items. The former would relate to individual data items from any one of the four content areas; the latter would relate to items from one or more content areas.

Targets and test items that are established along these lines and are then analyzed in relation to one another fall within one of four configurations:

1. Single-item targets, single test items
2. Composite targets, single test items
3. Single-item targets, composite test items
4. Composite targets, composite test items

To use the scanning approach at its maximum, i.e., systematically and comprehensively, the relationship between specific test items and specific targets would be analyzed with respect to all four configurations.[5]

In carrying out this analysis we would focus on the same questions that were asked relative to the preselected-targets approach. Thus, with configuration 1, the first question would be: Are successful target programs more likely to receive one type of rating than another, on this test item (e.g., work status at intake)?[6] The second question would be: Is there a significant difference between the ratings obtained in successful as compared with unsuccessful target programs, for this test item? The same type of question would be asked for each remaining configuration.[7]

Answers to these questions would result in lists of items similar to those described in the preselected-targets approach. Relative to all configurations, these lists would consist of continuous variables (e.g., IQ and frequency of contacts), plus features or characteristics that are readily subdivided (e.g., sex, ethnicity, and physical condition of setting). For configurations 1 and 2, they would not include test items that either have not been or, for particular analytic purposes, should not be subdivided, namely, discrete items such as day care centers or milieu therapy.[8] However, special lists could be developed that would reflect the results of comparisons between these items, e.g., between milieu therapy and group therapy or between milieu therapy and other modalities combined. Finally, discrete items could be included in lists that relate to composite test items; i.e., they could appear in connection with configurations 3 and 4.[9]

As with the preselected-targets approach, these lists could be further developed through a process of target expansion—unsystematic or otherwise. Unsystematic expansion would occur when one or more studies that are relevant to given targets are added to other studies that relate to previously analyzed targets. These combinations would not be based on any consistently implemented plan. Expansion by rule, i.e., systematic expansion, might ordinarily occur when immediately adjacent targets are added to one another. It could also occur on other preestablished grounds, structural and substantive alike.

Through either form of expansion, lists could be produced that relate to an increasingly broad range of studies and, therefore, an increasing percentage of available targets. The analytic procedures mentioned on pp. 122-125 would remain applicable and could be repeated at various stages of either expansion process. At any level or stage, the resulting lists could be compared, contrasted, and generally integrated with one another on the basis of specific questions or for particular purposes. Thus, lists could also be developed in relation to target combinations which, while not necessarily broad, happen to be of special interest.

For practical reasons, it would make sense to initially place a limit on the number of data items that can comprise any one target or test item. Such a limit—say, six items—would hold down the total number of composite targets and test items. It would therefore reduce the number of statistical tests that would otherwise be carried out relative to configurations 2, 3, and especially 4. It could, in fact, easily make a difference of thousands of tests, yet still leave room for the systematic analysis that characterizes the present approach. (See n. 10 for further discussion.)

Cluster and Factor Analysis

Systematic scanning can lead to products other than lists. For example when used with cluster- and factor-analytic techniques, it can help isolate various staff, setting, offender, and operations dimensions that are associated with successful target programs, dimensions that underlie the test items described above. These techniques will now be briefly reviewed.

When using cluster- and factor-analytic techniques in the context of systematic scanning, the basic procedure would be as follows: (1) targets, not test items, would be systematically scanned; and (2) test items, not targets, would be clustered or factored in order to identify the preceding dimensions. Thus, a separate cluster or factor analysis would be carried out for each target or combination of targets. In each analysis, all available and appropriate test items would be used to produce the clusters or factors in question.

More specifically, cluster and factor analyses could be carried out relative to configurations 1 and 2 for continuous variables and other test items that are capable of subdivision.[11] Each analysis could be performed on an across-areas basis, e.g., in connection with variables from such content areas as staff and operations. However, the most productive and methodologically appropriate use of these techniques would probably involve a within-area focus. This focus would probably make it easier to interpret the resulting clusters and factors as well [19,20]. To allow for the emergence of several rather than a greatly restricted number of dimensions, a substantial number of variables would be used in each analysis.[12] (For present purposes, we can now focus on factor analysis alone.)

Thus, in the case of successful programs that relate to a specific target (say, 16- to 18-year-old females on standard probation), we might, for example, intercorrelate 20 variables that fall within content area IV (operations), subdivision C2 (treatment processes). Area IV-C2 includes such variables as exposure to adult models, preparing client for specific life situations, ego bolstering via success experiences, use of positive peer culture, etc. Analysis of the relationships that exist among 20 such variables could result in the identification of three or four broad factors—possible underlying dimensions of treatment that are associated with successful programs for the target in question.

If the identified factors are consistent with results obtained via the model-programs approach or the preselected-targets approach, or both, this could represent converging evidence as to certain key ingredients of success for that particular target. If the factors make sense relative to a theory-based approach (if, for example, they can be directly predicted from the behavior-modifying or growth-promoting forces that are postulated by given theories), this, too, would enhance their validity and overall significance.

Identical analyses could be carried out relative to unsuccessful programs. Similarities and differences that exist between factors which are associated with unsuccessful and successful programs could provide support for and, in any event, shed more light on findings associated with the latter programs themselves.

Two entirely different applications of factor (and cluster) analysis will now be mentioned. These may be thought of as adjuncts to standard scanning itself (pp. 137-140). In the first case, this technique would be applied immediately prior to systematic scanning; in the second, immediately afterward.

1. Factor analysis may be used as an initial step in the standard scanning process. Specifically, it could be applied to a basic list of data items (original item list) in order to sharply reduce the number of potential link variables that would be tested for statistical significance relative to a given target or combination of targets.[13] For example, say that area IV-C2 of an item list consists of 40 separate data items. By factor analyzing these 40 items relative to a particular target, it might be possible to delineate, say, five factors. Once this is done, three or four items that are found to have "high loadings" on their respective factors might be used to represent the original item list in all subsequent stages of scanning—again, in relation to that same target. No other items would be analyzed. This application might be called *prescanning factor analysis*.

2. If prescanning analysis is not carried out, postscanning might be used to pare down the number of statistically significant items that appear on a given list which has been produced by the standard scanning approach.[14] If the factors that emerge from a postscanning analysis are consistent with or similar to the shared elements that have been identified across two or more model programs, this, too, would represent converging evidence regarding key elements of success for the target or targets in question.[15]

Multiple Regression

One other major technique might be introduced at this point: multiple regression. First, this technique could be used in a way that parallels the prescanning factor-analysis approach. Here, it would be applied to an original data list in order to reduce the number of potential link variables that would be tested for statistical significance as part of the standard scanning process.

Specifically, multiple regression would be used to analyze an original data list relative to a particular target or combination of targets. It would be applied at one of three main levels of analysis (the set of data items that could be included as predictors is shown in parentheses for each level of analysis):

Level 1: Within areas/within subdivisions (may involve items that comprise each subdivision within each of the four content areas)

Level 2: Within areas/across subdivisions (may involve items that comprise each content area regardless of subdivision)

Level 3: Across areas/across subdivisions (may involve all items taken together regardless of content area and subdivision).[16]

The product of a level 1, 2, or 3 analysis would be a shortened data list for the target or targets in question (see below). This list of data items (potential link variables) could then be substituted for the original data list in all subsequent steps of the standard scanning process.

For instance, in the case of a level 1 analysis, 5 of the originally listed data items that are singled out by the multiple-regression technique might be substituted for the 15 originally listed items (potential link variables) that comprise subdivision A of area I. Similarly, 4 of the original items that are singled out might be used in place of the 12 that comprise subdivision B of area I, and so on. In a level 2 analysis, 8 of the original data items might be substituted for the 27 that comprise area I, subdivisions A and B combined; 7 might be substituted for the 22 that comprise area II, subdivisions A, B, and C combined, and so forth. In all analyses, the substitute items would be those which, collectively, best predict the outcome measure in question, for the target(s) under consideration.

At any level of analysis, prescanning multiple regression would be applicable to all four configurations. It could be used with continuous variables and other data items that are capable of subdivision.

Next, multiple regression could be used as a partial substitute for systematic scanning, not just as a prescanning adjunct. For instance, by applying the "stepwise" version of this technique to an original data list at an across-areas/across-subdivisions level (level 3), we could directly produce a relatively short list that contains only those variables which, collectively, account for the largest proportion of all "outcome variance," relative to the target(s) under consideration. The items, i.e., the *set* of variables, which comprise this abridged list could be called *key item combinations*.

In carrying out this approach, each target or combination of targets would be analyzed separately. In each multiple-regression analysis, all available and appropriate, originally listed data items would be focused on collectively, in order to identify the most predictive combination. Thus, targets, not data items, would be systematically scanned; data items, not targets, would provide the raw material for any combination of key items [18].

When applied as a partial substitute rather than an adjunct, multiple regression could greatly simplify—perhaps oversimplify—systematic scanning as a whole. More specifically, when applied at level 3, this technique may result in overly condensed lists, i.e., a loss of potentially useful information. However, when applied at level 2 or especially 1, the chance of oversimplification would be greatly reduced. Together with this advantage, the latter applications may also be methodologically more appropriate than the former with respect to the range of psychometric properties that would exist across any set of predictor variables. Finally, whatever level is focused on, multiple regression should not be used with configurations 3 and 4.[17] (See n. 18 for further details.)

Scanning with All Targets Combined

Here, our goal is the identification of link variables for all targets combined, e.g., for all offenders within and across all settings. To achieve this goal, test items and composite test items would be used as the basis for organizing a complete, standard set of scanning analyses. That is, potential link variables would play the same role as before, both structurally and substantively.

However, in carrying out each analysis, all available studies (therefore all targets) would be focused on simultaneously. Specifically, all successful studies would be analyzed at the same time, with respect to potential link variables. Separate but identical types of analysis would be performed relative to unsuccessful studies. Thus, for every analysis, all offenders, staff, settings, and operations would be handled as one undifferentiated mass.

Link variables that are identified by this procedure would be those most applicable to corrections as a whole, i.e., to targets in general. As a result, they might serve as a basis for broad generalizations, perhaps even major policy decisions. Yet, the following should be kept in mind. Many of these link variables would be less applicable to any particular target than those variables which are identified via the specifically targeted procedures described thus far. In addition, many significant findings may be obscured by the masking phenomenon already described. Still, at the present level of analysis, patterns may emerge that would not be apparent at any other level.

In any field, there are advantages and drawbacks associated with analyses and integrations that occur at a very broad level or, for that matter, at any level. The present approach to scanning—"global targeting"—should be recognized as simply the terminal point of the target-expansion process which was described earlier. From this perspective, it can be seen as complementing but not substituting for specifically targeted analyses themselves.

Additional Observations

First, cluster analysis, factor analysis, and multiple regression can each be applied to the preselected-targets approach described in chapter 13, and to the global targeting level of systematic scanning.[19] In both cases, cluster and factor analysis would be used to directly isolate staff, setting, offender, and operations dimensions that are associated with successful or unsuccessful programs. Similarly, multiple regression would be used to isolate key item combinations that relate to greater or lesser success. These techniques could also reduce the number of potential link variables that might be used in any preselected-targets analysis. Alternately, cluster and factor analysis could pare down lists of link variables that have been produced by such an approach.[20] Other applications of these techniques need not be specified.

Second, where possible, number of prior arrests or convictions might be used as a primary basis for grouping or equating various offender samples with respect to risk. Specifically, this item might serve as a major control variable relative to likelihood of future offending, in the case of any set of target programs. Number of arrests or convictions might serve in this capacity, even though it may well produce useful information if handled as a potential link variable instead. (Separate analyses might be carried out in which this item *is* handled like any other potential link variable, not as a control variable.[21]) At any rate, special emphasis should be placed on length of prior record in view of its rather clear relationship to future offending, age being held constant. These considerations are of relevance to the preselected-targets, model-programs, and systematic-scanning approaches alike.

Third, the approaches described in the preceding and present chapters require, above all, large quantities of data, uniformly and routinely collected on an across-studies basis. This information can best be acquired through a long-term, consistently implemented effort by correctional researchers, academicians, practitioners, and policy makers, acting in concert. Advanced statistical techniques and computer technology would also be needed to efficiently handle the numerous interactions that would exist among given data items. Only with these techniques and technology could we comprehensively assess the role of composite test items, especially with respect to the systematic-scanning approach. Individually and collectively, these data-collection and data-handling tasks represent a major challenge for the future.

Finally, we should empirically explore not just effectiveness, but humane intervention as such. Eventually, it will be possible to specify and quantify key components of the latter concept relative to corrections as a whole. Once this is done, correlates and preconditions of humane correctional intervention (interaction and atmosphere included) could be objectively determined. This subject could be explored independently of, or in addition to, that of effectiveness itself. Thus, such questions as the following might be asked: What ratings on which test items are related to above average humane intervention for specified targets—hopefully, most targets? Which ratings are related to a combination of above average humane intervention and above average effectiveness? To carefully explore this subject, many new data items might have to be generated. Similar questions and tasks would apply to other possible subjects as well, e.g., cost, efficiency, and social adjustment, apart from recidivism itself.[22]

**Part IV
Final Observations and
Conclusion**

15 Reality Factors and Closing Remarks

Concrete Challenges of Offenders

Adolescent and adult offenders have many hurdles to clear, perhaps more than nonoffenders. It is often quite difficult for them to mobilize the strengths that are needed to deal with these social or personal hurdles, particularly on a sustained basis. To cope with these challenges on a manageable scale, offenders must focus on the specific circumstances in which they find themselves, and must respond in terms of what they have "going" for them at the time. In this respect, they must build their lives, and sometimes pick up the pieces, exactly like most people do: they must make decisions, then take action, largely in relation to what is concretely facing them and available to them at the time. This also includes what they believe they have going for and against them, and what they think they can count on in the relatively near future.

Given this situation, it would be a mistake to expect that offenders either can or should develop their personal plans around broad societal changes that may or may not take place several years in the future, i.e., their future. This is despite the fact that these changes might result in expanded vocational and educational opportunities for offenders and nonoffenders alike.

Similarly, it would be unrealistic to expect that the personal well-being or social adjustment of offenders would be well on its way to improvement, let alone automatically ensured, if sweeping organizational changes and substantive improvements were made within the correctional system itself. This would apply especially but not exclusively in the absence of concrete personal plans on the part of offenders.

True, expanded social opportunities and intrasystem changes would almost certainly increase most offenders' chances for improvement and success—at least if they were to occur in the present (the offenders' present) or could be counted on within the relatively near future. For some offenders, such changes and improvements might even make a decisive difference in terms of removing given hurdles or adding specific supports.

Nevertheless, despite the relief or boost that could be provided by these large-scale, external changes, the vast majority of offenders would still have a difficult road to travel. (First-time and perhaps second-time offenders are excluded from this vast majority.) This situation would exist chiefly as a result of hurdles that remained unchanged, and supports or strengths that were still undeveloped, insufficient, or unavailable. In short, it would reflect the fact that, boost or no boost, most offenders would still have to deal with their specific life circumstances or personal pressures on much the same basis as before.

The decisions that offenders make with respect to these circumstances or pressures will determine the general direction in which they travel, along their particular road. Here, too, offenders and nonoffenders are very much alike. Specifically, some decisions can bring offenders closer to satisfying their personal desires and social requirements; others can lead them farther away or may produce little movement at all. Decisions that lead in the former direction can often be very difficult to make, and stick to. This would apply even if expanded social opportunities, and intrasystem changes, had in fact occurred. It would also apply if relatively low crime rates happened to exist in the geographic area within which the individuals reside or to which they would eventually return.

Opportunities and Intervention

Relative to the decisions and reactions of offenders, a few words might be said about vocational and educational options that are available within society at any point in time, though seldom to an optimal degree. These options will be called *conventional social opportunities* (CSOs) since they are available outside the correctional system itself. Decisions that may be made in connection with CSOs can have considerable bearing on correctional programs themselves.[1]

Vocational and educational options are often seen as means to an end, i.e., as legitimate opportunities to develop a stake in conformity. (Conformity can be defined on a relatively broad basis, and it need not be viewed in a negative light.) At one point or another CSOs are almost certain to play a central role in the adjustment of all individuals, at least they retain the potential for doing so.[2] In this respect, they may be viewed as a dependable or potential "plus," an asset that is linked to the basic objectives of intervention. First, however, certain limitations should be kept in mind.

1. The availability of conventional social opportunities does not, by itself, preclude the occurrence of illegal behavior. For instance, a great many offenders—often serious offenders—come from middle-class backgrounds.[3] It would be difficult to argue that legitimate opportunities were not available in ample quantity to most of these individuals prior to their involvement in illegal activities. However, if one wished to assume that such opportunities were, in some sense, not available after all, one would then have to ask: To whom have legitimate opportunities been available, if not middle-class individuals? These considerations do not imply that conventional social opportunities have been almost entirely unavailable to offenders with lower-class backgrounds. At the same time, they do not suggest that CSOs have been equally available to the former and latter individuals.[4]

2. The availability of conventional social opportunities does not in itself guarantee the reduction of illegal behavior. Even where readily available, CSOs are bypassed or halfheartedly attended to by many individuals who, through time, maintain their particular level of involvement in illegal behavior. In the case of other, equally involved offenders, CSOs are more openly and firmly rejected. Similar responses or decisions are often observed in connection with vocational and educational opportunities that are available to these and other individuals within the correctional system itself.

3. Where specific vocational and educational options are pursued, and seriously so, this effort may still be countered or undermined by external and internal pressures with which many offenders cannot cope. Such difficulties can occur before the individuals have experienced much positive reinforcement in connection with these options, and before new patterns of adjustment have begun to stabilize. Under these conditions, the original effort may be abandoned and less desirable responses may be made instead. The latter may be accompanied by the reestablishment of previously relinquished, illegal patterns of adjustment. Similar processes are often observed among nonoffenders, although the specific content of the adjustment may be somewhat different.

Indifference, halfhearted pursuit, undermining, and abandonment are observed in relation to every type of offender—all personality groupings and all levels of social-psychological maturity. These reactions and developments are in no way the exclusive property of middle-class versus lower-class offenders. Nor are they monopolized by individuals from nonminority versus minority groups.

From this perspective, a major goal of intervention would be to increase the motivation and/or ability of all groups of offenders to pursue socially acceptable opportunities and to do so for extended periods of time.[5] To achieve this goal, some offenders might need little more than encouragement or practical advice in terms of using the strengths or supports they already have. However, many others (mostly multiple offenders, regardless of social class) might need additional resources to deal with pressures that could weaken their resolve or prevent them from making a serious effort in the first place. Still others might need a combination of these approaches or an emphasis on specific incentives instead.

These forms of intervention—like conventional social opportunities themselves—need not be accompanied by an implicit or explicit message that there is something wrong with anyone who attempts to use them. In fact, whether in or out of prison, intervention can be offered on the basis of what may be thought of as a positive social right, a right on the part of any individual who wishes to learn more workable, perhaps more satisfying ways of coping with today's demanding and often frustrating environment. In short, programs of intervention can be presented not as ways of curing illness, but as resources that may help an individual broaden his social opportunities and personal horizons, mainly by (1) increasing his practical skills and/or interpersonal strengths, and (2) where necessary, casting off ghosts of the past and worthless stereotypes as well. The fact of having undertaken such an effort can itself be recognized as a sign of strength, not defect, by many offenders. The fact of having achieved some of the goals in question can be experienced as even more meaningful and self-enhancing.

People, Programs, and Relationships

When working toward short- and long-range goals, nonoffenders typically make use of available social opportunities, noncorrectional programs included. When dealing with problems that relate to these goals, they sometimes seek the assistance of, and derive benefit from, various individuals as well. Inasmuch as nonoffenders and offenders (1) are essentially the same, as human beings, and (2) must deal with a core of identical social-psychological challenges, it should come as no surprise that many offenders can themselves become interested in, and derive benefit from, programs or relationships that are directed toward similar goals. This applies despite important differences in the noncorrectional versus correctional approaches, and despite the added obstacles and complexities that these differences produce. At any rate, there would be little point in maintaining that offenders, simply because they are or have been offenders, do not at times genuinely seek assistance. In this respect, they are people first and offenders second.

This does not mean that most offenders express a strong desire to become involved in correctional programs or relationships, especially at the outset.[6] They are likely to express ambivalence, specific reservations, or no more than moderate interest instead. Moreover, they are likely to do so despite the sizable hurdles that sometimes lay ahead, and despite their oft-expressed feelings of dissatisfaction with their life, or themselves.[7] Nevertheless, three points might be kept in mind:

1. Doubt and anxiety in the face of challenge or uncertainty is not the monopoly of offenders. Many offenders are very similar to nonoffenders when it comes to experiencing and expressing initial reservations about their possible or impending involvement in activities that may later be of value. For these individuals, the most difficult step is often the first. (See n. 8 regarding some of the reasons for these reservations or difficulties.)

2. Encouragement by others, relative to an individual's taking the first step, need not automatically be equated with coercion. Nor is encouragement invariably resented. On the contrary, it is often appreciated by offenders and nonoffenders alike and is not automatically categorized, or responded to, as a form of benevolent paternalism. As in most areas of human interaction, a good deal depends on the spirit in which something is offered—on whether messages of interest and concern come through. This can often apply even when the offender (and nonoffender) has approached the situation in question "with a chip on his shoulder."

In the absence of a humane overall environment (an atmosphere of interest and concern), these messages would probably have little chance of coming through, inside as well as outside a justice system framework. Within such a framework, the problems of communicating these messages and maintaining a belief in their relevance are greatly compounded regardless of how humane the atmosphere may be, and regardless of the offender's underlying attitude.

Fairness or fair treatment by the justice system can help create a tolerable, believable, sometimes supportive atmosphere for involvement and decision making by offenders. Yet, by itself, fair treatment does not supply the direction, does not arouse the motivation, and does not provide the feedback or personal reward that must exist before realistic, satisfying decisions are generated and maintained. Thus, for many offenders, fairness without programmed assistance can be empty, even blind, and programs without fairness can be futile, even pathetic.

3. Initial reservations usually diminish as soon as individuals (offenders and nonoffenders alike) begin to experience concrete benefits or personal satisfactions from involvement. This, of course, assumes that the individuals have been willing to "get their feet wet" and give the program or relationship a try—and that administrators and policy makers have been willing to let them do so. However, for these benefits and satisfactions to occur, the program itself—and the staff who try to assist—must be able to "deliver." In this respect, concrete gains and positive experiences are not the responsibility of offenders alone. Programs, like other tools, must be worth their salt.

Once again, some offenders need little or nothing by way of carefully focused assistance; others need a great deal. Most offenders probably fall somewhere in between. Here, as elsewhere, offenders and nonoffenders are very much alike. Here, as elsewhere, what is unneeded or even decried by some may still play an important role in the lives of others.

Finally, in the mind of nonoffenders, intervention is not inevitably associated with the concept of personal defect, e.g., with the idea that "there would be something wrong with me if I sought assistance or wished to involve myself in a certain program." Here too, insofar as nonoffenders and offenders are essentially the same, as human beings, it should come as little surprise that a great many offenders are quite capable of recognizing the potential value of intervention, and of keeping this awareness uppermost in their mind despite possible messages and stereotypes regarding personal defect. To assume that youthful and adult offenders cannot recognize, or be brought to recognize, the potential value of educational, employment, or other forms of intervention would be to look upon them as defective, or thoroughly indifferent, indeed. To assume that most multiple offenders perceive intervention as having little or no relevance to the lives they might wish to lead would be to regard them as quite far gone, or superhuman, as well.

Closing Remarks

If the input that society provides to known offenders must contain something "bitter," e.g., punishment, this does not mean it can include nothing that is "sweet," e.g., experiences that are perceived by offenders to be personally useful and oriented toward a better future. From the standpoint of most offenders and from a humane perspective in general, the addition of this latter element would not seem like a great deal to ask. Quite apart from this, there is little reason to believe that programmed assistance, when implemented with care, would negate the impact of punishment itself.

Despite their shortcomings, today's programs of intervention are the only vehicles that show promise of helping a substantial portion of known offenders focus on their needs and life circumstances in concrete, individualized terms, on other than a fleeting or tangential basis. Programs that carefully focus on these areas should receive the support of society and its key decision makers, especially if they show promise of meeting such needs (educational or vocational, for example), and/or of reducing recidivism, in a humane and relatively efficient way.

Society has no humane grounds for abandoning such programs as long as it has nothing to substitute for them. This fact is in no way diminished by today's heightened interest in punishment, regardless of how uniformly and fairly it might be administered in the absence of the above programs. Nor is it altered by the inability of these programs to clearly reduce today's widespread problem of crime. This is apart from the added fact that crime rates can scarcely be expected to drop in response to an elimination or reduction of the more promising intervention programs, i.e., in response to the withdrawal of practical and personalized assistance to offenders.

In short, regardless of present-day circumstances and needs, society still has a responsibility for making at least some assistance available to offenders as human beings. This obligation reflects particular traditions and ideals. This social responsibility might be easier to recognize or accept during less emotion-filled (not to mention financially strapped) times, e.g., in the event crime rates were considerably lower than they are. The justice system in America can be tough on offenders, yet responsible in a broader sense as well. We need not become callous and indifferent, in the name of firmness, justice, or fair and equal handling of all.

Given this responsibility, and/or given its immediate self-interest alone, society has the practical task of making this assistance as effective as possible within the limits of its resources and priorities. Relative to this task, researchers, practitioners, and others should pool their experiences and build on the leads that have been sorted out thus far. This exchange of ideas could help corrections get better mileage from programs or approaches that have already shown promise. It could highlight the importance of developing new and improved approaches as well. In so doing, it could help avoid an artificial and largely unproductive polarization of past and present efforts along these lines.

Within this context, researchers should use their most powerful and flexible data-handling techniques, however complex or inelegant these may be.[9] When applied to individual studies and groups of studies, such tools and strategies could help make optimal use of the data sources and research findings at hand, and could increase the overall rate of progress as well.

In closing, corrections can and should take the next step forward in terms of reducing recidivism rates and making assistance available on a relatively individualized basis. It can take this step within a framework of humane interaction and exchange, despite the inevitable need for some degree of social control. Researchers, practitioners, academicians, and key decision makers should recognize that progress can be made within this area without hampering the search for practical solutions to today's problem of crime. However, they should be equally clear that the pursuit of reduced crime rates must not stand as an obstacle to the pursuit of offender-centered goals and reduced recidivism rates themselves. Insights that are gained in relation to either area can in fact contribute to progress within the other.

We have emphasized the process of differentiation and integration since we believe it is at the heart of scientific growth. This cyclic yet open-ended process draws heavily on past experiences and insights. However, it paves the way for more precise or powerful concepts and for the identification of new relationships as well. This evolution of ideas and linking of diverse events can help corrections become as deeply and broadly based as possible. It is this process and evolution which represents solid strength.

Appendixes

Appendix A:
A/B Quality Rating, Weighting, and Sample Size

A/B Quality Rating

The A versus B categorization (A/B rating) was a way of describing the scientific quality of individual studies. This rating, which was presented in *Correctional Effectiveness,* indicated the extent to which certain "research shortcomings" existed within a given study. As described by Lipton et al., each rating was made as follows (no further details were provided):

> ... Experienced professional researchers in the social science and criminological fields read and prepared an annotated summary for each study. These annotations included the following information: (1) treatment method (independent variable); (2) desired area of change (dependent variable); (3) setting for treatment; (4) *nature and size of the population studied*; (5) *research design*; (6) time in treatment; (7) time in follow-up; (8) outcomes; and (9) *research shortcomings* (Research shortcomings refer to those aspects of the research methodology that may call to question the results the researcher obtained. These may include faults in the selection or allocation of subjects, experimental design, use of statistics, generalizations from and interpretations of data, and specification of methodological detail.) The annotations were then reviewed in committee and each study was allocated to one of three categories: "A" studies, acceptable for the survey with no more than minimal *research shortcomings* [i.e., category 9, above]; "B" studies, acceptable for the survey with research shortcomings that place reservations on interpretation of findings; and "Other Studies". Under "Other Studies" are reports and articles excluded because two or more of the following [eleven] conditions existed. . . .[1] [27, emphasis added]

Weighting

After the A/B rating was completed, it was used, together with research design (category 5 above), sample size, and other factors, to weight the given study in relation to each remaining study that fell within the same treatment category. The purpose of weighting was to determine how much "confidence [is] to be placed in the findings of the studies analyzed," i.e., how much confidence in terms of developing sound generalizations concerning the effectiveness of the treatment category into which the studies fell [27]. In short, the goal of weighting was to determine how much of a contribution these studies could make in terms of developing knowledge (valid generalizations) about the effectiveness of any given approach.

The A/B rating focused on the scientific adequacy of each study, taken by itself. It was made entirely apart from, and prior to, any weighting. Sample size (category 4 above) did not contribute to the A/B rating. It entered the picture only in relation to the weighting of each study in relation to all remaining studies within the treatment category. The latter investigations had, of course, also received an A or B rating prior to any weighting.

"Other Studies" were not weighted; they were excluded because they failed to satisfy preestablished scientific standards. Thus, weighting was carried out only in the case of scientifically acceptable (A or B quality) studies. Only these investigations were seen as contributing to the development of valid generalizations.

To better understand the weighting process, and the role of sample size in particular, the following should be kept in mind. In approaching the question of how to weight any particular study, *Correctional Effectiveness* staff first combined the A/B quality rating with a specific number that was also given to the study, a number that was the product of a particular "ranking system." This system was based on three factors, and each A or B quality study was evaluated with respect to all three factors (the items that comprise each factor are shown in parentheses):

1. "Type of research design" (pure experimental, ex post facto, or simulation)
2. "Method of obtaining the subject pool" (probability sampling or nonprobability sampling)
3. "Method of allocating subjects to experimental and control groups" (matched or random allocation versus nonmatched or nonrandom allocation) [27].

The rank that was given to each study reflected the particular way in which these factors—more specifically, the items that comprised these factors—were combined. These combinations, and their corresponding rankings, can be illustrated as follows (numerically lower ranks represent methodologically stronger studies; as will be seen, research designs of the pure experimental type were considered the most important single item[2]):

Rank 1: Pure experimental (E) design, probability sample, random allocation

Rank 2: Pure E design, nonprobability sample, random allocation

Rank 3: Pure E design, probability sample, nonrandom allocation

Rank 4: Pure E design, nonprobability sample, nonrandom allocation

Rank 5:   Ex post facto design, probability sample, random allocation

Rank 6:   Ex post facto design, nonprobability sample, random allocation

. . . . . .

Rank 9:   Simulation design, probability sample, random allocation

. . . . . .

Rank 12: Simulation design, nonprobability sample, nonrandom allocation

Although this design/sampling/allocation system contained 18 possible rankings, most studies (i.e., findings or entries) fell within the top four categories. Specifically, ranks 1 through 4 accounted for 65 percent of the more than 280 entries that appeared in *Correctional Effectiveness*; rank 2, alone, accounted for 49 percent. Ranks 9 through 18 accounted for only 14 percent.[3] Focusing on the 138 recidivism entries alone, the figures for these ranks were 51, 44, and 7 percent, respectively.[4] (If studies rather than entries are used, the figures change by a negligible amount.) This ranking system:

> . . . was applied in the survey as one measure of the confidence that can be placed in the various studies included. The number [specific ranking] assigned to a study was *combined* with an "A" or "B", A signifying a higher quality than B, to indicate in a gross way the extent of the reservations placed (by the survey team) upon interpretations of the findings due to *research shortcomings.*[5] [27, emphasis added]

The combined "rating system"—namely the A/B quality rating, together with the 18-point ranking—was then used as one of the factors that entered into the weighting of each study. These factors, and their interaction, were referred to in a general way by Lipton et al. (details were neither supplied nor referenced):

> . . . Any summary [of disparate studies] requires the application of individual judgments as to the confidence to be placed in the findings of the studies analyzed. When the studies are grouped in categories (by intersection of independent and dependent variables), the survey team must make judgments as to whether one study should be given more weight than *another* within a given category.[6] In this survey such judgments were based in part on the rating system described above [i.e., the combined rating system] and in part on the sizes of the sample population involved, evaluation of the *methodology* used (for example, sophistication of statistical techniques[7]), and all of the other factors that enter into an inductive process of arriving at conclusions. [27, emphasis added]

(The closing sentence is somewhat unclear in view of the fact that "methodology" was already reflected in the A/B quality rating, and in the design/sampling/ allocation ranking as well.)

Sample Size

The following bears on the role of sample size. By tabulating the sample size of all recidivism studies that appeared in *Correctional Effectiveness,* we found a strong inverse relationship between both quality and strength, on the one hand, and sample size, on the other. Among A quality studies, average sample size was 459; among B quality studies it was 900. For pure experimental studies, the average was 435; for ex post facto and simulation studies combined, it was 1033. Among A quality and pure experimental studies combined, the average was 291; among B quality and ex post facto and simulation studies combined, it was 1101.[8] In short, the better the study (scientifically speaking), the *smaller* the sample size.[9] To be sure, 459 (even 291) is far from small in absolute terms. In addition, it is more than adequate by most statistical standards, particularly in well-designed studies.[10] (Average sample size for all recidivism studies was 698.)[11]

With respect to weighting, the main implication of this inverse relationship is that, other things being equal, if sample size were considered just as important as the combined rating described above, studies which received a poorer combined rating (e.g., ex post facto, B quality studies) could be given as much weight, possibly more weight, than those which received a better combined rating (e.g., pure experimental, A quality studies). Stated differently, less powerful or lower quality studies could, by virtue of their far larger sample size, easily end up playing as large a role as the more powerful, higher-quality studies.

Such a situation—lower-quality studies in effect negating the advantages associated with higher-quality studies—would hardly seem defensible, especially if sample sizes were already quite substantial among the latter investigations. The questionable appropriateness of any such hypothetical outcome leads us to believe that, in actuality, the survey team probably gave much less weight to the factor of sample size than to those of technical and qualitative strength. This inference is also consistent with the following, indirect evidence (we use such evidence because *Correctional Effectiveness* contained no direct or specific statements regarding the relative importance of sample size in the context of weighting):

1. Sample-size comprised a single factor or item, whereas technical and qualitative strength, as reflected in the combined rating, was the product of several items. 2. Most or all of the latter items could easily have been considered as important as sample size. This possibility is consistent with the fact that almost no space was given to a discussion of sample size, whereas considerable space was devoted to items that comprised the combined rating. More directly, as implied by Lipton et al., the merit and generalizability of scientific findings is ordinarily evaluated in relation to items that comprised the combined rating. This would suggest that it is not primarily assessed on the basis of sample size.

Appendix B:
Inaccuracy and
Reasoned Discourse

"California Research at the Crossroads" ("Crossroads") contains numerous inaccuracies and potentially counterproductive techniques of discourse. A few examples will now be given, together with comments regarding their main implications for corrections. In this appendix, "Martinson Revisited" will be referred to as "Revisited."

Inaccuracies: (A) General Factual Errors

1. Martinson stated: "Palmer notes no basic flaw in my brief discussion of CTP findings in 'What Works?' " This statement is only partly correct. For instance, Martinson had asserted that "experimentals were actually committing more offenses than their controls." In response, Palmer, in "Revisited," pointed out that this statement "holds up only if one has included, in the overall analysis, offenses which are of a minor nature—more specifically, technical violations . . . and various infractions; e.g., 'uncooperative attitude toward program,' 'missed group meeting,' [etc.] ." Palmer also indicated that when these offenses were eliminated, "the monthly rate of arrests was . . . *equal* among E's and C's."[1]

To stick with the main theme of "Revisited," Palmer chose not to mention four inaccuracies that appeared in "What Works," relative to the Community Treatment Project:

a. Martinson referred to CTP youths (experimentals) as "probationers," and to CTP agents/workers as "probation officers." In line with this, experimental subjects "were released directly to probation status" and "were permitted to remain on probation" subsequent to various arrests [31]. However, CTP was conducted, not in a probation setting, but in a parole setting; this applies to experimentals and controls alike. (See n. 2 for details.) The difference between parolees and probationers is substantial. During the 1960s (collectively) no more than 1 in every 7 juvenile probationers was sent to the Youth Authority; those who were sent had continued to get in trouble with the law.[3] Moreover, parolees (but not CTP experimentals, although they, too, were parolees) had ordinarily spent 8 or 9 months in a large-sized YA institution before being released to parole.[4]

Martinson's view of Community Treatment Project youths as "probationers" may be one source of his hypothesis about CTP, and of his related questions as well: "CTP beefed up what amounted to a *probation-like* status for

young people with a very expensive and complicated set of 'programs.' If
probation placement alone had a 'positive' effect, would this embarass any and
all community 'treatment' . . .? Would the public demand that research separate
the effect of *probation* placement from the effect of those expensive 'programs' . . . which Palmer and his allies insist on adding to everything that
exists?" [Emphasis added]

As suggested, in evaluating Martinson's comments, it is important to
distinguish between most probationers and most multiple offenders, i.e., parolees. (This distinction was very clear in *Correctional Effectivenes* with reference
to CTP. In the 1960s, few parolees had fewer than three police contacts prior to
their Youth Authority committing offense; typically, the number of priors was
five. In the early 1970s, this figure rose to seven.) Thus, in CTP, a relatively
expensive program was not added to probation, since all youths who were sent to
the YA (of which CTP was a part) had already been removed from probation by
local judges, and had been sent to the state system for long-term institutionalization. Instead, a community-based program for multiple offenders was *substituted* not only for YA *parole,* but for the expensive alternatives of long-term
institutionalization and large-scale capital outlay relative to the construction of
still other institutions. There was in the 1960s, and there still is today, little need
for embarrassment in this respect. At any rate, Martinson's description may well
have led many readers to believe that CTP was essentially a beefed up (or in
perhaps more positive terms, an enriched) probation program. His hypothesis
concerning CTP may be evaluated accordingly.

b. Martinson also stated: " 'Success' in this experiment was defined as
favorable discharge by the Youth Authority." (This, in itself, would indicate
that CTP youths were not on probation.) However, favorable discharge was only
one of the measures used in CTP;[5] and despite its recognized importance, it was
clearly never the primary one. As of the data cutoff for *Correctional Effectiveness* and, therefore, "What Works," assessments of CTP were based on a range of
criterion measures. These included not only standard 15- and 24-month parole
followups (the primary measures), but favorable and unfavorable discharge
cohorts, and attitudinal or psychological change as well. Findings that related to
each of these outcome measures were presented in considerable detail in
Correctional Effectiveness. Cost data were also reviewed.

c. Martinson stated: "Fewer of the experimentals as compared with the
controls had been judged to have successfully completed their program of
supervision and to be suitable for favorable release." This statement directly
contradicted the favorable discharge results that were presented in the CTP
report which was reviewed in the source document, *Correctional Effectiveness.*
The CTP report stated: "A four-year parole-followup showed that *56* percent of
the Experimentals and *42* percent of the Controls had received a favorable
discharge within this period of time. [These 86 E's and 131 C's were] . . .
equated with regard to total amount of community exposure time. Statistically,

this difference is significant in favor of the Experimentals."[6] [41, $p < .05$; computed from table 11 of CTP report]

d. Martinson stated: ". . . None of the controls had been directly released to their regular supervision programs instead of being detained first [in YA institutions]." However, the fact is that a certain portion of the controls did get released directly to parole, as indicated in CTP reports.[7] This was specified in *Correctional Effectiveness* as well: "Approximately 20 percent of the C's were placed directly on parole by the board about one month after they had been committed to the Youth Authority. All remaining C's spent between eight and nine months in a Youth Authority institution."

2. Martinson stated: "By some incredible trick of fate, Palmer seems to have found but one [method that really works]: CTP." This statement is inaccurate. First, CTP reports routinely indicated that this program worked for certain offenders only, not on an across-the-board basis. This was amply illustrated in *Correctional Effectiveness* as well. Second, in "Revisited," positive or partly positive results had been noted by Palmer in connection with no fewer than 48 percent of all individual studies (programs) that were mentioned by Martinson in "What Works." CTP was only one such study, and in "Revisited" as well as in "What Works," neither Palmer nor Martinson described CTP as a "method" (independent variable category).

3. Martinson referred to questions which "Palmer thought he had settled, like deterrence." This statement is inaccurate, since Palmer, in "Revisited," in no way focused on the concept of deterrence. Even the term did not appear. Nor did Palmer ever deal with the issue of deterrence, prior to "Revisited."

4. Martinson stated: "All [one] gets from Palmer is the dry crust of 'middle base expectancy' and interminable intramural bickering about . . . significance tests." However, "Revisited" touched on many topics and factors other than that of base expectancy, and it contained relatively little material and almost no discussion regarding the latter itself. It contained no discussion of significance tests.

Inaccuracies: (B) Altered Meanings

1. In "Revisited," Palmer made it clear that the positive or mixed-positive studies which Martinson reported were by no means isolated exceptions:

> Martinson originally referred to 39 studies—48% of the total—as having yielded positive or partly positive results. In light of this, it was surely amiss to have elsewhere characterized these same studies as being "few and isolated exceptions." This inaccuracy would continue to exist even if his characterization had been in reference to all 231 technically adequate studies which had been located. . . . This issue . . . relates to the proportion of *individual studies* that yielded favorable or differentially favorable results. . . ." [38]

In his summary, Palmer again referred to this issue in the following context:

> ... Methods of treatment which had been of value to only *some* offenders were of necessity classified as unsuccessful. This was entirely aside from Martinson's rather inaccurate description of *individual studies,* whose results had been favorable or partially favorable, as being "few and isolated exceptions." [38]

Now, in "Crossroads," Martinson altered the meaning of the phrase *inaccurate description.* He did this by indicating that Palmer's evaluative comments referred to studies not on a collective but on a strictly individual basis:

> Palmer can uncover no single case of "inaccurate description" of a study in "What Works?" He is obliged to admit this or to document his assertion. [30]

Again, it is apparent in "Revisited" that Palmer's remarks referred to studies collectively, i.e., to the fact that 48 percent of all studies could not reasonably be considered a small or isolated group, and that it was inaccurate to describe them as such. His remarks did not reflect on the accuracy with which the findings of each individual study had been reported. With few exceptions, individual findings were reported accurately.

(Before proceeding, it might be noted that elsewhere in "Crossroads," Martinson stated: "[Palmer] asks what *proportion of the total studies* have 'positive or partly positive results.' ... The answer is '48%' " [emphasis added]. Thus, Martinson did recognize that Palmer had referred to studies in a collective sense within the context under consideration.)

Since the issue of accuracy has been raised at the level of individual studies, it might be pointed out that in "What Works," Martinson stated: "And Schwitzgebel (1963, 1964), studying other, different kinds of therapy programs, found that the programs *did* produce improvements in the attitudes of his boys—but, unfortunately, not in their rates of recidivism." However, a review of the source document, *Correctional Effectiveness,* shows that this is an essentially inaccurate account of the findings. Specifically, "counseled subjects did not differ significantly from controls in the percent returned to reformatory or prison (the return rate for experimentals was 35 percent; for C's, 45 percent) but they had significantly fewer arrests (average of 2.4 versus 4.7), and significantly fewer months of incarceration (average of 3.5 versus 6.9)." That is, "Schwitzgebel's findings indicate reduction in arrests and in months of incarceration for youths given individual counseling, although no difference was obtained between experimentals and controls in proportion returned to physical custody" [27].

It might also be noted that in "What Works," Martinson stated: "The one study of a non-institutional skill development program, by Kovacs (1967), described the New Start Program in Denver, in which offenders participated in vocational training, role playing, programmed instruction, group counseling, college class attendance, and trips to art galleries and museums. After all this, Kovacs found no significant improvement over incarceration." This summary conveys a rather different message than that which appeared in the source document: "Kovac's findings indicate that at three months, a smaller proportion of experimental subjects were in jail (33 percent; detained or convicted) than controls (53 percent) $[Z < 0.10]$; at one year, the experimentals maintained a significantly higher success rate [specifically, "E's once more had a significantly higher success rate (61 percent) than C's (47 percent) $(Z < 0.10)$"]. These differences between experimentals and controls were not significant at the 5 percent level. However, they could not be expected to occur by chance more than one time in 10 given the size of the groups tested.... It is difficult to draw conclusions from these [six] studies since two of the studies (Sullivan, 1967 and Kovacs, 1967) combined special educational programs with vocational programs, two of the studies ... evaluated standard institutional education, one study ... involved both a special educational program and special education combined with standard institutional education. In general, the special educational programs seem to be more successful, especially when combined with vocational training, than standard institutional education."[8]

Finally, in "What Works," Martinson stated: "Three of the four 'phases' of this experiment [Special Intensive Parole Unit (SIPU) experiment] produced 'negative results.' ... The only phase ... for which positive results were reported was Phase Three." However, according to *Correctional Effectiveness,* major, positive results were reported relative to other phases as well. For example, in Phase Four, "Subjects in small (15-man) case loads and medium (30-man) case loads performed significantly better than subjects in large (70-man) case loads in proportions of no arrest (37.5 percent versus 38.8 percent versus 24.8 percent) and in proportions of minor arrest (21.2 percent versus 24.4 percent versus 34.6 percent) $[F < 0.05]$." Also, "subjects with whom agents said they felt 'comfortable' at initial interview had significantly fewer arrests than those rated otherwise $[X^2 < 0.05]$" [27]. (See n. 9 regarding positive findings in Phase One.)

2. In "Crossroads," Martinson explained that his phrase/concept, "a sure way," referred to whether or not a program was accomplishing "anything at all." (See n. 10 for details.) Despite this explanation, a review of "What Works" indicates that "a sure way" was used to convey just what this phrase would ordinarily be expected to convey. It was used relative to the question of whether any treatment method could be recommended on an across-the-board basis, i.e., as an approach which would work under a wide variety of conditions. (This usage is illustrated in n. 11, together with the contradictory nature of Martinson's assertion.) There is no evidence to suggest that "a sure way" was

used relative to the question of whether any given program, or even method, was "doing anything at all." Moreover, unless one broadens the meaning of all key words that appear in both phrases, the concepts in question seem only minimally related to one another in the first place.

3. Martinson stated: "Suppose all [six weak ex post facto, group-method studies] had positive findings and the [one massive experimental study] showed 'no effect.' Using Palmer's innovative method, one would say that 'group methods' are six-sevenths 'effective.' " Despite this assertion, a review of "Revisited" shows that Palmer did not use the ratio of positive-to-no effect outcomes, or any variant thereof, as the basis for a quantitative-evaluative statement regarding any treatment method as a whole. For instance, Palmer neither indicated nor implied that probation was 7/14ths effective, that casework and individual counseling was 6/8ths effective, or, for that matter, that rehabilitation in general was 39/82nds ("about half," or 48 percent) effective. Instead, he spoke of positive outcomes for specified individuals within specified settings, etc. Since there is no evidence to support Martinson's assertion, the latter may be thought of as a very loose application—an application by analogy—of the 48 percent finding to other findings that were associated with specific categories of treatment. Obviously, it would be senseless to state that rehabilitation is about half effective or that casework and individual counseling is about three-fourths effective. Nevertheless, this would be quite different from saying that a given program reduced recidivism in approximately 50 percent of the cases, or (as Palmer stated) that 48 percent of all studies showed positive or mixed positive results.

Potentially Counterproductive Techniques of Discourse

1. In "Crossroads," Martinson presented a case for plain speaking: "To advance the field of criminal justice research, we must look closely at the sources of [Palmer's] confusion without mincing words. Plain speaking will be painful. We are all mired in jargon, ornament, and Aesopian subterfuge, but only temporarily till we get on our feet." With this in mind, he then addressed the reader in a manner that involves a good deal more than what is ordinarily thought of as plain speaking. His techniques of discourse included name calling, ridicule, prejudicing the reader via emotion-arousing phrases, ad hominem argument, etc. These may be illustrated as follows.

"Palmer and his cronies"; ". . . the research community will not follow the Pied Piper [i.e., Palmer] into the river"; "with [Palmer's] answer and thirty cents you can buy a cup of coffee in New York. It is meaningless"; "only a person [viz., Palmer] liberated from his normal senses by polemical fury . . ."; ". . . if research is to get out of the straight jacket Palmer wishes to impose on it"; "[we did not commit the obvious error of] adding camels and coat hooks as

Palmer managed to do"; "to review one of Palmer's research reports is . . . something like translating the Moscow telephone book into Swahili. Why is this? . . . If the truth be known, correctional research is about nine-tenths pageantry, rumination, and rubbish, and about one-tenth useful knowledge"; "Palmer's interminable intramural bickering"; ". . . not a peep from Dr. Palmer during these years"; "the series of reports which gushed forth from CTP"; "the narrowest and meanest of questions"; "[the economists] will help put an end to the rank opportunism, theoretical and analytic barrenness, and downright fraud which pervades the field of correctional research"; "Only the troglodytes opposed probation for the first offenders when it was first introduced"; "I ask Palmer to leave the 'treatment' Philistines to their idle chatter. . . ."

Examples and discussions of ad hominem arguments will not be presented right now. However, in this connection, see p. 85 and Appendix G of the present volume; also see the quotation on p. 53.

Martinson also presented speculation as though it were fact. This included an attributing of specific intentions, actions, or abilities to others, without suggesting the possibility of alternate explanations, alternate intentions, etc.

For example, "[Palmer] is *intent on fudging* this issue along with a phalanx of others"; "[Palmer] *carefully refrains* from defining this circumlocution";[12] "Why is it [that Palmer] . . .*cannot bring himself* to say whether any existing treatment method should be abandoned. . . ?"; "Why not admit that [Palmer] *conveniently ignored* the ex-attorney general's error?"[13] "Insiders like Palmer knew about it [*Correctional Effectiveness*] and its essential conclusions [despite the fact that "it was resting securely in the vaults of the Division of Criminal Justice Services of the State of New York"];[14] "Palmer wishes to reduce this discussion to a quibble over research methods" [emphasis added].

Despite their irrelevance or unproductiveness from a logical and substantive point of view, the preceding techniques do not always pose a serious problem. Indeed, their occasional use can sometimes enliven a complex or dry discussion. (There are, of course, other ways to accomplish that end.) In point of fact, their presence within correctional reviews and debates is by no means rare.

However, when used even half as often as in "Crossroads" (a 12-page article), such techniques can be counterproductive. For instance, they can make it difficult for many readers to remain focused on substantive issues.[15] They can easily shift the readers' attention to the occasionally entertaining and often compelling level of personalities instead [15].

Thus, however appropriate it might be to liven up discussion and ease the readers' burden,[16] these particular techniques—again, used en masse—run a large risk of precluding carefully reasoned discourse. (This term emphasizes the clarification of issues via an inspection of premises, evidence, and conclusions.) This risk is probably greater if the readers' or discussants' emotions have been aroused (see below).

Although plain speaking can play an important role in the clarification of issues, the correctional community might still consider the following question: If used on a large-scale basis (not simply in an occasional article or discussion), to what extent would Martinson's particular form of plain speaking contribute to an atmosphere of reasoned discourse? In answering this question, it might first wish to address two others: Does the given approach help focus attention on substantive issues, underlying assumptions, and specific evidence? Does it shed more light than heat? In addressing each question, the correctional community can assume that the earlier-mentioned inaccuracies and internal contradictions are not inevitably bound up with plain speaking, heated or otherwise. That is, the former do not necessarily go hand in hand with the latter.

Debate, like plain speaking, is also to be desired, again as a way of clarifying issues. However, when used at almost every turn, debating techniques such as name calling, ridicule, and ad hominem argument often preclude dispassionate or relatively objective discussion—except perhaps among (1) participants who are fairly unflappable and difficult to embarrass or intimidate, and (2) participants, readers, or audiences who are not easily diverted from the issues and evidence at hand.

In all likelihood, dispassionate discussion is even more difficult to achieve if the techniques in question appear to reflect an attitude which extends beyond that of good-natured humor, caricature, or even ridicule, e.g., one that involves intolerance or disdain for alternate points of view. Such an attitude (often a forerunner of invective) can sometimes arouse emotions which detract from the task at hand.[17] In this connection, Walter Miller's observation would seem particularly apt:

> None of us can free himself from the influence of ideological predilections, nor are we certain that it would be desirable to do so. But the purposes of effective policy and practice are not served when we are unable to recognize [or perhaps do not choose to acknowledge] in opposing positions the degree of legitimacy, validity, and humane intent they may possess. It does not seem unreasonable to ask of those engaged in the demanding task of formulating and implementing criminal justice policy that they accord to differing positions that measure of respect and consideration that the true ideologue can never grant. [35]

Miller's observation is valid despite the fact that name calling, ridicule, etc.— good-natured or otherwise—may be an individual's principal and preferred way of expressing his deepest convictions on specific subjects. In short, directness of expression, however desirable, refreshing, or painful, ordinarily can and should be integrated with the need for reasoned discourse. It should not dominate the scene at the latter's expense.

Finally, Martinson's particular form or extension of plain speaking is probably not the only route of escape from the jargon, ornament, and subterfuge to which he refers. In any event, however important it may be to minimize these three factors, it is equally important not to generate new factors or conditions whose impact can be at least as far-reaching. More specifically, when dealing with the former set of factors, it is important not to lose sight of the principal method, goal, and advantage of reasoned discourse itself. The reason for this is that in the long run, it is the careful inspection of evidence and the clarification of issues that can serve as the most objective basis for action. Honest emotion and candid expression can contribute to, but should not interfere with, this end.

As implied above, the present considerations are separate and apart from questions of accuracy and internal consistency. The latter features constitute indispensable building blocks of reasoned discourse. As such, their presence must be taken for granted or ensured.

Appendix C:
Efforts, Studies, and
Substantive Realities

In response to Palmer's critique of "What Works," Martinson placed special emphasis on the following:

> Palmer based his critique on grounds of research method. In doing so he makes an interpretation error by construing as "studies" the "efforts" Martinson mentions in his conclusion. In fact, "effort" represents an independent variable category. . . . Let me quote what I said: *"With few and isolated exceptions, the rehabilitative efforts that have been reported so far have had no appreciable effect on recidivism."* Palmer translates "efforts" as "studies." The term "effort" was used so that I would not have to say "independent variable category" [i.e., method of treatment], an awkward phrase in a piece which was to be free from jargon.[1] . . . The "few and isolated exceptions" do not refer to studies but to "independent variable categories." [30]

Martinson's assertion that *effort* represents *independent variable category* (IVC)—and by implication, nothing but IVC—does not square with his key statements in "What Works."[2] There, for example, *efforts* appeared to be synonymous with *individual studies.* (These studies are, of course, the specific components of any given IVC.[3])

First, take the summary statement or conclusion which, in Martinson's view, Palmer misinterpreted (this oft-quoted statement appeared in the opening pages of "What Works," subsequent to Martinson's description of the literature survey and selection criteria, and prior to any presentation or discussion of given treatment methods; for convenience, it will now be repeated): *"With few and isolated exceptions, the rehabilitative efforts that have been reported so far have had no appreciable effect on recidivism"* [31].

Now, it was obviously not Martinson's independent variable categories that had been "reported so far" (*report* relates to the literature survey); it was individual studies as such. This is also apparent from the sentence that immediately followed the preceding statement: *"Studies* that have been done since our survey was completed do not present any major grounds for altering that original conclusion" [emphasis added]. The fact that Martinson's summary statement focused on individual studies (efforts) was also apparent from the overall context in which the statement appeared. (This is illustrated in n. 4.)

Second, in his summary assessment of rehabilitation, Martinson used the term *instances* in the same sense in which he had used the term *efforts* in the preceding quotation. Here, he conveyed the clear impression that the instances in question were individual studies, and that these studies (not IVCs) formed the real basis of his overall conclusion. The summary assessment is as follows:

> Do all of these *studies* lead us irrevocably to the conclusion that nothing works, that we haven't the faintest clue about how to rehabilitate offenders and reduce recidivism? . . . I am bound to say that these data, involving over 200 studies and hundreds of thousands of individuals as they do, are the best available and give us very little reason to hope that we have found a sure way of reducing recidivism through rehabilitation. This is not to say that we found no instances of success or partial success; it is only to say that these instances have been isolated, *producing* no clear pattern to indicate the efficacy of any particular *method* of treatment. [31, emphasis added]

In the final sentence of this assessment, *instances* was not synonymous with *method of treatment*, i.e., with *independent variable category*. This is logically indisputable since, in the given statement, it was these instances which failed to *produce* the "pattern" that might otherwise have indicated the efficacy of any given method. Taken literally, and in context, "instances," i.e., "isolated" instances of "success or partial success," clearly referred to particular studies that belong to one "method of treatment" or another (i.e., to a given IVC). This was not simply a matter of avoiding an awkward phrase.

In sum, in Martinson's earlier conclusion, *efforts* did not refer to methods of treatment. As in the case of *instances* (in his summary assessment), it referred to the technically adequate individual studies that were surveyed in the large-scale literature review. Thus, *efforts* and *studies* were synonymous in the statements under consideration, and no error of interpretation was made by equating the two terms in this regard.[5] This applied despite the crucial role that had indeed been played by independent variable categories in the actual implementation of Martinson's analysis.

Clearly, in some contexts, *efforts* can be used to represent *studies*; in other contexts, it can represent *independent variable categories*. In "What Works," *efforts* was used in both senses, not just the latter. With regard to *studies*, it was used explicitly; in the case of IVC's, it was used implicitly. Palmer's critique ("Martinson Revisited") focused on both the former and latter meaning, as needed. This was in spite of the way that Martinson had presented the given terms.

Thus, regardless of context, it is important to separate questions that relate to (1) which specific terms can and/or should refer to which specific concepts, analytic units, or approaches (CUAs) from questions which focus on (2) the relationships among, and the actual utilization of, CUAs themselves. (CUA's will be called *substantive items* or *substance*.) *Substance* includes the specific subject matter, the methodological structure, the procedures,[6] and the underlying logic of a given analysis. It provides the basis for systematically and objectively responding to various issues or questions, e.g., the question of "What works in rehabilitation?"

The validity of any given conclusion—that is, the empirical justification for, and logical appropriateness of, any response to a substantive issue—can be determined via an examination of the CUAs that are involved in the given analysis. This determination can be made regardless of the specific terminology that is used to communicate the concepts and relationships in question.

Now, Palmer's critique assessed the validity of Martinson's overall conclusion regarding rehabilitation. It did so by examining the relationships and interactions that existed in connection with the subject matter, the structure, etc. of the latter's analysis. It found that Martinson's conclusion did not adequately represent findings that were present within the full range of technically acceptable to excellent, individual studies. It also found that the given conclusion reflected his negative assessment of almost every independent variable category (IVC) instead.

In short, by focusing on specific subject matter, structures, etc., this critique took into account not only the role of (1) studies, viewed as individual efforts, but that of (2) treatment methods (IVCs), viewed as central units of analysis, and obviously, as a different level of effort than that of studies. Thus, from a substantive perspective, the equating of studies and efforts reflected only one aspect of the critique in question (namely, item 1 above). Moreover, as suggested in the following quotation, this aspect was handled separate and apart from that of treatment methods per se (item 2 above):

> Martinson evaluated these claims [viz., success-claims which existed, implicitly or explicitly, relative to each method of treatment]· specifically in terms of the presence or absence of substantial differences, or inconsistencies, among the results of the several studies that had been reported for any given method. However, because of the heterogeneous nature of these studies it was probable, from the start, that a certain percent of all results would turn out to be mutually inconsistent, as, in fact, they did. Because the criterion of "inconsistency" was then applied in a fairly rigorous manner, the related concept of "success" barely seemed to admit of degrees. As a result, methods of treatment which had been of value to only *some* offenders were of necessity classified as unsuccessful. This was entirely aside from Martinson's rather inaccurate description of *individual studies,* whose results had been favorable or partially favorable, as being "few and isolated exceptions." [Here, the final sentence refers to individual efforts (item 1 above), whereas preceding sentences are focused on structural and logical factors as such (item 2 above).] [38]

In sum, Palmer's critique focused directly on the substance of "What Works." It did so at each of two main levels of analysis, and regardless of the specific terms that had been used in Martinson's summary assessment and oft-quoted conclusion. As a result, it was neither limited nor led off the track by the specific use that Martinson had made of such terms or concepts as *efforts* and *studies.* Thus, the latter's point about the erroneous equating of these particular terms or concepts was of little relevance to the thrust and outcome of the critique itself.

The conclusion that Martinson drew in "What Works" was largely a product of the interaction between given analytic structures, on the one hand, and a specific assessment criterion, on the other. This interaction did not allow numerous, positive, individual studies to formally contribute to the assessment of rehabilitation as a whole. Palmer's review of the "What Works" conclusion focused on factors or substantive realities such as these. These factors or realities remain unchanged regardless of the terminology that he and Martinson may have used in specific contexts,[7] and regardless of which words were actually synonymous with which, irrespective of context.[8]

Thus, even if one substitutes the term *independent variable category* for that of *efforts,*[9] Martinson's conclusion in "What Works" still fails to represent the promising leads that were observed in numerous individual studies. It therefore fails to reflect the leads which were present relative to various treatment methods themselves. In short, even if *efforts* and *studies* had not turned out to be synonymous—in the earlier-mentioned quotations and else-where—this would in no way alter the status of his overall conclusion with respect to rehabilitation.

Appendix D: Approaches Used at the Community Treatment Project

At the Community Treatment Project (CTP), approximately three of the following general approaches were used with any given offender during one or more phases of his parole experience: individual counseling, group counseling, family counseling, pragmatically oriented planning discussions, individual psychotherapy, and/or control or deterrence (e.g., limit setting, surveillance, and/or short-term detention[1]). The three that were selected varied from one offender to the next. One or more of the following program elements were also likely to be used: project-based school (with individual tutoring), social and recreational activities plus cultural enrichment, and/or out-of-home placement. Other elements were used as well.

With one minor exception, the full range of approaches and elements was available to youths who fell within *any* base expectancy, maturity, and subtype classification.[2] However, certain general approaches (e.g., group counseling), and a number of rather specific techniques, were more likely to be used with some subtypes and levels than with others.[3] As a result, the overall treatment-and-control strategy that was used with the former subtypes and levels often seemed rather distinct from that which was used with the latter. (Methods used at CTP are described in an upcoming book, separate for conflicted, power oriented, and passive conformist youths [42].)

Nevertheless, even within any one subtype or level, any specific pattern of treatment was seldom used with more than a single offender. This was largely because the earlier-mentioned interests, abilities, and life circumstances (factors which varied a good deal within each subtype and level) had played a major role in determining the specific combination of approaches and elements that was used, and the relative emphasis that was placed on each.[4] (Emphasis was reflected in the number of monthly contacts, the total duration of usage, etc.) In effect, a fairly distinctive pattern of treatment and control was thus developed for most individuals on the project. This was despite the above-mentioned similarities in approach that often appeared at the levels of individual subtype, subtype grouping, and overall maturity.

Appendix E: Measures of Adjustment, Achievement, and Change

Collectively, the studies that were surveyed in *Correctional Effectiveness* used a wide range of measures to assess vocational adjustment, educational achievement, community adjustment, and personality and attitude change. Included were the following (this list is not exhaustive).

Vocational Adjustment

Part-time or full-time employment rate (e.g., percent of the sample employed during followup), percent of time employed during followup, number of part-time and full-time jobs, average wages, average monthly earnings, total earnings during followup, salary increases, job stability, reasons for job change, percent of sample in dead-end jobs, "employment outcome rated by two groups of vocational experts on basis of vocational achievement compared to individual potential," and percent of sample contributing to support of dependents.

Educational Achievement

Average gain in grade level (net grade level achieved, all academic subjects combined), highest grade completed, attainment of grade level 6.5 or more, grade point average, achievement and improvement in vocabulary, comprehension, and arithmetic, on standardized educational tests (e.g., Stanford Achievement Test Battery; Metropolitan Achievement Tests), and reading achievement and improvement (e.g., using the California Achievement Test and the Gates Reading Survey).

Community Adjustment

Improvement in "(1) drinking behavior, (2) health, (3) work, (4) family relations, (5) social functioning, (6) insight, plus an 'overall' index"; "(1) marital status, (2) quality of marital relations, (3) church attendance, (4) organizational membership, (5) friendship relations, ..."; "interpersonal competence, family and social activity, and general community participation"; "Mandel Social

Adjustment Scale: ratings on 'movement' toward adjustment in the areas of occupation, family, economy, health, religion, residential stability, community, and social adjustment, and a total score"; "Community Adjustment Scale" [27].

Lipton et al. pointed out the following with regard to community adjustment:

> In this survey, community adjustment was conceived as a residual category—that is, a study or a finding from a study was placed in this outcome category only when it was unclassifiable under recidivism, institutional adjustment, drug or alcohol readdiction, or vocational or educational achievement. . . . From the point of view of post-adjudicatory rehabilitation, community adjustment measures alone would appear to be the weakest and most unreliable outcome measures. However, when used in combination with recidivism measures, or when used for the purpose of understanding how a specific treatment accomplishes a reduction in recidivism, appropriate community adjustment measures may be quite useful. [27]

Personality and Attitude Change

Lipton et al. summarized this outcome area as follows:

> This dependent variable refers to changes measured by means of standardized projective and objective personality tests and attitude inventories or by the judgment of "treatment" personnel. . . . Personality dimensions frequently used as dependent variables are ego strength, maturity, dependence, alienation, social introversion-extroversion, impulsivity, aggressiveness, authoritarianism, delinquency proneness, and anxiety. Attitude changes are also frequently examined, especially changed attitudes toward family, work, authority, and self. [27]

Specific instruments and scales included: TAT, Rorschach, Sacks Sentence Completion, MMPI, Human Relations Inventory, Edwards Personal Preference Scale, Jesness Inventory, California Psychological Inventory (CPI), Haggerty-Olson-Wickman Behavior Rating Scale B, Butler-Haigh Q-Sort for Self and Ideal-Self Concepts, Semantic Differential, Pd Scale of MMPI, Asocial Index of Jesness Inventory, De Scale of CPI, C scale of Minnesota Counseling Inventory, and Delinquency Scale of Inventory of Personal Opinion.

Other scales and areas included time perspective scale, alienation scale, "illegitimate means acceptance scale," "attitudes toward teachers, schooling, self . . . ," ratings of progress by judges listening to recorded therapy sessions, remission of "target symptoms," and improvement in symptomatology: reduction of depressive and anxiety states [27].

Appendix F:
Independent Forces
and Conditional
Opposition

We do not view the public's attitude toward level 1 approaches as exclusively a product of forces which are largely unaffected by its specific and immediate desires, e.g., for protection against known offenders, and by various information inputs as well. For example, we do not regard its "conditional opposition" as essentially a product of large-scale or long-term social-historical forces which relentlessly sweep the public and its decision makers along with them (in the sense of shaping the latters' attitudes, then holding them in its grip) but which, in turn, are only minimally influenced or controlled by them (i.e., by the public and its decision makers.)[1]

In "Crossroads," Martinson did not postulate the existence of any such overpowering, unresponsive, or essentially independent forces—large-scale, long-term, or otherwise. Nor did he present the "social planning epoch" as essentially a product of external forces that are largely beyond the control of the public and its decision makers.[2] His overall portrayal seemed to suggest that the public is, in effect, involved in its own inexorable or essentially irreversible course of action instead.

Two technical points should be noted in connection with these remarks. First, the above-mentioned attitude relates to the conditional level in particular, e.g., product-centered opposition or, for that matter, support. It does not focus on the unconditional level, i.e., that which relates to the public's view and feelings toward treatment approaches as such. However, the point regarding large-scale or long-term social-historical forces can be applied to the conditional and unconditional levels alike. Second, the information inputs in question can include research findings; statements or position papers by policy makers; program descriptions by offenders, practitioners, and administrators; etc. These can help modify the public's expectations regarding level 1 approaches.

179

Appendix G:
Ad Hominem
Arguments: A Two-
Edged Sword

Relative to front-line decision makers, most ad hominem ("directed at the man") arguments would center around the factors of vested or self-serving interests in correctional programs as they currently exist. Others might focus on ego involvement, or on overidentification with offenders, with particular programs, etc. Such arguments cannot settle specific issues, whatever these may be. This is so because they do not relate to the substance of those issues, namely, the premise, the evidence, or the conclusions. Instead, their thrust is on discrediting the objectivity, judgment, etc. of the individual(s) who has taken a given position on the issue at hand. They usually attempt to do this (1) on grounds of the latter's presumed personal motives (e.g., material gain or security), ego needs, or role-related obligations, and (2) by suggesting that certain possibilities (e.g., possible selfish motives and possible resulting biases) are, in fact, probabilities or virtual certainties.

Ad hominem arguments can be used literally anywhere, and in relation to anyone. (They are repeatedly observed in "Crossroads.") For example, they can be directed against major decision makers who, it might be claimed, see their primary role in terms of developing, supporting, or promoting a strategy for the future, and who (presumably for self-serving reasons or, perhaps, ego needs) might therefore be biased against, or somewhat blind to the value of, whatever may have occurred in the past. Similarly, members of the previous generation could automatically be dismissed as having somewhat clouded judgment when it comes to evaluating most programs of the present and future; their "diminished capacity" might simply be attributed to a continued ego involvement with programs of the past. Yet, by the same token, an identical argument could be applied to members of the newer generation in terms of their presumed inability to properly evaluate most programs of the past. Finally, many academicians could be charged with being (1) functionally (not intellectually) unable to draw seemingly obvious or logically called-for conclusions with respect to given issues, or (2) unable to support almost any position at all. Here, the ad hominem claim might relate to their presumed investment in the self-serving role of neutral observer, unbiased referee, etc.

By now, the futility of ad hominem approaches should be apparent. However elaborately presented, they remain, at base, a logically irrelevant form of argument—one among several that fall within the broader category of material fallacies [50]. At best, these approaches might be considered a variant of overgeneralized and stereotypic thinking. Unfortunately, despite their irrelevance and specious nature, they remain a very common and often influential substitute for logical and objective discussion. For this reason, they deserve special attention.

Appendix H:
Life Span and Systems
Approaches

Investigations which involve "the sociology of the life span and the analysis of systems" are relative newcomers to the correctional scene [30]. As a result, their long-range contribution to level 1 objectives can hardly be predicted with certainty. However, the following may be noted. First, few though they may be, findings to date do not suggest that these investigations will, in the near and intermediate future, lead to the development of programs or approaches that can provide an effective substitute for a wide range of present-day intervention strategies. (The latter refers to treatment-control programs which attempt to focus direction on the specific, often powerful, here-and-now problems and desires of offenders as individuals, and which do so for the express purpose of achieving level 1 objectives.) It seems more likely that these investigations will eventually lead to supplementary approaches and to program modifications, instead. Second, considerable practical value may be derived from adequate followup studies of offenders, staff, and setting, regardless of the short-, intermediate-, or long-range products of these investigations.[1]

The following is essentially independent of the conclusions presented above. Investigations of the life span and (especially) systems may well provide some assistance with respect to the elimination of today's "plague." This potential contribution would appear to justify a significant investment of energy in these investigations, entirely apart from the fact that at the present time, there is little reason to believe that the approaches which may result from these investigations will provide substantially more than their share of assistance with regard to this level 2 objective—e.g., more, or substantially more, than that provided by studies or programs of correctional treatment itself.

Appendix I:
The Public and The
Goals of Correctional
Treatment

We will briefly state our general view regarding the public's attitude toward the goal of "bringing offenders closer to their personally desired and/or socially required destinations," and of doing so with a minimum of wear and tear on everyone concerned. From a strict scientific perspective, our view should be considered neither more nor less than speculation and hypothesis since it is not based on scientific investigations or formal surveys. As far as we are aware, no such investigations or surveys have been conducted on this particular subject. As a result, speculation is all that one can present today. It is in this spirit that we offer the following view, a synthesis of observation and readings, for what it may be worth. We might add, however, that it would not be very difficult to determine, by scientific means, what in fact the general public does believe at any point in time.

In our view, the public does not dispute the appropriateness of the offender-centered and socially centered goals of correctional treatment. It usually accepts the idea that someone should be concerned with the needs and, especially, the future behavior of offenders—partly for the sake of offenders themselves. Its acceptance of this concept coexists with the earlier-mentioned attitude of conditional opposition to, or disinterest in, many of today's treatment programs. In this respect its overall attitude is somewhat complex, mixed, or dynamic, rather than unidirectional, 100 percent consistent, black and white, or static.

We believe that large segments of the public more or less accept the view that punishment, however harsh or humane, might not in itself provide enough stimulus or input to alter certain behavior patterns which may be related to future recidivism.

Finally, we believe that the public largely accepts or implicitly assumes the correctness[1] of the view that many offenders, at least most repeat offenders, are more likely to modify various behavior patterns and improve their ability to cope with the environment[2] if (1) they become involved in a directed activity and/or put forth effort with respect to a challenging task or interaction, than if (2) they "sit around and do nothing in particular," e.g., participate in few if any structured activities or pragmatically oriented learning situations.[3] This applies within as well as outside institutional settings.

This composite view suggests that a sizable portion of today's public is usually prepared to accept the concept of intervention or programming—not only on its own merit, but in the face of specific alternatives such as punishment alone and noninvolvement as well. We would add that this acceptance or support seems to derive from motives of a self-protective and altruistic nature alike, in that specific order.

A closing observation. As in other fields, e.g., education, the public's willingness and ability to finance what it believes in, or what it may consider reasonable and acceptable, has a history of its own. For the most part, its meaning should therefore be interpreted separately from the issue of acceptance or support. However, if one does choose to (1) set aside the factor of ability and (2) maintain that the public's "unwillingness" to foot the bill for many more intervention programs constitutes clear evidence that it does not believe in the value of such programs, one should then be prepared to (3) maintain that the public's unwillingness to pay for many more prisons is, itself, prima facie evidence that it rejects the idea of locking people up. Clearly, the public's limited ability to foot the bill is a factor that cannot realistically be set aside in the first place.

Appendix J:
Differentiated Analyses
and Hypothesis
Testing: An Illustration

Differentiated analyses, e.g., analyses in which the study sample has been subdivided as to personality type, can often provide an efficient way of partially testing certain hypotheses, assumptions, and generalizations. Take, for example, the following hypothesis: "greater use of external controls will reduce the illegal behavior of offenders." (Among parolees, these controls may include limit setting, surveillance, short-term lockup, etc.) While this statement may seem true beyond all doubt to many people, differentiated analyses which were carried out at California's Community Treatment Project suggest that it requires considerable qualification at the very least.

During 1961-1969, "power oriented" CTP males received limit setting and surveillance from their parole agents five times more often, per month, than "conflicted" CTP males.[1] In addition, they were placed into short-term detention three times more often than the latter individuals (again, time on parole and size of sample were held constant)—for a total of more than twice as many detention days during their overall parole experience.[2]

Results. Increased utilization of external controls was associated not with less, but with more illegal behavior. During parole, power oriented males had an arrest rate 62 percent higher than that of conflicted males.[3] During a 4-year postdischarge (postparole) followup, they had an arrest rate twice as high as that of conflicted males.[4] As indicated on p. 45, similar parole and postdischarge rates were obtained in connection with court convictions that related to these same arrests.

Appendix K:
Offender Intervention
Scales[1]

1. *Reducing Delinquent or Criminal Self-Image*

   Involve client in activities and interests which show promise of reinforcing a nondelinquent or noncriminal self-image.

   Try to extinguish, in client, the value of a delinquent or criminal self-image.

   Expose client to adequate males/females who are neither impressed nor taken in by "tough" or "delinquent" mannerisms.

2. *Modifying Attitudes toward Adults*

   Show client that there are many adults whom he can trust.

   Show client that many adults are worthy of his respect, e.g., genuine appreciation, positive regard, or esteem.

   Try to convince client that you represent more than "the man," or more than an extension of "the establishment."

3. *Increasing Internal Controls*

   Try to get client to start "thinking twice" before he acts.

   Teach client to cope with delay-of-gratification of his needs and wants.

   Try to instill in client certain basic social values and standards.

   Instruct client on basic do's and dont's, as though he were a child.

4. *Increasing Self-Awareness/Self-Acceptance*

   Help client understand some of the early sources of his present self-image.

   Help client change some of his beliefs regarding what and who he "should" be or "ought" to be.

   Help client resolve doubts about his basic adequacy and worthiness.

5. *Countering Apathy/Indifference*

   Try to get client to be more evaluative and responsive to his social world.

   Encourage client to more actively care about what happens to him.

Try to get client to be more reactive to the events in his life, to take a more active stance in determining what happens to him.

6. *Family/Parental Relationships*

Help client become aware of how the personal problems of parental figures can interact with, or have interacted with, his own development.

Get client to see his parents in a realistic light—their strengths, weaknesses, and individual personalities.

Increase client's understanding of the role he has played in his family (as child and sibling), and of the particular ways this might have influenced his life.

Get client to see his present family (wife, children) in a realistic light—their strengths, weaknesses, and individual personalities.

Increase client's understanding of the role he has played in his present family (as father and husband), and of the particular ways this might have influenced his current behavior, especially illegal activities.

7. *Peer Influence/Pressure*

Explain to client specific ways in which peers may set him up to meet their own needs at his expense.

Discuss issue of "the price of loyalty" to, or "the price of going along with," peers, in various situations.

Suggest to client alternatives to conforming behavior on his part when he is confronted with peer pressure, especially in relation to possible illegal activities.

Serve as a counterforce to negative effects of peer influence.

8. *Everyday Practical Adjustment*

Teach client how to take care of himself and meet his needs on a practical basis.

Work primarily with performance, e.g., school, employment, living arrangements, rather than with emotions and psychological issues.

Actively help client find job opportunities and obtain actual work.

9. *Client/Worker Relationship*

Talk with client about how you and he are relating to one another, about the nature and quality of your relationship.

Encourage client to begin actively thinking about the nature of, and changes in, his relationship with you.

Use your relationship with client to illustrate, to client, themes and problems in the way he relates to others.

Emphasize to client that you expect him to relate to you on a personal basis.

10. *Gaining Client's Confidence in Worker as Understanding/Capable*

Gain client's confidence as someone who is skilled in understanding interpersonal problems.

Demonstrate to client that you can understand very personal feelings and needs on his part.

Gain client's confidence in you as a worker (person, treater) who can in fact help.

11. *Expressing Personal Concern for and Acceptance of Client*

Help client feel you really do care about him in more than a formal, "it's my job" fashion.

Help client feel that you accept and care for him as an individual, not only in terms of his uniqueness, but independent of his particular problems and behavior.

Help client feel that his personal happiness is quite important to you.

Help client feel that you do not see him as "sick," "weird," or undesirable.

12. *Exposure to Adult Models*

Expose client to same-sex, adult models whom he cannot regard as weak, incompetent, etc.

For male workers with male clients, behave in a masculine manner that the client can recognize and accept or respect as such. For female workers with female clients, behave in a feminine manner that the client can recognize and accept or respect as such.

13. *Preparing Client for Specific Life Situations*

Teach client how to handle specific difficulties he may experience when he's on his own and you're not available to him.

Review with client his plans for handling difficult situations, e.g., temptations, pressures, that may arise when you're not around.

Teach client specific ways of "avoiding trouble," e.g., fights or narcotics.

14. *Ego Bolstering via Success Experiences*

Expose client to situations in which he can "win."

Expose client to probable success experiences, even if they represent menial challenges.

Make sure the client gets ego-bolstering recognition from others, even for menial successes or accomplishments.

15. *Using Positive Peer Culture*

Encourage client to interact with nondelinquent or prosocial peers.

Encourage client to interact with delinquents or offenders who wish to communicate nondelinquent or prosocial views.

16. *Using Authority (Legitimate Power or Force)*

Give client a relatively specific set of terms or conditions which he must meet or live up to.

Make client responsible for failure to follow through on his agreements with you by taking privleges or freedom from him.

Provide support for those who live with client and/or are responsible for helping to control his behavior.

Keep "on top of" client; don't accept any "shining-on"; let him know you're usually around and interested in what he's doing.

Make sure the client sees you as the main source of power with whom he must deal when making decisions and plans.

Make sure the client does not succeed in "power plays," intimidation tactics, or manipulation efforts when interacting with you.

17. *Using Internal Stress as Stimulus/Motivator*

Capitalize on distress or anxiety in the client, as a stimulus for change.

Capitalize on internal pressures, e.g., anxiety or guilt, as stimuli for motivating the client in the direction of treatment or change.

18. *Doing the Unexpected*

Maintain an element of unpredictability in how you react to client under particular circumstances.

Intentionally relate to client in ways that will not readily fit into his usual manner of perceiving and interpreting others.

Try to prevent client from thinking he can predict, using simple formulas, your responses to his behavior.

19. *Client's Participation in Case Planning and Decision Making*

Discuss with client your treatment rationale, plans, and goals.

Involve client as an equal in case decisions.

Thoroughly discuss with client any challenges and objections he has to your decisions concerning his case.

Allow client to significantly determine the extent of your involvement in his life.

Allow client to make nearly all his own decisions, largely without your participation.

Allow client to pretty much run his own life.

Discuss and review the progress of treatment, with client.

20. *Concreteness versus Abstractness of Verbalizations and Interpretations*

Avoid using adult-level concepts or explanations when talking with client.

Speak to client in very concrete terms, avoiding abstractions.

Repeat (more than once) any expectations you have of client, so that he will be less likely to forget them as soon as you're gone.

21. *Increasing Interpersonal Sensitivity*

Encourage client to perceive, appreciate, and respond appropriately to more individual differences among other people.

Encourage client to consider new ways of perceiving and interpreting the behavior of others, and their motives and needs for acting as they do.

Give feedback and clarification to client about the reactions of others to him.

Teach client more mature ways of influencing others.

22. *Expression of Feelings*

Help client verbalize and more adequately express his feelings and emotional reactions toward others.

Serve client as a source of catharsis, listening to expressions of pent-up needs, emotions, or fears.

Show client it is all right to direct reasonable emotion and anger at their true source, rather than displacing, suppressing, etc.

Emphasize to client the importance of expressing his inner feelings directly to those whom they involve, e.g., parents, spouse, peers, yourself.

23. *Self-Understanding*

Try to get client to begin asking questions (at least of himself) regarding inner sources of his behavior.

Use review of past life and social history events to help client better understand his behavior and feelings.

Increase client's awareness of how such factors as guilt or feelings of inadequacy can be a destructive force in his life.

Discuss with client particular ways in which his unique needs and response style can manifest themselves in his interpersonal relationships.

Develop what may approach a professional counseling or therapy relationship with client.

24. *Recreation, Socializing*

Encourage client to participate in any of several recreational activities, e.g., fishing, sports, or group field trips.

Involve client in group recreational activities.

25. *Frequency of Contact*

Make sure that you and the client are in frequent contact.

Maintain a regular schedule of frequent contacts with client.

26. *Informality—Lack of Social Distance*

Minimize social or personal distance between yourself and client.

Talk with client about yourself and your feelings in order to let him know you on a fairly personal level.

Invite client to your home, much as you would a friend.

27. *Client's Commitment to Treatment*

Let client know that he must meet you half way in the sense of committing himself to treatment, e.g., showing reasonable willingness to work on whatever main goals have been established for him.

Let client know that your support of him is largely contingent upon his making a reasonable commitment to treatment objectives and goals.

28. *Expressing Warmth, Friendliness, Affection*

Relate to client in an interpersonally warm or affectionate manner.

Express, to client, positive affection that you may feel for him.

Give client warm, friendly, physical contact, e.g., pat on back or arm on shoulder.

29. *Protecting, Minimizing Demands and Pressures*

Expose client to supportive, nonthreatening, social situations.

Make only minimal demands on, and establish only minimal expectations for, the client.

Allow client to be childish and immature, including childish dependency.

Avoid exposing client to harsh, direct, personal encounter-group situations.

Avoid exposing client to sophisticated, aggressive, or manipulative offenders.

30. *Being Forceful, Blunt*

Be willing to "tell off" the client when you feel he needs it.

Be verbally forceful, even harsh, during necessary confrontations.

Be willing to yell at client during confrontations.

31. *Associating Concern with Control*

Try to convince client that controls, by you, reflect real concern for his well-being.

Make sure the client understands that discipline of him, by you, is not a sign of personal rejection.

Emphasize to client that his being controlled by you is not the same as his being emasculated by you.

32. *Familiarizing Client with Authority Figures*

Expose client to police, probation officers, and judges as individuals, by means of informal meetings and onsite tours.

Via meetings, lectures, and onsite tours, familiarize client with the goals, philosophies, and rules that underlie the thinking, and govern the activities, of police, probation officers, and judges.

Appendix L: Psychosocial Development: An Illustration

The following will illustrate a type of theory that focuses on major stages in the establishment of person-society links, and that postulates specific forces which help promote those links. The structure and constructs that are presented comprise only the first part, albeit the main features, of a "developmental-adaptation" theory. This account will focus on later childhood, adolescence, and the transition to early adulthood [37].

Basic Concepts and Stages of Development

The basic concepts of this theory, and the relationships among these concepts, are as follows:

1. *Era.* Each era is subdivided into a number of distinguishable *stages.*
2. *Response-Adaptation Sequence.* Each sequence is subdivided into a number of separable *phases.*

Three main eras will be distinguished. Simply labeled, they are:

II. Later childhood[1]

III. Socialized relationships

IV. Role establishment, Commitment[2]

Within contemporary American society it is appropriate to (1) roughly equate era II with the ages of approximately 5 to 10 (era I would refer to early childhood); (2) think of era III as encompassing not only several aspects of preadolescence, but much of what is commonly termed adolescence (ages 10-11 to 16-17); and (3) think of era IV as primarily a period of early adulthood, commonly beginning around age 17 or 18.

Era is thus used as a generic term. In its reference to later childhood, to preadolescence together with adolescence, and to early adulthood, it signifies a set of actual[3] as well as perceived,[4] interrelated opportunities, expectations, activities, challenges, and themes. Viewed as separate entities, each era usually extends over a period of years, and each can be distinguished from the other on the basis of differences in the observable content and quantity of social opportunities, expectations, and challenges.

197

Five stages of psychosocial development will now be outlined. This description largely relates to normal, i.e., typical or modal, development within contemporary society.

Era II (later childhood) consists of two main stages:

Stage A: Familiarization, Coping. This is a period in which the child learns many new things about what the external world is like and what it expects of him or her. He learns the permissible and nonpermissible ways of expressing a number of feelings and impulses. He is highly involved in coping with external demands and with attempting to master as well as reduce anxieties. He is quite concerned with being able to control the actual and perceived power of "significant others" by whatever methods seem acceptable to those individuals or at least seem to work (e.g., by complying, by being "good," by direct or more subtle demanding, by intimidation).

Stage B: Stabilization, Repetition. This stage is reached when a pattern of activities has been established for and/or by the child, one which brings predictable satisfactions and which the child usually enjoys repeating. He is generally satisfied with his role as child and with the opportunities that seem open to him. His expectations and thoughts seldom extend beyond hoping for more of the same, or for variations and exciting elaborations thereof. Insofar as it connotes a time of adventure, fun, fantasy, and games, the term *high childhood* could be applied to this period.

The shift from later childhood to the era of socialized relationships occurs gradually, not overnight. This transition comprises a distinctive stage in itself.

Stage C: New Awareness, Suspension, Assessment. The stage C youth has begun to recognize the existence of a rather extensive, new world of expectations, opportunities, different possible activities, and privileges. He associates many of these features with the approaching years of adolescence; that is, he recognizes, if only intuitively, that a person must be of at least adolescent age in order to participate in many such activities. He generally begins to curtail and redirect some of his childhood activities in light of his new awareness of "what the bigger guys (or girls) do and don't do," and in relation to skills and traits that seem to be desired (strength, courage, self-control, endurance, etc.). This is generally a period of rising uncertainty and anxiety, with the youth having neither (1) fully relinquished the most pleasurable aspects of later childhood, or of the childhood role, nor (2) having "bought into" the world of adolescence in an intense and involved way, or in much detail.

Era III (socialized relationships) consists of two main stages, the latter of which is often a transition to era IV:

Stage D: Reorientation, Assimilation of Social Values. Stage D youths are consciously concerned with taking on a set of standards or participating in groups of activities which they recognize as being different than those of later childhood. They consciously seek new people to emulate or new activities to master, largely as a way of gaining a sense of social or personal status, esteem, or acceptability. This process involves a beginning "redefinition of self," relative to newly recognized sources of potential status, power, and/or pleasure. It also involves a generally conscious repudiation of or nonconformity toward previous standards and roles. It frequently involves a propensity toward thinking of others (and oneself) as being either categorically worthy/good or else unworthy/ bad, largely on grounds of whether they live up to certain all-encompassing standards of behavior, or else in terms of the particular beliefs, attitudes, and motives they appear to have. This process usually occurs in the following context:

1. A minimally discriminating conformance to—in fact, often a direct copying or attempted assimilation of—a new set of social expectations, opportunities, or significant others. Although this new level of conformity appears internally directed when compared with stages A through C, it may be characterized as primarily an "external" approach to reorienting oneself and/or defining one's worth.[5]

2. Relatively little awareness, by the youth, of the longer-term implications of many such external standards, i.e., implications with regard to (a) his newly emerging personal interests or convictions and (b) the more individualized needs, traits of personality, and personal/social limitations of which he is first becoming aware.[6]

Stage E: Self-Responsibility, Personalization of Attitudes and Values. Individuals at this stage are no longer vigorously copying or assimilating the attitudes, traits, or expressed values of people who have usually been their first or second set of postchildhood friends and/or "heroes"—people who may have appeared to possess considerable social and interpersonal power, influence, or status.[7] Instead, stage E individuals are likely to feel that their own experiences or beliefs (1) ought to lead them toward interpersonal or personal satisfactions of an ongoing or longer-term nature, and (2) are, at least in principle, capable of guiding their everyday affairs.

These youths have a fairly clear idea of the way in which a number of people generally view or respond to their expressed attitudes and/or traits of personality. They have several definite ideas regarding the apparent differences and similarities between themselves and others. These perceptions and beliefs help give them a clearer picture, and often a stronger feeling, as to who they are, where they stand, and where they ought to be moving—clearer, that is, than in the case of stage D youths. This development takes place despite the fact that their views and assessments of self and others continue to be characterized by a large segment of stereotyping and overgeneralizing.

Stage E youths feel they have identified many, possibly most, of the major social or personal choices that they will need to make in the near and intermediate future. They also feel they have identified the principal, personal implications of the differing choices in question. They generally, though not always consciously, expect to build their life around some of the attitudes, traits, or values which they have assimilated subsequent to childhood and have personalized or integrated in the form of a moderately self-consistent self-image, or at least a set of priorities. This is not to say that they are free of occasional confusion, uncertainty, or even intense anxiety.

The temporal and formal relationship between eras II and III, on the one hand, and stages A through E, on the other, is shown in figure L-1. The relationship between the three stages of era II and the six phases of the era II adaptation sequence is also shown. The temporal and formal relationship between the two stages of era III and the eight phases of the era III adaptation sequence is shown in figure L-2. For present purposes, we need not elaborate the latter phases.

Era IV (Role-Establishment, Commitment) individuals take on at least one of the more or less positively sanctioned, adult or young adult roles that are available within the society. Their activities and self-image come to be centered around role involvements of this nature. For now, we need only note the following with regard to this era:

1. In normal development and within most present-day societies, stage E may be viewed as a transition between eras III and IV. Many individuals remain in this stage for several years prior to entering era IV.

2. Many individuals move into adult-type roles, e.g., marriage and/or parenthood, without having reached stage E^8 in terms of psychosocial development. (See n. 9 regarding the difference between movement and development.) Their involvement in these roles may be largely voluntary or involuntary.

3. The number of conceptual differentiations that are made between self and others, and among others, does not automatically increase in connection with, or as a precondition to, the transition from era III to era IV.[10]

At this point, we will turn to the concept of response-adaptation sequence. This sequence is positively though not perfectly correlated with the above-mentioned stages.

Response-Adaptation Sequence

Insofar as it involves a set of complex social conditions, each era undergoes very little modification as to content and scope during the life of any individual.[11] Individuals, on the other hand, are usually able to produce a range of responses and a series of adjustments to the opportunities, expectations, and challenges of the given era. By and large, then, it is the individual who in some fashion responds and adapts to the era, not vice versa. In this connection, the *response-adaptation sequence* is a way of describing the changing and developing relationship between the individual and the main stages of any given era, i.e., the changing nature of the person/society link. For present purposes, we need not review each and every phase of the era II and III adaptation sequences. However,

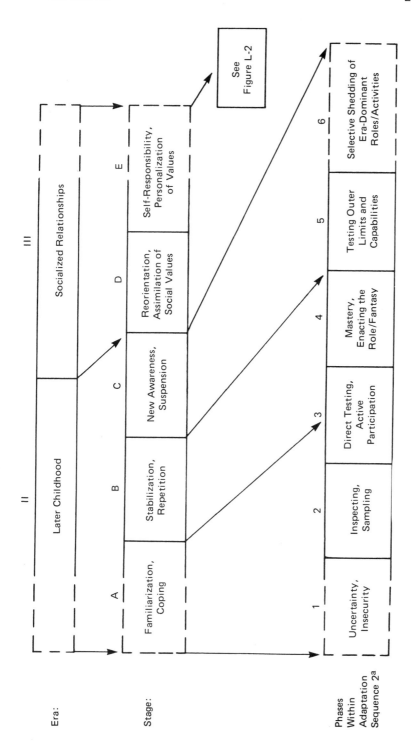

[a]Adaptation sequence 2 is that which corresponds to era II; adaptation sequence 3 (corresponding to era III) is shown in Figure L-2.

Figure L-1. Temporal and Formal Relationships between Selected Eras, Stages, and Phases—Emphasis on era II.

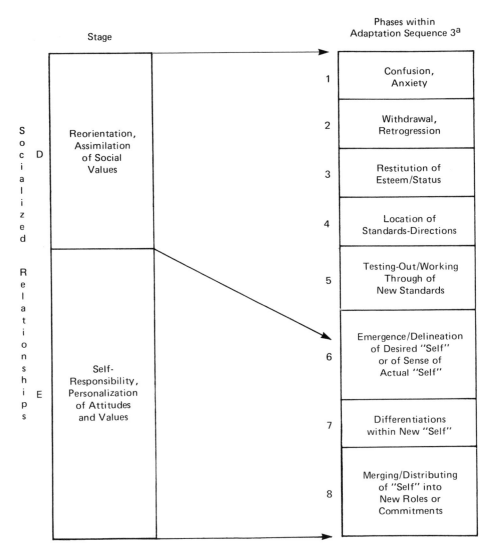

aParts of this adaptation sequence are sometimes repeated (recycled) during era III, each time around somewhat different content, e.g., new identification figures or shifting social expectations. This is most notable in connection with phases 1 through 5.

Figure L-2. Temporal and Formal Relationships between Era III Stages and Era III Phases.

certain aspects of phases 4, 5, and 6 of era II will be described by way of background for later discussion.

Phase 4: Mastery, Enacting the Role/Fantasy. The phase 4 child has been able to apply some of his abilities or skills to a slowly increasing number of social and/or family-centered contexts. As this phase progresses, he becomes increasingly aware of the relationship that generally exists between being strong, powerful, skilled, or cool, on the one hand, and being able to participate with peers or adults in a number of known (though, in many instances, not personally experienced) activities, on the other. He often regards these activities as being, actually or potentially, at least as enjoyable or exciting as many of those with which he is already familiar. Much of his energy is invested in elaborating upon desired activities or fantasized roles in this area. Thus, in a sense which is of direct significance to his everyday activities, ongoing interests, and emerging personality, the youngster begins to form certain ideas about (1) types of people whom he would like to emulate and (2) areas of participation, i.e., ongoing activities, in terms of which his own life differs in fact or fantasy from that of individuals who have become of increasing interest to him.

Phase 5: Variations, Testing the Outer Limits and Capabilities of One's Present Adaptation/Role. At this point, the youngster begins to express his skills and fantasies in ways which he recognizes may (and, at times, probably do) go beyond previous levels of acceptability to others. He sometimes allows himself to participate in a number of selected, "way out" activities. In so doing, he is (1) checking the limits, and value to self, of his present range of era II options, alternatives, and priorities, and is comparing these with what he believes to be those of era III; he is also (2) checking on the interest value, and level of acceptability to others, of his changing set of primary interests. During this process, he is hardly cognizant of the concepts described in (1) and (2).

Phase 6: Selective Shedding of Era-Dominant Roles or Activities. At this point, the youth becomes increasingly reluctant to interact with peers or adults in ways that may be labeled "babyish" or "childish" by those individuals, and which might lower his standing in their eyes. He attempts, both personally and vicariously, to find out whether his emerging areas of skill and information will allow him to participate in what appear to be the more legitimate, available activities of early adolescence. Although he still holds on to several aspects of his era II adjustment, his explorations relative to era III activities are often quite conscious and deliberate. He begins to feel (and often worry) that he might not be able to participate in desired or interesting activities relative to the broader social environment, if he does not possess the needed skills or does not have certain accoutrements and privileges that others appear to have.

Factors Related to Change

We will now review several factors that relate to psychosocial development through all phases of era II. Era III will not be reviewed since many of these factors operate in similar ways during eras II and III.

The responses and longer-term activities of era II youths are chiefly a result of expectations that come from the external environment—mainly parents and (to a lesser extent in most environments) peers, together with relevant others such as siblings, relatives, or teachers. Significant others—primarily parents—

usually remain in firm possession of the capacity or power to take a number of critical and at times decisive steps in connection with the child's exposure to many opportunities, activities, and challenges of era II. In broad terms, they may (1) permit, encourage, channelize, and generally support; (2) be largely indifferent or perhaps ambivalent toward; and/or (3) discourage or prohibit much of the preceding exposure or ongoing experience. They can, for instance, be supportive of, indifferent toward, or in opposition to the child's attempts to inspect and sample the opportunities and activities of his era II world (phase 2). They can do likewise with respect to his later attempts to test the outer limits of the era II roles that he may previously have accepted and enjoyed (phase 5). Generally speaking, the way in which significant others can effectively utilize their power varies somewhat from phase to phase.

The era II child senses that he will need the approval of others if he is to participate fairly regularly in era II activities and, in a general sense, stand up to its challenges. Particularly during phases 1, 2, and 3, he will gladly align himself with individuals who appear willing and able to use their strength and authority to help him obtain, or gain access to, the things he wants. In effect, he would like to participate in, comply with, or even come to possess the external "power" of these individuals. This is so because he assumes, generally and implicitly, that he will be able to benefit from these forms of relationship with this type of strength and authority.

This type of actual or perceived power, on the part of others, can be termed *wanted* or *supportive, outer power.* Usually, this form of power or influence is willingly assimilated by, and becomes ego syntonic to, the era II youngster. On the other hand, environmental influence which markedly discourages, opposes, or oppresses the youngster will be termed *unwanted* or *nonsupportive, outer power.* To the era II youth, this form of influence, or perceived influence, is often frightening or overwhelming. It is often evaded, fought against, and/or unwillingly submitted to.[12]

The environment can exert influence on the era II youngster in a supportive and/or oppositional direction. Relative to any given youth, it generally exerts influence in *both* directions. This influence can be thought of in terms of force, i.e., in a quantitative way. Thus, for example, at any given point such influence would consist of, or result in, a specified amount of support as well as a particular quantity of opposition.

Support and opposition comprise two of the six broad factors that are integrally related to movement along the era II adaptation sequence. These factors, together with their labels, are as follows:

1. Support-approval from environment (esa)
2. Opposition-disapproval from environment (eod)
3. Individual's own accomplishments-abilities (iaa)[13]
4. Difficulty of tasks/goals invested in by the individual (itg)[14]

5. Difficulty of social requirements/opportunities (sro)[15]
6. Major or sudden trauma and overwhelming events (ote)[16]

Individually, these factors operate in one of two basic directions. Two of the factors (esa and iaa) can promote or accelerate continued development; the four remaining factors (eod, itg, sro, and ote) can hinder or decelerate such development.

To assess the prospects of continued development or forward movement on the part of any given youth, one must evaluate both the separate contributions and overall product of these six factors. This product, the end result of an often intricate balance of forces, may be conceptualized in terms of the following general formula (the product in question would represent the total effective power, e.g., developmental power, that may be ascribed to a youth at any point in time):

$$\text{Total effective power} = \frac{(esa)\,(iaa)}{(eod)\,(itg + sro)\,(ote)}$$

The higher the ratio of numerator to denominator, the greater are the chances of continued movement or development through the several phases of era II.[17] Specifically, the smaller the product of eod, itg + sro, and ote, the higher is the overall ratio of movement-promoting forces (esa and iaa) to those which would generally impede, restrict, or oppose such movement or development. Under these conditions, total effective power would also involve a greater total quantity of force, other things being equal. This force would have meaning relative to the challenges, expectations, and opportunities of the given society.

Similar numerators and denominators operate in eras III and IV. However, within contemporary American society, the specific content of most such factors is rather different and more complex than in the case of era II.

The differing types of power, ability, or positive potential that an era II youth may come to feel relative to himself can be termed *developmental capacities*. They may be described in terms of seven postulated items or general categories:

1. A general competence with regard to objects and activities, including an ability to adequately utilize his body, apply his mind, and/or perform well in physical or social activities that are defined as important or good.
2. An ability to influence other individuals.[18]
3. An ability to (a) resist what others define as "bad" activities or individuals, and/or (b) avoid or neutralize situations that appear physically threatening.
4. An ability to help other individuals and/or "do a friend a favor."
5. An ability to understand or predict what is happening around him.
6. An expectation that enjoyable activities will occur, and a belief that he, the youth, will be able to participate in several of them.

7. A feeling of being, in the main, unhampered in his desires to seek varied experiences; a sense of having received permission/approval to try things out.

Developmental capacities 1 through 5 are major components of the iaa factor, whereas 6 and 7 are products of the esa factor. Few youngsters can be expected to score high on all or nearly all capacities, at least with regard to large slices of era II time. Nor is it essential that they do so, i.e., essential in terms of continued movement or development. This is because some capacities can partly substitute for others.

Most of these capacities are also of considerable relevance to eras III and IV. However, with respect to these capacities, there are several important differences between the latter eras and era II. These relate to (1) specific content and overall complexity; (2) rules that informally govern their application or expression in given situations; (3) significance or implications, e.g., consequences of a relative lack or perhaps nonutilization of given capacities. Eras III and IV include other capacities as well, e.g., those which help individuals respond and adapt to challenges and opportunities that rarely exist in era II.

For present purposes, these capacities need not be reviewed in detail. However, it might be hypothesized that in all eras, personnel, settings, and program operations that promote these capacities are those most likely to be seen as relevant by a wide range of youths and clients. In effect, these particular staff, settings, and operations are the ones most likely to be seen as useful means to ends which the individuals in question are likely to desire.

As chronological adolescence approaches, many era II youths begin to feel they may not have enough by way of usable and/or useful accomplishments/ abilities (iaa factor), or enough by way of support from others (esa factor) in connection with developmental capacities 6 and 7. This change in perceptions often occurs because these individuals have, to an increasing degree, begun to compare themselves to, and/or be compared with, new reference groups or new sets of standards. At about this time, many youths are likely to experience new or increased pressures with regard to social requirements and opportunities (sro factor). Beyond this, they generally begin to recognize new areas of opposition as well as pressure, from parents and/or significant others (eod factor).

It is at about this time that the first three phases of era III get underway, namely, confusion-anxiety, withdrawal-retrogression, and attempted restitution of esteem/status. It is under the preceding conditions and during these phases that a number of significant personal compensations and social adjustments often occur. Developments of this nature are of particular relevance to the formation and/or reinforcement of structures and response patterns commonly observed among several groups of delinquents.

The eight phases of era III will not be reviewed. The central themes and products of these phases can be inferred by relating the respective phase names shown in figure L-2 to the stage D and E descriptions that appear on pp. 198-200.

Observations Regarding Intervention

This theory suggests that, to be considered relevant by many clients, a program may have to work toward one or both of the following goals: (1) reduce pressures or change perceptions that are preventing individuals from developing areas of genuine competence, or from using skills and assets they already have; and (2) increase present skills and assets or assist in the development of new abilities, thereby helping individuals evolve a power base that can help them attain legitimate satisfactions and pleasure, or genuine esteem.[19] This means that a program may have to address not only one or more of the denominator items mentioned above (e.g., eod or itg), but one or both of the numerator items as well (esa or iaa).

This type of theory can help us focus on the possible why's of change, and lack of change. It can help us conceptualize the movement-promoting and movement-hindering factors that might best be, or may have to be, worked on with specific clients in specific social settings.[20] It can also suggest several target areas (e.g., developmental capacities and elements thereof) that might be of relevance to particular clients at certain points in their life, regardless of social setting. This type of framework would apply not only to relationships between individual clients and workers, or between individual clients and their treatment group, but to programs and intervention settings as a whole, inside and outside the justice system.

Notes

Introduction

1. This principle not only embraces the concept of fairness, it implicitly prescribes an extension of it. It does this by linking the idea of fair treatment to (1) the often difficult process of decision making by individual offenders, and (2) the specific content of the offender's involvement in today's complex, often frustrating world. Realistic decision making is a key ingredient in any offender's socially acceptable and personally satisfying adjustment to his environment. However, to complement this process, fair treatment on the part of the justice system can help create a tolerable, believable, sometimes even supportive atmosphere for decision making itself. By itself, fair treatment does not provide the feedback or personal reward that must exist before realistic, satisfying decisions are generated and maintained. Thus, for many offenders, fairness without programmed assistance can be empty, even blind, and programs without fairness can be futile, even pathetic.

Chapter 1
The Years of Decline

1. At the time, no one claimed to have any detailed, broadly based comparative data as to how much treatment, and what quality of treatment, was occurring in these and other, less problem-ridden environments.

2. Certainly not as a principal or exclusive basis for obtaining various rewards, for example, time cuts.

3. One key question was: of all decisions made by staff, what would be the maximum acceptable percentage of mistakes? From an ethical standpoint, the question of overuse might assume a substantially different tone if inmates themselves were to give final approval to the idea of extending or continuing their stay. This might at least apply to those who were not violent, bizarre, or suicidal in the extreme, and to extensions or continuances which were not primarily or exclusively related to specific offenses that are committed within the prison itself.

4. Time extensions were still possible on the grounds of punishment—for example, if an individual had committed specific offenses or infractions during his prison stay. While such extensions also grew more difficult to obtain, the difficulty was less substantial than for extensions which focused on the concept of treatment need.

5. Practice has lagged far behind this principle and ideal. To date, a somewhat different objective has been more reachable—namely, that of physi-

cally separating these youths from (1) some of the harsher conditions that exist in many institutions, (2) some of the harshest institutions themselves, and (3) sophisticated offenders as a whole.

6. Many policy makers and administrators were also concerned about the possibility that an increasing volume of lawsuits would be directed against state and local agencies, or agency officials, if immediate changes did not take place.

7. Within institutional settings, milieu and group therapy have been the most common exceptions.

8. The former discussions go beyond the more specific or pointed question of mandatory versus voluntary participation in treatment. A wide range of programs can be operated on either basis.

Chapter 2
Almost Nothing Works

1. In the original survey by Lipton et al., the 231 studies were discussed under slightly different headings (see chap. 5, n. 1). However, the treatment methods to which these headings referred were identical.

2. These 39 studies comprised 48 percent of 82 investigations that were tabulated in "Martinson Revisited." In "What Works" Martinson had presented an additional 11 studies under the heading, "The Effects of Sentencing." These studies were not tabulated in "Martinson Revisited," relative to the question of whether few or many investigations had produced favorable results. This was because the context of all such studies, when combined with the research design that was used, made it unlikely that anything other than partially positive results could possibly have been obtained. (Results of this type were in fact observed in almost all sentencing studies. If these 11 investigations had been included in the tabulation, the figure of 48 percent would have become 53 percent.) The 93 recidivism studies that were mentioned in "What Works" comprised 74 percent of the 126 that were included in *Correctional Effectiveness.* Martinson, in "What Works," did not describe how these studies were selected from among the 126. However, the former investigations do appear to have been reasonably representative of the latter, at least in relation to the percentage of studies with positive results (see table 3-1). The somewhat complex relationship between the 126 studies and the 231 which provided the basis for the survey as a whole is reviewed in chapter 3, n. 9 of this book.

3. There is a positive but by no mean one-to-one relationship among many of these categories.

4. Bailey reported the following: "Regardless, then, of rigorousness of the research procedures employed, roughly one-half of the [100] outcome studies evaluated reported considerable improvement (marked improvement plus statistically significant improvement). . . . Experimental studies [22 of the 100]

reported a successful outcome in roughly 60% of the sample; systematic-empirical studies [26 of the 100] reported successful outcome in roughly 46% of the sample, while non-systematic studies [52 of the 100] reported favorable outcomes 42% of the time." Bailey went on to caution: ". . . When one recalls that those results, in terms of the success or failure of the treatment used, are based upon the conclusions of the authors of the reports, themselves, then the implications of these findings regarding the effectiveness of correctional treatment become rather discouraging. A critical evaluation of the actual design and the specific research procedures described in each instance would substantially decrease the relative frequency of successful outcomes based upon reliably valid evidence." However, Bailey did not carry out this evaluation (at least he provided no further statements, quantitative or otherwise) and, as far as we can tell, did not actually test his hypothesis regarding a substantial decrease—in effect, an implied assumption concerning inflated reports of success. The fact remains that "43% [of the 22 correctional outcome studies classified as experimental] provided statistical evidence that the changes which occurred in the experimental group were not due to chance" [5,6]. This figure was similar to the one reported by Palmer [38] in connection with 82 studies described in "What Works." These studies were derived from the 126 investigations (138 separate recidivism findings) reported in *Correctional Effectiveness*. In reviewing the 126 investigations, Lipton et al. independently checked every finding that was presented by the authors of each study. Lipton et al. apparently found no more than an occasional discrepancy between the originally reported findings and the results of their own calculations. This independent check may lead to a more critical assessment of Bailey's implied assumption regarding inflated reports of success.

5. These types or characteristics were not invariably associated with a reduction in recidivism.

Chapter 3
The Defense of "What Works"

1. In "What Works," Martinson himself referred to differences among offender types when accounting for contradictory results that were observed across individual studies which fell within single categories of treatment, for example, individual counseling.

2. This was in addition to the fact that different combinations or mixtures of offenders may sometimes have been involved from one study to the next.

3. Only certain subcategories of treatment, for example, intensive probation supervision, came close to passing the across-the-board test. Generally speaking, subcategories involved far fewer studies than did overall categories; therefore, they provided less opportunity for interstudy contradictions.

4. Despite its substantial promise, probation (as an entity, that is, an overall category) was not recommended as "a sure way" of reducing recidivism. It, too, contained interstudy contradictions.

5. Similarly, the relatively low percentage of interstudy contradictions that was found within some subcategories of probation was matched by that which was found within the subcategories of certain other treatment approaches. Here too, probation was not unique.

6. Despite its five separate entries in connection with probation [27].

7. If the Warren study is counted as five separate entries, 39 percent of all studies (7 of 18) that were categorized as probation efforts showed essentially no reduction in recidivism.

8. In the analysis that is represented in table 3-1, *reduction of recidivism* (positive outcome) meant that, for any given study, the recidivism rate which was observed among experimentals was at least 15 percent lower than that observed among controls (or other comparisons). This 15 percent criterion, i.e., 15 percent (not necessarily percentage points) reduction in recidivism, was used so that the distinction between positive and nonpositive studies would be rather clearcut. In other words, it was used so that the positive and nonpositive studies, around which the analysis itself was organized, could be differentiated from one another better than they would have been if a less conservative criterion had been used. Had such a criterion been used, say, a 5 to 10 percent reduction in recidivism instead of 15 percent, the percentage of studies that would have been classified as positive would, of course, have risen. Yet, by the same token, studies classified as positive and nonpositive would have been less clearly differentiated from each other in terms of an absolute drop in recidivism. As indicated, the latter factor—clear differentiation—was the central consideration in the present analysis. It might be noted that in a large majority of cases, the 15 percent criterion represented more than just a substantial absolute drop in recidivism rates; it represented an experimental/control difference that only occasionally could be accounted for by random fluctuations. That is, a strong relationship was found to exist between reduction of recidivism, as defined by this criterion, and the presence of a nonchance difference in recidivism rates between experimentals and controls. Specifically, 81 percent of all studies that (1) involved at least a 15 percent reduction in recidivism and (2) for which Lipton et al. had reported a significance test, also produced a statistically significant difference $(p \leqslant .05)$ between experimentals and controls. (For $p < .10 > .05$, the 81 percent figure rises to 88 percent.) Despite this relationship between absolute drop in recidivism, on the one hand, and statistical reliability, on the other, several studies that involved a *smaller* reduction in recidivism produced statistically reliable differences as well. Generally speaking, these differences resulted from the comparatively large sample sizes that were involved. The substantial relationship between sample size and statistical significance was also seen in cases where the 15 percent criterion was used. Here, the

presence of relatively small sample sizes was sometimes related to the absence of statistically reliable differences between experimentals and controls. For this and related reasons, in our approach to the present analysis we did not look upon statistical significance as the sole or even primary determiner of whether a study should be considered positive, with respect to outcome. This was despite the obvious importance of statistical significance.

9. As indicated by Lipton et al., extensive search of the correctional research literature, combined with the numerous selection and exclusion criteria which they used, yielded a total of 231 "accepted studies," relative to 11 treatment categories combined [27]. Accounts of these investigations appeared in the 174 reports that were listed in a section of *Correctional Effectiveness* entitled "Studies Referred to in This Survey." The 231 studies contained 286 separate findings; this difference in numbers arose from the fact that "in several studies, more than one independent variable [treatment category] was tested for its effect upon a dependent variable [outcome measure, e.g., recidivism], or the effect of an independent variable was measured on more than one dependent variable" [27]. Of the 286 findings, 138 involved the dependent variable of recidivism; each of the 148 remaining findings was distributed across one of six other dependent variables, e.g., educational achievement. The 138 recidivism findings were derived from 126 separate studies; and the 93 studies that were mentioned in "What Works" were selected from these 126 exclusively. In *Correctional Effectiveness*, specific information was presented regarding the type of research design and the overall quality rating that was involved in each of the 138 findings (later called studies, for convenience) in tables 3-2, 3-3, and 3-4. In the case of tables 3-1 and 3-5, the reasons for including only 115 of the 138 findings (126 studies) may become apparent from notes c, d, and 3 of table 3-1. At this point, suffice it to say that a major reason for the reduction in question was the fact that these tables either focused on or were organized around the distinction between positive and negative outcomes; and when tabulating these outcomes, it was important not to repeat any studies which had been included, in *Correctional Effectiveness*, in more than one of the 11 treatment categories. Moreover, sufficient information was not always present to allow for a clear determination of whether a study should be categorized as positive or negative (nonpositive) in the first place.

10. Since all studies met basic scientific standards, it was clearly not the case that Palmer's 48 percent figure represented, in Martinson's words, an adding together of "camels and coat hooks," qualitatively and methodologically speaking [30]. This was apart from the fact that, in *Correctional Effectiveness*, ex post facto plus simulation studies were not automatically regarded as weak, and pure experimental design studies were not invariably looked upon as strong. Thus, 30 percent of all ex post facto plus simulation studies were given a quality rating of A, whereas 36 percent of all pure experimental design studies were given a rating of B. In addition, positive findings were obtained no more

often (proportionately, that is) in connection with ex post facto plus simulation designs than they were in relation to pure experimental designs, and negative findings were obtained only slightly less often than positive findings (42 percent versus 51 percent of all studies) in relation to ex post facto plus simulation designs.

11. Martinson drew his conclusion regarding given methods despite the emphasis that was placed on the factor of research quality by Lipton et al. (See Appendix A regarding research quality.)

12. When all entries rather than all studies were tabulated, the figures were: B quality, 51 percent; ex post facto plus simulation, 42 percent; A quality and pure experimental combined, 34 percent.

13. Another study did not directly compare experimentals and controls on parole success.

14. Four of the 42 entries were excluded from this analysis. One was a repeat; i.e., it appeared in more than a single treatment category. (We counted this study only once.) For three other entries, the information available in *Correctional Effectiveness* was insufficient or too ambiguous to allow for classification as either positive or negative (nonpositive). For the 38 studies in question, average sample size was 291.

15. As in table 3-1, positive results meant that for any given study, the recidivism rate which was obtained for experimentals was at least 15 percent lower than that obtained for controls (or other comparisons) (see n. 8).

16. If the 10 percent rather than 15 percent criterion had been used in the present analysis, 53 percent of all studies would have yielded positive results (see n. 19 regarding the 10 percent criterion).

17. These combinations were pure experimental, A quality; pure experimental, B quality; ex post facto plus simulation, A quality; ex post facto plus simulation, B quality. The 82 studies in question included 15 of the 38 investigations that were used in the present analysis.

18. This figure relates to the above-mentioned behavioral measures. It might be noted that there was a slight, positive relationship between the overall quality of each investigation and the average reduction in recidivism: A rated studies, 36 percent reduction; B rated, 29 percent; pure experimental designs, 37 percent reduction (A rated, 39 percent; B rated, 34 percent); ex post facto plus simulation designs, 28 percent (A rated, 31 percent; B rated, 27 percent). As before, all quality ratings and all categorizations as to type of design were made by Lipton et al.

19. Relative to the 48 studies in question, positive results were defined as those in which the rate of recidivism for the experimental group was at least 10 percent lower than that of the controls or comparison group. Here, we are referring to percentage differences, i.e., percent reductions in recidivism. (Multiple results were sometimes reported for any given study; in such cases, these results, as presented in *Correctional Effectiveness*, were averaged together to produce a single figure for the study in question.) The criterion of 10 percent difference between experimentals and controls was, obviously, somewhat differ-

ent than the earlier-mentioned criterion of 15 percent (n. 8). The 10 percent figure was chosen so as not to exclude from consideration those studies which had produced results that many people might consider less than striking or other than clearcut—but which were in a positive direction nonetheless. Moreover, if a 15 percent criterion had been used, i.e., if only clearcut studies had been included, the 32 percent reduction in recidivism that was obtained (in connection with the 10 percent criterion) would necessarily have risen. However, it would only have risen to 34 percent, mainly because no more than 6 of the 48 studies would have been eliminated from consideration.

20. For the studies under consideration, the average reduction in recidivism was 28 percent among adults and 35 percent among juveniles and youths combined. (For juveniles—individuals under 16—the figure was 31 percent; for youths—ages 16 through 20—it was 38 percent.) Mean length of followup was 19 months among adults and 19 months among juveniles and youths (14 months for juveniles, 21 months for youths). For all treatment categories combined, the average drop in percentage points was 17. Thus, the following might be considered typical of the results from any given investigation: 36 percent of the experimentals and 53 percent of the controls were rearrested, on 19 months followup. This finding would reflect both a 17 percentage point drop and a 32 percent reduction in illegal behavior.

21. The figure of $400 may be conservative. It is about one-half of the $805 that is obtained by dividing (1) direct expenditures by state and local government for police protection in all reporting jurisdictions within the United States by (2) all reported and estimated arrests within the United States. These expenditure and arrest figures—$7,290,166,000 and 9,055,800, respectively—relate to 1974. Expenditures exclude all intergovernmental costs, plus state and local costs, for "judicial," "legal services and prosecution," "indigent defense," "corrections" (incarceration beyond 48 hours is included here), and "other criminal justice" activities. They include the cost of lockup or "tanks" for holding prisoners less than 48 hours. See Hindelang et al., pp. 60, 524, and 810-812 regarding expenditures, arrests, and definition of terms [21].

22. Glaser estimates the per-arrest social cost of "damage done by known and inferred offenses" as $50 per misdemeanor, $500 per nonviolent felony, and $2500 per violent felony. (For juveniles and youth, the figures are $50, $300, and $2000.) He estimates the cost of court or parole violation hearings as $200 each, and the cost of production foregone as $300 per month. Glaser presents "confinement costs"—$333 per month, for adults—separate from these categories [17].

Chapter 4
Global Portrayal and the Basis of "What Works"

1. The distinction between individual studies/subcategories and total categories was also apparent in Lipton et al. There, however, the positive leads that

appeared in connection with individual studies/subcategories were not abstracted out, in line with particular criteria and objectives. Nor were they considered relatively unimportant in terms of the overall picture. Largely for these reasons, the portrayal of corrections that emerged in *Correctional Effectiveness* was a good deal more positive than that presented by Martinson. Specifically, serious efforts were often made to directly incorporate and reflect the major subunits (subcategories) of analysis, e.g., specific combinations of age, sex, and type of treatment setting. The following might also be noted: As we have seen, Martinson, in "What Works," did not utilize a differential weighting approach; he placed heavy emphasis on the factor of interstudy contradictions instead. Partly for this reason his conclusions regarding the effectiveness of correctional treatment approaches were much more negative than those presented by Lipton et al. Judging from their methodological review in *Correctional Effectiveness*, the latter, as compared to Martinson (in "What Works"), did place emphasis on differential weighting when evaluating the effectiveness of treatment approaches as a whole. (The amount of emphasis they placed cannot be determined, since differential weighting was not discussed in relation to specific studies and actual weights were never presented for any set of studies.) This suggests that a differential weighting approach may indeed allow positive leads to emerge at the level of overall treatment categories. At any rate, it may be far less likely than the interstudy contradictions approach to obscure many leads that do exist. This may largely be due to the fact that it does not, in effect, pit each study against all remaining studies within the given treatment category, or even subcategory.

2. In a strict methodological sense, individual studies were the ultimate units on which Martinson based his assessment of each treatment category. In turn, individual treatment categories were the principal operational units on which he based his overall assessment of rehabilitation. The former evaluation called for a within-category analysis; the latter required an across-categories approach. Martinson, however, did not carry out the latter type of analysis.

3. This is independent of any differential weighting that was utilized in *Correctional Effectiveness* relative to the A or B quality rating of each individual study. Each quality rating was utilized at the within-category level only, and was therefore subsumed under its particular treatment category alone.

4. Subcategories rarely functioned as independent or additional sources of power, in "What Works." Instead, they were operationally subsumed within the broader, total category itself.

5. One can readily understand the difficulties of conducting a massive review of correctional research on a dual basis, i.e., both within and across categories, or across selected categories. Thus, on practical grounds, it was not unreasonable to choose at least a primary basis for organizing the numerous research studies in question. The within-category/independent-category approach that was selected by Lipton et al., and then by Martinson in "What Works," did have certain advantages in this and other respects. It was also

directly related to the basic mandate of the survey: to assess treatment methods as such, not to evaluate rehabilitation as a whole. Nevertheless, the absence of an across-categories analysis was associated with specific limitations which became especially significant in light of the standards and objectives that were emphasized by Martinson. Under other conditions, these disadvantages would have been less critical or far-reaching.

6. Especially, but not exclusively, at the across-categories level, e.g., across the categories of casework and individual counseling, individual psychotherapy, and group therapy.

7. In "Crossroads," Martinson described these categories as the "legitimate comparison" or basic "unit of analysis."

Chapter 5
Offender Classifications and Treatment Modalities

1. These categories were probation, imprisonment, parole, casework and individual counseling, individual psychotherapy, group methods, milieu therapy, and skill development. The minor categories were partial physical custody (e.g., halfway houses), medical methods, and leisure-time activities. The latter categories consisted of four, five, and one study each, relative to the outcome measure of recidivism [27]. In one of the five medical methods studies, the independent variable was castration. This study was omitted from the analyses presented in tables 3-1 and 3-5 because of Martinson's sharp objection to this type of investigation [30]. It did not qualify for inclusion in table 3-6 since it did not involve a pure experimental, A quality design.

2. Because of random assignment, experimentals and controls were closely matched on age, IQ, race, level of parole risk (base expectancy), etc.

3. Results were essentially the same when "minor" offenses (e.g., traffic and incorrigibility) were added to this combination.

4. Rates of court conviction were excluded from table 5-1 in the interest of space.

5. For a brief review of eligibility, see [43]. In most respects, youths included in CTP were representative of those within the Youth Authority as a whole. This applied to the conflicted, power oriented, and passive conformist classifications as well.

6. During 1969-1973, the figures were 74 and 10 percent, respectively. This shift was largely an indirect result of California's Probation Subsidy Program, which produced a higher average age among Youth Authority first commitments beginning in the later 1960s. Among juvenile offenders there is a moderate, positive correlation between maturity level and age. The higher maturity category includes conflicted youths; the middle maturity category contains power oriented individuals.

7. During parole, monthly rates of arrest were much lower among passive conformist E's than C's for moderate and severe arrests combined. However, on postparole followup, no significant differences were observed. Thus, the results for this group were somewhat different from those for either conflicted or power oriented youths.

8. It might be noted that neither Martinson ("What Works") nor Lipton et al. had characterized the middle-risk, treatment amenable, and prosocial offenders as being rare or in other respects exceptional.

9. Similarly, its value would not necessarily be increased, or at least greatly increased, by the existence of any such specializations.

10. His statement could conceivably have applied to any single though unalterable combination of modalities as well. However, primary if not exclusive emphasis did seem to be on the concept of one modality alone.

11. A number of these concepts were implemented at the Community Treatment Project.

Chapter 6
The Call for Sweeping Reform

1. The post-1967 studies had presumably not been reviewed as of early 1976; at least Martinson gave no indication to the contrary, subsequent to his 1974 suggestion.

2. By itself, the analytic structure in question was logically incapable of representing the areas of overlap that existed among any of the 11 treatment categories. (These areas were intrinsic to the operations which define these categories in the first place. As such, the areas of overlap exist independent of the particular studies that were used as a means of focusing on one or another of those categories.) Thus, in order to allow for even the possibility of bringing to light the across-categories information in question, that structure had to be supplemented by one which allowed for a linking of categories and for a subsequent combining of studies across those categories. Only in this way could the basic data—individual studies—be resifted, and then appraised, from an across-categories perspective.

3. In Lipton et al. and in "What Works," the across-categories information in question was never developed in the first place. It was therefore untapped rather than overlooked or omitted.

4. These ground rules were logically independent of the above-mentioned, analytic structure; they could have been used with any other structure as well. Moreover, a very different set of rules could have been used in relation to the very same structure.

5. In this context, *conditions* included restrictions as well as opportunities.

6. For example, "Only when we devote 20 per cent and less [of our institutional manpower] for institutional care and 80 per cent and more for community supervision can we begin to rehabilitate. Only a dedicated community supervision staff properly trained with high skills can cut recidivism substantially" [8].

7. For instance, as seen in Lipton et al., several dozen research studies had produced positive or mixed-positive findings during 1945-1967. Those which contained a behavioral measure of program impact showed a recidivism drop that was far from insubstantial. By 1970, numerous correctional scholars and decision makers, Clark included, were probably familiar with the basic results of many such studies. During 1968-1970, additional leads emerged. Reports from California's Community Treatment Project contained similar and, in some respects, even more encouraging results for certain types of youth.

8. In other contexts Martinson maintains a sharp distinction between recidivism rates and crime rates. In "Crossroads," for example, he rejects the former index in its entirety, on grounds that it is wholly irrelevant to the new tasks of correctional research and that only the latter index is relevant.

9. The rare exceptions would theoretically apply to situations in which the sample of offenders that was involved in relation to a given recidivism rate was, quantitatively, rather similar to the sample which formed the basis of a given crime rate. In real life, situations of this type are seldom even approached, at least within the United States. If given countries (e.g., rather small-sized or sparsely populated nations) or specific regions are characterized by very low crime rates and little population movement, the relationship between recidivism rates and crime rates should be substantially closer than it usually is within the United States.

10. These individuals were often drawn from, and later returned to, more than one geographic area. One or both processes usually took place over a period of several months, sometimes even years.

11. Nonprogram offenders may or may not be taking part in, or have already taken part in, other rehabilitation programs instead—programs that may or may not be relevant to the geographic area, and crime rate, under consideration.

12. The programs in question may be similar or dissimilar to one another, in terms of focus and scope.

Chapter 7
Unrealistic and Realistic Expectations of Treatment

1. Thus, as of the present, little or no evidence can be presented to support the view that such programs can reduce, or have reduced, *crime rates* within the United States. This would also apply to the overall category of probation status.

2. In this latter connection, it might be noted that Martinson did indicate that two approaches show promise in terms of reducing recidivism: "One exception [to the consistently negative findings] is probation—not probation *supervision*, but the status of probation when there is the choice of such placement in lieu of incarceration. . . . There is also the category of *intensive probation supervision* for younger offenders" [30]. However, he did not suggest that these approaches had demonstrated an ability to reduce the *crime rate*, either significantly or to any extent at all, and could therefore be used as a way of responding to the public's overriding concern with crime.

3. On this score, level 2 reductions would presumably involve a direct and not unduly large extension of level 1 reductions. In this regard, Martinson had implied, by commission and omission, that level 2 phenomena are to a substantial degree a product of illegal behavior on the part of program-exposed offenders.

4. For example, "The public (and those sharp-eyed budget analysts) now tend to ask the questions: Has your 'program' overall reduced the crime rate? What specific aspect of your 'program' *accomplished this*? Was all this *worth it*, given the tremendous expense of these programs?" [30, emphasis added]

5. But not necessarily every individual program that falls within any one modality.

6. As indicated in chapter 6, n. 9, there are theoretical exceptions which, even if actualized, would make no more than a slight difference relative to the broad picture of crime. These exceptions would relate to crime rates within lightly populated geographic areas, areas that contained, for one thing, very few undetected as compared to detected offenders. In addition, these would be areas to which a high percentage of all local, convicted offenders would be returned subsequent to their program exposure (assuming actual incarceration and removal). In addition, depending on how effective or ineffective the factor of general deterrence appeared to be, these offenders might have to be returned to the community fairly rapidly, for instance, prior to the emergence of a new set of offenders, detected (and perhaps convicted) or otherwise. Within contemporary American society, this combination of events or conditions is hardly likely to occur, except by specific design.

7. School systems may be thought of as belonging primarily within this area; however, they would be of considerable relevance to other areas as well. Utilization of volunteers could also be included here, insofar as it did not involve direct interaction with known offenders.

8. In the long run, earlier apprehension could theoretically result in fewer actual crimes to detect.

9. It is recognized that some level 2 approaches, e.g., those which relate to earlier apprehension of offenders and court reforms, can have impact on level 1 objectives.

10. That is, promising in terms of level 1 objectives. To the extent that

there exists a generally positive relationship between level 1 and level 2 outcomes—and despite the overall weakness of this relationship in absolute statistical terms—the specific level 1 treatment programs which seem most appropriate with respect to level 1 objectives would (other things being equal) also be those most likely to make the largest *relative* contribution to level 2 objectives themselves. This applies regardless of how small the latter contribution may happen to be in absolute terms. It would also apply regardless of whether the programs in question had been modified substantially, in light of level 2 objectives.

11. In this as well as the preceding sentence, the terms *small* and *modest* are used primarily in a relative sense. Thus, in the first sentence, the impact of level 1 approaches is compared to that of level 2 approaches with reference to level 2 objectives; in the second sentence, the impact of level 2 approaches is compared to that of level 1 approaches with respect to level 1 objectives. Second, these terms can be taken in an absolute, statistical sense; that is, they can also be understood to mean that the relationship or correlation between given approaches and given outcomes (namely, between level 1 approaches and level 2 objectives in the first instance and between level 2 approaches and level 1 objectives in the second) is, in all probability, numerically rather low. Finally, neither the primary nor secondary usage of these terms is intended to suggest that the roles and impact in question should be disregarded from a social/personal frame of reference. Thus, in relation to the public's concern with today's level of crime, and with regard to the needs of offenders as individuals, whatever "helps" *is* important—in terms of making a positive contribution to legitimate needs and values. As such, it should be considered more than welcome and should not be disregarded. Still, this is not the same as saying that one should rely heavily on low correlation approaches, and that other methods should not be utilized to the fullest extent possible.

12. In one way or another, most treatment programs attempt to focus on some of the more immediate causes—the apparent triggering and perhaps sustaining conditions—of an individual's illegal behavior. This reflects an implicit assumption that is frequently made regarding the longer-standing, cultural-historical factors that ultimately (1) may have been responsible for the overall conditions within the individual's social environment, and (2) might have helped set the stage for his legal and personal difficulties in particular. This assumption is that, within most segments of contemporary American society, few such cultural-historical factors and related social conditions can be changed or improved rapidly enough—either by level 2 programs or by broader approaches—to make any decisive difference to *his* (the individual's) immediate future, or to substantially modify his already established, often self-reinforcing pattern of delinquency or adjustment. (This assumption relates especially to the preponderance of multiple offenders. As a result, it is possible that a decisive difference could perhaps be made with some individuals.) For this reason, it is

often taken for granted that most of the changing or adapting will have to come from the individual himself, and from influential members of his immediate environment. Thus, it is on these latter areas (the individual, etc., and the triggering or sustaining conditions in particular) that most treatment programs implicitly or explicitly attempt to focus. This is apart from the fact that few present-day programs are capable of focusing on these areas in both an intensive and extensive way, i.e., in a comprehensive manner.

13. Here, and in the next few pages, the term *approach* should not be taken to include, indiscriminately, all programs that fall within any one treatment modality (e.g., group counseling). As seen earlier, only some programs appear to be effective in the case of any one modality. In the present context, *approach* will be used to place special emphasis on the latter, more effective programs.

14. Approximately three-fourths of the 30 studies (programs) were designed to focus specifically on one or more areas (e.g., education); these programs, of course, also measured offender progress within the given area(s). The remaining programs were not designed to focus on any one or more areas in particular. For instance, they contained no elements for dealing specifically with vocational training. Nevertheless, these programs measured offender progress within the given area(s), and were therefore included within the Lipton et al. survey of that area. (All programs that were classified under educational achievement did focus on that particular area.) If all 30 programs had been designed to focus specifically on a given area, the preceding percentages might have been somewhat different.

15. For all 92 entries in the areas of vocational adjustment, educational achievement, community adjustment, and personality and attitude change combined, results were as follows: strong positive or clearcut gains, 46 percent; mixed positive or moderate overall gains, 30 percent; and no positive results (or, in a few cases, change for the worse), 24 percent. The 92 entries related to 81 separate studies (several studies appeared in more than one area). Focusing on these 81 studies—that is, omitting all 11 repeat entries—the percentages were 43, 32, and 25, respectively. Figures shown in tables 7-1 and 7-2 are based on our tabulations of the results presented in *Correctional Effectiveness* for each individual study.

Chapter 8
Correctional Treatment in Its Own Right

1. Martinson used this phrase in the context of level 2 objectives, but not in connection with level 2 approaches as we have described them [30].

2. Factor (2) has already been reviewed in relation to the present issue, and in terms of its being based on defensible assumptions. To a lesser extent, this also applies to factor (3).

3. It is also due to the intensity of these forces. For present purposes, the intensity factor need not be focused on.

4. That is, by virtue of there being too few "airplanes" available to carry them. Relative to the broader picture, it would be useful to separate this issue from that of "single airplane capacity," i.e., average number of passengers that can be handled by individual treatment programs or types of treatment programs.

5. Martinson expresses no disagreement with the descriptions or interpretations that he presents, i.e., with the opinions which he assumes are held (or knows are held) by each of the following groups relative to the present issue: "neighbors in the 20th precinct," "the public," "budget analysts," "the economists," "state planning organizations," "LEAA." His statements also imply that these groups are in essential agreement with one another as to the relative importance and absolute value of crime rates and recidivism rates [30]. Finally, the statements in question reflect the assumption, or knowledge, that no significant differences of opinion exist within any of these groups, relative to the present issue.

6. With or without an actual purge, large-scale implementation of the suggested requirement would strip most treatment programs of the principal role for which they were originally designed. It would probably eliminate their ability to make an independent and, in many cases, significant and unique contribution relative to their present area of focus, namely, level 1 objectives. It might also be noted that since this requirement is virtually impossible to satisfy in real life—by treatment programs alone—few if any such programs would end up justifying their existence in the first place. Thus, implementation of this requirement would be tantamount to setting these programs up for failure. Under this condition, level 1 programs would soon have no role to play in connection with level 2 objectives, either.

7. According to Martinson, it would also free us from such "narrow" questions as "Which methods work best for *which* types of offenders, under *what* conditions or in what types of setting?" [30].

8. Indirect communications include those which may be transmitted in terms of the presumed or definitely known opinions of individuals or groups whose position (as reported) on a given issue is specifically supportive of, or generally consistent with, one's own. In this respect, these communications can be a way of expressing one's personal views through the voice of others, as it were.

9. This would apply especially but not exclusively when these programs are viewed in the aggregate.

10. Once out of the way they would presumably be allowed to dwell in the background, like survivors from an era that no longer exists or matters.

Chapter 9
The Public, Decision Makers, and Treatment

1. This distinction was not made by Martinson.

2. Despite its specificity, this reason is important. However, despite its importance, it does not relate to any quality or factor that is intrinsic to the nature or composition of treatment programs themselves, i.e., any feature that is fundamental to what these programs are or represent. As a result, this specific reason does not constitute a condemnation or unalterable rejection of level 1 approaches as such. By the same token, it neither reflects nor constitutes a rejection of the underlying concepts of treatment and intervention. In short, it represents a form of conditional, not unconditional, opposition.

3. More specifically, in Martinson's account, the means of production are not singled-out as a decisive factor or indispensable ingredient from the public's point of view. In this regard, the "something else" (lower crime rates) can presumably be produced by treatment programs or by any other approach, as far as the public is concerned. If this is indeed the case, there would appear to be no bias in favor of or against any given means of production, assuming, of course, that it is not looked upon as cruel and unusual, etc.

4. This would apply from a quantitative perspective as well. The objection that Martinson describes is not presented as a total objection, a direct and/or indirect opposition to all aspects of the program.

5. This may be restated in somewhat more detail. As mentioned on p. 79, Martinson never went so far as to suggest that the public was unconditionally opposed to treatment programs. However, by adding no qualifications or elaborations to the statement that the public does not care, he left the door open for considerable misinterpretation regarding the extent to which the public is no more than conditionally opposed to such programs, i.e., opposed to them for a specific reason or reasons alone.

6. For example, the consummation or seemingly inevitable result.

7. These reactions go well beyond alienation or estrangement.

8. That is, forces which are largely internal or external to the public itself. Internal forces would include the desires or motivations in question, e.g., those which may directly relate to the preferences that comprise part of factor (2) above.

9. To bring about this shift, factors (1) and (2)—in conjunction with the underlying acceptance mentioned above—would have to partially offset the psychological impact of factor (3), namely, current crime rates. In all likelihood, the public could make this shift without at the same time minimizing the actual significance and impact of factor (3). In essence, this process would be based on a broadening of perspective or a deepening of understanding. It would not involve a denial or repudiation of something else, namely, the reality and impact of crime rates or the actual and potential importance of level 2 approaches.

10. We assume that the basic preconditions already exist (see p. 83). For present purposes, there is no need to elaborate on these conditions or outline related factors and conditions.

11. Martinson's position leaves little if any room for serious investment in the above-mentioned goal and method. For example, in "What Works," his overall conclusions regarding rehabilitation clearly pointed away from, not toward, an increased investment in this goal. This position was largely repeated in "Crossroads," albeit in highly condensed form. In "Crossroads," the question of increasing the public's interest in and support for treatment programs was never broached. Instead, without directly saying so, Martinson left little doubt that he considered the public's present level of interest and support (actually, its disinterest or opposition, as reported) to be an appropriate and essentially adequate response, one that called for no modification in an upward direction. Given this context, there was no reason for him to suggest (and accordingly, he did not suggest) that it would be important for decision makers and others to supply information which might help the public recognize the specific, positive contributions of level 1 approaches. (Martinson may have assumed that little or no such information exists.) Beyond this, and perhaps of central importance, the idea of increasing the public's investment in the above-mentioned goal and method would have been completely at variance with the unidirectional proposal that he had clearly and firmly stated—one which urged that virtually all energies be focused on the promotion of what we have called level 2 objectives, instead. It might be mentioned at this point that the impact on the public of Martinson's conclusions regarding rehabilitation was not just a result of such factors as polarization and stereotyping. The latter factors were especially prominent in "Crossroads," but not in "What Works."

12. This portrayal, or polarization, was communicated via a combination of explicit assertions and tacit assumptions [30].

13. The following might also be kept in mind relative to front-line decision makers: (1) their responsibility to the general public is neither more nor less than that of other decision makers; (2) they, like most other decision makers, do regard crime rates as important.

Chapter 10
Treatment-Centered Research Today

1. To quantitatively compare this group of studies with a subsequent group (see text), each may be thought of as having been conducted during comparable intervals of time.

2. It is recognized that the vast majority of replications are inexact and incomplete, at least in the applied sciences. These features do not invalidate the point in question.

3. In this context, negative findings would help one single out unworkable alternatives. They would not necessarily mean that the objectives themselves are impossible to achieve.

4. In a sense, it has done what most individuals, offenders included, intuitively do in order to better integrate their own reality with that of their environment.

5. Even the long-established sciences do not leave inefficiency and trial and error completely behind, however much these may be reduced. Still, when it comes to corrections, this fairly typical mode of scientific progress remains difficult for many people to accept, even in part. In this connection, the demands that are made on correctional research have been rather intense. Similarly, the standards by which it is judged have sometimes been very rigid. In both cases, this may largely be a reflection of today's (and yesterday's) disquieting social realities and pressures. At any rate, these demands and pressures often reflect an understandable desire for sweeping solutions, a desire which is probably beyond the capacity of any one science to satisfy, especially within the time frame that has been presented. In a sense, this desire (or demand) is somewhat like asking an 8- or 10-year-old to do the job of Paul Bunyon. From this perspective, it would make limited sense to call such a youngster inadequate because of what he cannot produce.

6. For example, within the applied sciences, the medical profession has long recognized the importance of prescribing "different pills for different ills." (Few people would maintain that this is either an invalid approach or little more than a reflection of vested interests.) Apart from its relevance to the issue of complexity, this recognition reflects the principle of utilizing the best tools available at the time, however few or many they may be.

7. More specifically, because of the sizable differences that ordinarily exist between their own subject matter and that of previous investigations. Previous investigations are those which relate to offenders, staff, and setting.

8. This applies despite the small to moderate amount of content overlap that can exist between the former and latter types of investigation, at given levels of analysis. Former investigations are those which relate to offenders, staff, and setting.

9. Measures of community adjustment mainly included, e.g., "work record, family adjustment, church attendance, or participation in voluntary associations" [27].

Chapter 11
Challenge and Initial Response

1. That is, one which does not terminate with the identification of basic clues.

2. This applies despite relatively rare occasions on which the analytic structure was, in effect, temporarily overridden or ignored.

3. In itself, the independent-category approach makes sense with respect to the goal of evaluating each treatment category individually. However, by itself, it cannot serve as a basis for evaluating rehabilitation as a whole, if rehabilitation is taken to mean (1) all treatment categories collectively (here, *collectively* would refer to a synthesis of all components or categories, many of which may be relatively complex), rather than (2) an aggregate or simple sum of all such components (regardless of the relative complexity/noncomplexity of individual components). To argue from the individual to the collective in such a context would involve the logical fallacy of "composition" [15].

4. Regarding this lack of emphasis, it is not possible to precisely parcel out the relative contributions of factor 2, on the one hand, and factors 3, 3a, and 3b, on the other.

5. Martinson relaxed his strict application of this criterion relative to his overall portrayal of probation.

6. Under the circumstances, only the earlier-mentioned subcategories had a reasonable chance of satisfying the given criterion.

7. Differentiated analyses would have helped clarify and eliminate many of the contradictions that were in fact observed.

8. That is, this approach of Martinson's strongly implied that each treatment method ought to be accepted or rejected on some such basis. The specific interrelationships that existed among factors 2, 5, and 6 virtually ensured that each treatment would have to be accepted or rejected on such a basis.

9. Here, *correctional knowledge* refers to the pool of information that is associated with all treatment categories, and related correctional components, collectively. This information, e.g., research findings that relate to specific variables associated with given studies, exists independent of the particular analytic framework by means of which it has been organized. That is, the information would continue to exist even if the analytic framework were modified or abandoned, and if an entirely different framework were utilized instead.

10. To make such contributions, findings from individual studies would have to be organized along lines that cut across the present treatment categories. They would not be mediated by, or funneled through, the treatment categories as such. In "What Works" and "Crossroads," Martinson made no reference to direct contributions insofar as this is used (1) in the context of correctional knowledge as a whole, i.e., over and beyond that level of knowledge which focuses on individual treatment categories as such; and (2) in connection with the issue of realigning or redistributing the basic data pool (i.e., all individual studies) on the basis of an alternate analytic framework. By itself, this lack of reference to the concept of direct contributions does not force one to conclude

that Martinson would have taken either of the following positions if the given concept had been focused on in relation to (1) and (2) above. Alternate ways of organizing or processing the basic data pool are probably incapable of (1) yielding legitimate knowledge or valid and reliable leads, or (2) producing this knowledge or these leads in a practical and efficient way. Since none of Martinson's statements expressly or implicitly rule out either position, all that can be said for sure is (1) he simply did not refer to direct contributions in connection with the data-reorganization issue, and correctional knowledge, as described in n. 9; and (2) he accepted the idea of assigning individual studies a limited, exclusively subordinate role relative to the task of accumulating correctional knowledge, in the present sense of this term (see item (1) at the start of this note). In short, taken together, his statements and lack of statements or differentiations did not necessarily imply that correctional knowledge can only—or can best—be developed via the type of analytic approach that was used in *Correctional Effectiveness* and "What Works." Nevertheless, they suggested that he believes the accumulation of such knowledge should take place via this particular framework.

11. The presence of such a framework would allow the primary focus of the knowledge-gathering effort to be extended beyond, or shifted from, individual treatment categories. This does not mean the knowledge-gathering effort would have to be focused on individual studies as opposed, for example, to any of several subcategories.

12. This a priori narrowing or limiting also applies to the quantity—therefore strength—of all related, converging evidence. All analytic structures necessarily produce some limitations or restrictions. However, some involve far more than others and may hinder rather than facilitate the achievement of given objectives.

13. For example, the replication effort does not extend beyond the boundaries of the particular treatment category within which the former as well as latter studies happen to fall. Instead, it focuses primarily on the one characteristic or dimension which those particular studies share in common, and which underlies as well as defines the given category. Nor does the replication effort reflect additional characteristics which these and/or other studies share in common, characteristics that are observed within as well as across given treatment categories.

14. The latter investigations could be taken into account if an alternate or supplementary analytic framework were used. However, relative to the above-mentioned contribution to knowledge, such a framework, in itself, might still be unable to help a given set of studies overcome the criterion hurdle presented by factor 5, assuming this factor remained in effect.

15. In itself, this view does not inevitably lead to the difficulties in question.

16. For example, in the present case, operational or practical considerations

may have played a critical role relative to the lack of differentiation that was observed. As explained in *Correctional Effectiveness*, "the 11 treatment categories were designed to classify economically the findings of the survey." (Compare n. 20, below.)

17. Data integration thus involves something other than a formal or structural reorganization of the findings from individual studies, studies which had previously been presented in a different format. In itself, such a reorganization or format change reveals no new relationships or links among the given studies. This is because the formal structure (by means of which a pool of information is organized) does not, in itself, include a set of attributes in terms of which the items of information can be related to one another. These attributes are external to the formal structure. Similarly, data integration involves more than a cross-referencing of individual studies, on the one hand, and sets of criterion measures, on the other. Criterion measures may be distinguished from the preceding dimensions and factors not only on substantive grounds, but by the fact that the former are external, not intrinsic, to the studies or programs in question.

18. These analyses were made at the within-category (i.e., single-category) level alone.

19. This, too, applied at the within-category level alone.

20. This sharing of program features and related elements was clearly recognized in *Correctional Effectiveness*: "Studies of probation, parole, and casework and individual counseling presented classification problems because they inherently include aspects of other treatment methods. All 11 [treatment] categories were derived inductively; therefore, each involves a variety of specific techniques for changing behavior that share certain common elements" [27].

21. Statistically advanced techniques notwithstanding, no single framework can deal with all major components and factors (program features) at the same time. As a result, it is important to look at each study more than once, each time focusing on different program features or combinations thereof. Since these "looks"—comparisons and contrasts—would proceed (collectively) in terms of alternate analytic frameworks, such a process could be thought of as a "successive-bases, successive-opportunities" approach. Relative to this approach, and in connection with any single framework, each program feature or set of features would, of course, be counted only once in terms of its potential contribution to correctional knowledge.

Chapter 12
Tasks, Strategies, and Tools

1. Martinson forcefully rejects these more recent questions. For example: "Palmer would impose on the search for knowledge in criminal justice the

narrowest and meanest of questions. In his own words everything must come down to this: 'Which methods work best for *which* types of offenders, and under *what* conditions or in what types of setting?' " [30]. (It might be noted that an across-categories frame of reference is needed in order to systematically answer these questions.) Martinson's position is tantamount to saying that it would be positively wrong to ask: "Should such-and-such diets (or exercises/ vitamins/medicines) be recommended to such-and-such individuals; and if so, under what conditions or with what precautions should this be done?" His rejection of such questions would be easy to justify if, for some reason, one were obliged or otherwise forced to permanently abandon the concept or practice of individualized handling, and literally had to offer every person the same diet, the same medicines, etc. Short of this situation, Martinson's position would be difficult to justify. For one thing, it is virtually impossible to make progress within any applied science, corrections included, if increasingly specific questions are not asked. This is particularly true of questions such as the preceding, i.e., questions which focus on the functional relationship between variables or factors. (As suggested earlier, progress can occur relative to other specific questions as well. It need not occur only on the basis of these exact questions; nor must it take place within any one content area alone. In this connection, Palmer never did state or imply that "everything must come down to this." Instead, Martinson failed to distinguish between everything, on the one hand, and some things or many things, on the other.)

2. In upcoming years, correctional research will hopefully not just focus on the refinement and optimal utilization of today's more promising methods of intervention and their related settings, rather it will try to develop new and more humane approaches and environments as well. At the same time, additional research efforts might be focused on areas other than intervention.

3. These areas relate to strategies for developing comprehensive research efforts, broad organizational changes within the research community, etc.

4. Continuity with the past necessarily restricts one's freedom to frequently shift directions, especially on a major scale. In this respect, it sets an outer limit on one's flexibility, at least within the context of short-to-moderate intervals of time. From intermediate- and long-range perspectives, this type of limitation by no means represents an inevitable loss, either in principle or in practice. For example, in principle it is at least as important to avoid a scattering or frequent diluting of one's efforts as it is to avoid a marked reduction of flexibility. Stated differently, without the presence of continuity and focused efforts, comprehensive, indepth answers might seldom be developed with regard to specific, often complex issues. In this respect, satisfactory closure or at least relative closure might seldom be achieved. On the other hand, without flexibility, one's base of operations—and perspective—could become quite narrow, and important relationships could be overlooked. In terms of practice, a workable balance between the old and the new probably can be established. This

might be done by insisting on a high degree of continuity and detailed analysis, and, at the same time, by encouraging the introduction of new subject matter, refined methodologies, and more broadly based outcome measures.

5. The individual and collective levels of data handling are not mutually exclusive (see text). However, they can be distinguished from one another fairly easily.

6. In terms of specific content, the job of uncovering these relationships would ultimately require (1) the establishment of distinctions which had not been made in connection with the original analysis and (2) the addition of new variables or factors. In principle, this job could be carried out by means of supplementary analyses alone, all within the context of strategy A. However, to deal with the more complex relationships and interactions that are likely to exist across various studies, strategy B would probably be required instead. This requirement would not be based on the latter's advantage over the former with respect to efficiency and rate of progress. It would derive from the fact that it is very difficult for strategy A to uncover and integrate these relationships and interactions in the first place, with the precision and relative comprehensiveness that can be associated with strategy B. On a smaller scale, this fact is also reflected in the latter's marked advantage over the former in dealing with the "masking of significant findings" issue [38].

7. This difficulty does not negate the positive contributions that can be made by such an approach, particularly, but not exclusively, at the level of data analysis.

8. The following relates to the issue of representativeness, e.g., adequacy versus inadequacy of representation. The picture of correctional knowledge that is produced by an overly restrictive approach may not be representative of the findings from all studies or programs that comprise the given data pool. That is, the given account of correctional knowledge may portray not the full range of findings, but a particular segment alone. (In this connection, representativeness may be seen as a data-integration issue, not a data-analysis issue as such.) It is likely to be the result of specific structures and criteria which, when operating jointly, systematically highlight one type of finding, e.g., negative findings, and unduly limit or otherwise soften and restrict the impact of others. As such, it should be distinguished from a particular data-analysis problem that is also associated with overly restrictive approaches. Here, specific structures and procedures, also operating jointly, make it possible for only certain categories of studies or programs to be compared and contrasted with one another in the first place. This may be viewed as a problem of reach, or extent of influence. It may or may not be associated with that of representativeness as well, at a subsequent point in the data-handling process.

9. A relatively high percentage of these factors operated in a primarily restrictive manner. This applied mainly but not exclusively at the level of data integration. Again viewed collectively, and as a specific approach, these factors

were characterized by considerable differentiation at the analytic level of data handling, within though not across categories. At the same time, they were characterized by a general lack of differentiation at the integrative level, particularly across categories. In this respect, they represented a mixture of strategies B and A.

10. Data-handling approaches should be distinguished from research designs. The latter can and should influence the course of every program.

11. Or, from certain perspectives, "subsist"—prior to their being revealed.

12. We have used the following terms as synonyms for *data items: variables, factors, attributes, features, events, items, specific content*, and *defined content*. Of these terms, *variables, factors*, and *items* are probably the most common and useful.

13. The limitations in question would exist even if adequate data-processing techniques were available.

14. Use of these items and scales cannot guarantee an absence of overly broad generalizations. However, by reducing the amount of selective recall, wishful thinking, etc., it can markedly lower their chance of occurring.

15. For present purposes, there is no need to focus on issues that relate to adequacy of data reporting, maintenance of data files, and methods of obtaining information that has been collected by others, but either not analyzed or not reported.

16. Area I-B contains four subsidiary classes of items: developmental level, classification or personality type, trait clusters, and specific factors or generic variables. For each of the first two classes, researchers would categorize offenders with respect to at least one developmental level or classification system, e.g., the interpersonal and/or moral level system. For each of the remaining classes, researchers would make separate ratings on all dimensions that are listed, i.e., on communicative-alert, passive-uncertain, and so on. (The latter approach, namely, rate on all dimensions, also applies to areas II-B, IV-C, and the second section of II-C. It applies to the "social climate dimensions" item in area III-B as well.) For the first section of area II-C, researchers would focus on at least one orientation set, e.g., A type versus B type. Relative to that set, they would choose the specific orientation (e.g., A type) that best describes the staff or staff member in question. This approach, namely, select the most descriptive choice, also applies to the last two items of area III-B.

17. This would include (1) absolute number of arrests and/or convictions and (2) number of arrests and/or convictions, categorized as above average, average, or below average relative to offenders of the same age group. Other components could be added to this item, e.g., dominant type of offense history (against other persons, property, other). As an alternate approach, this and/or other components could be used as independent items.

18. The interpersonal, psychosocial, moral, ego, and conceptual level systems are described in the writings of Warren, Palmer, Kohlberg, Loevinger, and Hunt, respectively [55,37,25,28,23].

19. Each item in this subdivision represents a separate scale. This also applies to the last two items in area II-C. For details regarding these scales, see [39].

20. Each item in this subdivision represents a separate scale. These and other scales are shown in Appendix K.

Chapter 13
The Next Steps

1. For purposes of data analysis and data integration, we will handle each treatment modality as if it were a single, albeit complex, data item (see p. 116, area IV-B). In this respect, we will not accord it special status.

2. If the second but not the first suggestion were followed, several or (preferably) all treatment modalities would be combined, not just two or three. If the first and second suggestions were used on a complementary rather than independent basis, the modalities that would be established for both approaches would have to be identical as to type and amount.

3. For reasons which need not be specified here, it is often essential, or at least useful, to subdivide continuous variables (e.g., age or IQ) and to combine discrete items (e.g., prison and jail). In the case of age, the following might be used as standard subdivisions: 0-12, 13-15, 16-18, 19-21, 22-29, 30-39, 40 and up. For some purposes, 16-21 and 30 and up might be substituted for the more detailed breakdowns. For type of setting, the following combinations might be used: prisons or institutions and jails; camps, ranches, and farms; day care centers, other community centers, halfway houses, and group homes; and free community. For some purposes, it might be appropriate and feasible to separate day care and other community centers from halfway houses and group homes.

4. Items in which there is marked interest could be given priority if time and resources are limited.

5. The experimental groups that comprise the 40 target studies would probably have been established on the basis of a wide range of independent variables (items). In some studies the independent variable may have been vocational training; in others it may have been milieu therapy or group counseling. In still others it may have been living-unit size, postprogram contacts, or type of program orientation (e.g., behavior modification). If no control group is present for a given target study, we might compare the recidivism rates for that study with the average rate (baseline) for those control groups (in other target studies) that were used with offenders who were very similar to those in the given study. Here, too, a 15 percent or more reduction in recidivism rates would be used to define success. Nevertheless, studies that lack a control group should be used with considerable caution, even under the best of conditions.

6. When fewer than 20 programs are involved, the Fisher exact-probability test might be substituted for Chi square, regardless of the Yates correction.

7. Studies that lack a control group would not be included in these analyses, unless one wished to use the baseline approach suggested in n. 5.

8. Here, as in other analyses, leads may emerge if one were to add certain targets to the picture, e.g., 16- to 18- and 19- to 21-year-old males. This is apart from whether one were to combine any two or more independent variables in order to create broader categories of analysis. In the present example, no significant differences or statistical tendencies are observed relative to various combinations of modalities, e.g., individual counseling, group counseling, and milieu therapy. For exploratory purposes it is useful to include statistical tendencies (.10 level findings) rather than draw the line at .05.

9. We are assuming that these items and item combinations were—or would be—analyzed on the basis of a sufficiently large sample, since insufficient sample size may itself result in a lack of clarity.

10. This is apart from the fact that the impact of these unidentified factors may be other than negative when they are combined with still other data items, or used with different targets.

11. We would want this reduction to reflect a followup of at least 12 months. For community programs, followup would begin at point of program entry; for institutional programs, it would begin at point of release to the community. For halfway homes and work release programs, the starting point would reflect a combination of factors.

12. If positive models are found to have almost no data items in common with each other—at least none we can identify—this would suggest there may be several distinctly different ways of working successfully with the target in question.

13. The reason for this caution is as follows. Programs that represent negative models may nonetheless contain several positive factors. Some of these factors may be shared by several such programs but may not have been identified as positive in connection with the preselected-targets approach. Though positive, these factors may be suppressed and overpowered by negative factors, whether or not the latter have been identified as such via any given approach. Because of this possible swamping effect, we should not automatically assume that the common elements which are observed among negative model programs will in fact operate in a negative direction, within these programs. This position would be supported if we were to observe these same elements—especially in combination—in any two or more positive model programs.

14. This is not contradicted by the fact that the model programs in question would have been included among the target studies that were already analyzed via the preselected-targets approach, and would therefore have already contributed to the findings in question. We are assuming that the contribution made by these studies would be small to moderate, quantitatively speaking, since it would directly reflect (1) the number of model programs that have been included among the target studies, as compared to (2) the number of model plus

nonmodel programs (all target studies) that are present. The contribution made by model programs would probably remain about the same even if a differential-weighting approach were used to supplement the statistical techniques described on pp. 122-125.

15. This might be a more serious problem with some targets, or some categories of analysis, than others. For instance, with respect to categories of analysis, it might be more hazardous to generalize from (1) 13- to 15-year-olds to 16- to 18-year-olds than from (2) 19- to 21-year-olds to 16- to 18-year-olds, at least within contemporary American society.

Chapter 14
Systematic Scanning and Related Techniques

1. The item list in chapter 12 contains over 90 data items, and in several respects, it is incomplete. In addition, as seen on p. 138, most data items can produce two or more test items. Thus, the given item list actually involves far more than 90 potential analytic units. Finally, in this list, item components have not been counted separately from the data item to which they "belong." (See n. 3 regarding item components.)

2. If one were to use a significance cutoff of .05, five chance relationships could be expected to reach statistical significance for every 100 tests performed. Such relationships or findings may be described as spuriously significant. Given the many tests that are involved in the systematic-scanning approach, spurious significance could theoretically pose a problem. Yet in reality, the situation may be less serious than it seems. For example, the following guidelines could be used to help determine if, relative to given targets, an apparently significant finding or collection of findings is more likely to be genuine than a product of chance. First, expected significance levels could be compared with those actually obtained. For instance, by chance alone, one would indeed expect to find four .05 relationships and one .01 relationship for every 100 tests performed. However, one would not anticipate any .001 or .0001 relationships; nor would one expect, say, two or three .01 and two or three .001 relationships. Second, convergence of evidence could be considered. For example, if significant findings often appear with respect to similar or otherwise related items, or if these items seem to group together in an orderly way, the possibilities would be remote that most such findings are the result of chance. In deciding independently which items are likely to be related to other items with respect to outcome (especially to those items which have reached the .01 or .001 levels or which consistently reach or approach significance across a range of analyses), reference to a table of item-intercorrelations could be of considerable help. In factor-analytic terms, related findings often suggest the presence of "true variance," e.g., common and specific factors, not so much "error variance" or chance [19]. Convergence of

evidence would be particularly important if the number of target programs were not very large. This is due to the difficulty of obtaining .001 and especially .0001 relationships with samples smaller than 20. Given these guidelines (especially in combination), it would often be fairly easy to decide if individual findings, and/or the preponderance of significant results, are probably not a product of chance.

3. For some analytic purposes, items such as milieu therapy would be handled as one of several possible alternatives within a broad group, or set, of items. In such contexts, the group to which these alternatives belong (e.g., the group of treatment modalities, taken together) may itself be regarded as the item, and each alternative might then be thought of as an item component. These considerations are of particular relevance to test items that appear in configurations 1 and 2 (p. 138).

4. There are six possible two-area combinations: offender-staff, offender-setting, offender-operations, staff-setting, staff-operations, and setting-operations. There are four possible three-area combinations: offender-staff-setting, offender-staff-operations, offender-setting-operations, and staff-setting-operations.

5. Organization and implementation of the systematic-scanning approach is no easy matter, especially with configurations 2, 3, and 4. With these configurations, this approach would call for successive analyses at each level of increased structural complexity, e.g., complexity in terms of the number of data items that are allowed to comprise each target and test item. Compared to this task, the preselected-targets approach might seem relatively simple and, in several respects, more appealing.

6. Wherever possible, additional analyses should be conducted in order to focus on targets as such, not on the total program in which they appear. Such analyses would be advisable since any given program is likely to include offenders, staff, and/or operations that extend beyond the boundaries of the target itself, e.g., beyond the 22- to 29-year-old group that might perhaps be focused on. In general, we would expect to find considerable similarity in the results of target-centered as compared with program-centered analyses. We would also expect to find increasing similarity in the above results, as a function of increased number of target programs. Nevertheless, in any given instance (especially in the case of relatively few target programs), findings from target-centered and program-centered analyses may or may not be very similar. (It goes without saying that in any program-centered analysis, each program would be analyzed with respect to its main target and would be counted only once.)

7. For instance, with respect to configuration 4, the first question would be asked in the following form: Relative to 22- to 29-year-old males in prisons and jails, are successful programs more likely to contain (1) a combination of above average adequacy of services (AOS) and smaller than average living-unit size (LUS) than (2) all other combinations of AOS and LUS, taken together?

8. If two or more distinctly different types of day care centers or milieu-therapy approaches were established, such test items could be included on these lists. The reason is that once these items have been subdivided, e.g., into two hypothetical types, one type can be compared with the other, and the items would no longer be discrete.

9. The following would apply to all configurations and all types of variables or items. First, statistical analyses cannot be focused on rarely occurring targets taken by themselves. An example of such a target would be 13- to 15-year-old females in halfway houses or in camps, ranches, and farms. Second, some composite targets and test items are irrelevant or inapplicable under most or all conditions. An example of the latter would be self-contradictory combinations such as "living-unit size" in a "free community" setting.

10. As the number of data items that comprise a target or test item is increased from approximately five or six (say, it is increased by the addition of one data item at a time), the new target or test item that results from this increase would largely be a repeat of the previous one. That is, the content of the new composite item would be the same as that of the previous composite item, except for the one data item that was added. Thus, when a composite item already includes roughly half a dozen data items, it may have entered the area of rapidly diminishing returns with regard to changes that are likely to be brought about by the addition of any new data item. Yet, the following possibility might be kept in mind. Some individual data items may make an unusually large contribution when added to certain composite items. This may occur even though the content of the new composite items is largely the same as that of the old. For instance, when data item X is combined with a particular test item that already contains several individual data items, the contribution of X may be much larger than that which could have been made by most other individual data items, relative to that same test item. Despite this definite possibility, it might still be best (for practical reasons) to initially utilize no more than 6 data items at a time, relative to composite targets and test items. This would also apply despite the fact that targets and test items which consist of, say, 9 or 10 data items *would* be quite different in terms of content (and perhaps in many cases, in terms of significance or potential contribution) from those which consist of 5 or 6.

11. Each analysis would be based on intercorrelations among these variables, e.g., among such staff items as strength of feelings and opinions, sharpness-alertness, criticalness, and socially desired qualities. It would be methodologically inappropriate to use cluster and factor analysis with configurations 3 and 4 since these configurations involve combinations of test items, and the correlation between one combination and another would be spurious. More specifically, every correlation would be artificially inflated since each test item would be repeatedly correlated with a combination of one or more items and itself. In short, cluster and factor analyses should not be based on composite test items.

12. The earlier-mentioned limit of six items does not apply to the pool of

individual variables (all available and appropriate test items) that would be used to generate the correlation matrix from which these clusters or factors are ultimately derived. It refers to the maximum number of individual data items which should form the basis of any one composite item—in this case, a composite test item. As seen in n. 11, the present analyses would not, or at least should not, involve composite test items.

13. Here, cluster and factor analysis would be appropriate in the case of all four configurations. This is so because it would be based on an original item list, not on combinations of items that could be generated from such a list during the course of standard scanning. In effect, cluster and factor analysis would be used only to produce an abridged item list from an original item list. The abridged list would be derived from intercorrelations among individual variables alone, and would consist of individual items alone. In the present context, all combinations of items would be generated from the abridged list alone, using standard scanning procedures. They would not be a product of the cluster or factor analysis itself.

14. For the reason described in n. 11, postscanning factor analysis would be inappropriate in the case of configurations 3 and 4.

15. If the number of link variables is not very large, cluster analysis might be more appropriate than factor analysis.

16. Further analytic distinctions might be made within given areas or subdivisions, for various groups of items.

17. The reason for this limitation is the same as that described in the case of cluster and factor analysis.

18. Three points might be noted. 1. Each set of key items would be derived from (a) intercorrelations between variables that appear on the original data list and (b) correlations between each such variable and the particular outcome measure that is used. In the present discussion, the outcome measure has been level of success. Specifically, we have considered two levels: successful (S) and unsuccessful (U). Both levels of success—operationally, all S programs and all U programs—must be reflected in all outcome correlations that are computed. (The data pool that is used to compute any given outcome correlation would be comprised of all S and all U programs. Both groups of programs must be present in order to operationalize the specific outcome measure that is used—in this case, in order to generate the S/U dichotomy.) Since these correlations relate to S and U programs combined, key item combinations that are identified by the multiple-regression technique cannot be listed separately for either S or U programs. 2. As indicated, level of success refers, in the present discussion, to a simple dichotomy within the total range of target programs. This dichotomy is: S versus U programs. However, in real life, the first component of this dichotomy is comprised of programs which, collectively, have demonstrated not only moderate, but considerable success. The second component includes only those programs which have shown very little success, no measurable success, or

worse results than a control group. If these real-life distinctions within the S and U groups were reflected in our hypothetical analysis—if, for example, moderately successful programs were compared with highly successful programs—then it *would* be possible to list key item combinations separately for each type of program. In the preceding example, this would be possible because outcome correlations could then be computed with respect to S programs themselves, independent of any U programs. As seen on pp. 133-134, a possible differentiation was suggested in relation to S programs. However, to simplify the presentation, this distinction was not reflected in the discussion of systematic scanning. 3. One should not assume that the more there is of a given item, e.g., more supervision of staff or more treatment contacts, the better is the chance of success. For this reason, it is necessary to specify the positive-outcome pole of each item that is part of any key item combination. This issue—direction of relationship—should be distinguished from that of curvilinear relationships between predictor variables and outcome measures [58,18].

19. It might be kept in mind that the preselected-targets approach does not in itself require systematic scanning.

20. Under specified conditions, multiple regression could also be used in this context (see n. 18).

21. With respect to length of prior record (a component of offense history), two approaches might be used in turn. First, this item might be used as a control variable. As such, it would not be analyzed at all, i.e., statistically tested relative to any target. Second, it could serve as a potential link variable. In this context, it would be analyzed. In the first approach, all target studies might initially be divided into four risk groups, e.g., those whose clients are found to have the following average number of prior arrests, respectively: 0.00-0.99, 1.00-1.99, 2.00-4.99, or 5.00 and up. Separate preselected-targets analyses, systematic-scanning analyses, etc. could then be carried out, in the standard way, for each group of target studies. Eventually, one might use (as the major or exclusive control variable) a base-expectancy index that reflects (without absorbing and eliminating) not only prior arrests, but other potential link variables that help predict recidivism. If such an index were available, all individual predictors of recidivism could be released for exclusive use as potential link variables, despite their positive correlation with the control variable itself.

22. Relationships among these subjects or criteria might also be explored. Included would be (1) the cost of greater humane intervention, (2) the efficiency of greater humane intervention, and so on.

Chapter 15
Reality Factors and Closing Remarks

1. CSOs need not be thought of as programs, in the usual sense of the term.

2. It does not follow that options which are legal yet relatively unconven-

tional would be unable to play a similar role. (This assumes a relatively broad, nonprejudicial definition of conformity.)

3. Here, social class is defined on the basis of occupation or income—either that of the individual or that of persons responsible for him. For present purposes, upper-class offenders may be ignored.

4. It is recognized that gradations exist within any social class, and that lower- and middle-class groupings eventually merge.

5. Two points might be noted: (1) intervention may be supplied from within and/or outside the correctional system (however, the present remarks focus on the former source); and (2) the opportunities in question need not be entirely conventional.

6. Before they are willing to seriously involve themselves in given programs or relationships, many offenders seem to need an update on their view of adults as people, or of authority figures in particular. That is, they may need to have long-standing stereotypes broken down, at least in part. This update can lead them to rethink the role that specific adults might play in helping them attain, or even formulate, their personal goals.

7. Many offenders are not aware of the extent or immediacy of the hurdles in question. Here, too, they are not unlike many nonoffenders.

8. Initial reservations or difficulties may be the product of several factors. For instance, many offenders have received relatively little assistance during their life, focused or otherwise. Like many nonoffenders, they may feel uncomfortable with the idea of becoming involved in a process with which they are unfamiliar. In the case of other offenders, prior experience with adults or social agencies may make it difficult for them to believe that most programs or relationships can be other than superficial, short-lived, threatening, humiliating, or disappointing—or can actually make a difference in the long run. Here too, the net result is that these individuals may have definite reservations or even strong anxieties about becoming involved in any program or relationship, and may play down its possible relevance to their life. These views or feelings may be intensified in connection with what they might regard as a typical present-day correctional setting. A reputedly mediocre program—and threatening or indifferent staff—may further reinforce these views.

9. The present remarks focus on data analysis and data integration, not on research design. However, related principles would apply within the latter area.

Appendix A
A/B Quality Rating, Weighting, and Sample Size

1. The 11 conditions are described in *Correctional Effectiveness*. They need not be presented here.

2. These designs "require[d] an experimental situation in which the

researcher can effectively control the selection of subjects, the administration of treatment, the measurement of variables and physically control or restrict the interference of unwanted outside factors" [27].

3. Of the 18 categories, 4 contained no entries and 3 contained a single entry.

4. Ranks 13 through 18 involved before/after studies which did not have a control group. They comprised 6 percent of all recidivism and nonrecidivism entries combined, and 2 percent of all recidivism entries alone.

5. The A/B rating was a reflection of research shortcomings within major areas that were focused on in the design/sampling/allocation ranking as well. As indicated on p. 157, the former shortcomings related to "the selection or allocation of subjects, [and to] experimental design, ... " The extent of overlap between the A/B rating and the design/sampling/allocation ranking is difficult to determine in this regard.

6. The reader might note the following implication. Take any recidivism study (study R) in which more than a single treatment approach has been utilized—say, group counseling and milieu therapy. (Dual-approach or dual-comparison studies did appear in *Correctional Effectiveness*, not just in relation to recidivism.) When study R (its group counseling results, its research design, etc.) is compared with all remaining studies that fall within the group counseling category, study R would, of course, receive a particular weight. However, when study R (its milieu therapy results, its research design, etc.) is compared with all remaining studies that fall within the milieu therapy category, study R might very well receive a different weight.

7. As seen on p. 157, statistical techniques (use of statistics) were also focused on as part of the earlier A/B rating.

8. When entries rather than studies were tabulated, the changes in these six figures ranged between 2 and 4 percent.

9. Naturally, this finding only applies to the range of sample sizes that were represented in *Correctional Effectiveness*. In this connection, it might be kept in mind that Lipton et al. excluded all studies whose sample was too small to satisfy conventional scientific standards.

10. Given an acceptable to excellent design and methodology and a sample size of approximately 200 to 300, the mere addition of subjects plays a rapidly diminishing role with respect to increasing the soundness and generalizability of given findings and conclusions.

11. Relatively few recidivism studies (17 percent) had a sample of less than 100. Only 4 percent had a sample of less than 50. The smallest single study had a sample of 20.

Appendix B
Inaccuracy and Reasoned Discourse

1. These findings were based on CYA files, which, as was discovered in 1973, biased some statistical analyses against the E's. Central index rapsheets

were used to eliminate this and other biases to the extent possible, and to eliminate the factor of differential decision making. The latter factor had biased some analyses against the C's.

2. In California, "probation" is operated at the city/county level, by individual departments. "Parole" is operated at the state level only, by a single agency: the California Youth Authority. CYA represents the next (and final) step for youths who fail on probation.

3. By the early 1970s the figure reached 1 in 18 [13]. This was largely due to the statewide probation subsidy program which was initiated in 1967. Probation subsidy paid local counties *not* to send juvenile offenders to the Youth Authority, but to provide them with an enriched probation program instead.

4. Random assignment was used to determine which specific youths would enter the intensive, CTP program and which ones would be sent through the traditional Youth Authority program.

5. This is also apparent when one compares the favorable-discharge quote with Martinson's statement that "experimentals were actually committing more *offenses* than their controls" [emphasis added].

6. A 2-year followup had shown no significant E/C difference. (This, in itself, does not correspond to Martinson's statement that E's performed worse than C's.) Although its sample size was certainly adequate, Lipton et al. did not report the 4-year followup. They reported the 2-year followup alone.

7. Level of parole performance was very similar for these controls, on the one hand, and those who had not been directly released to parole, on the other. These groups were very similar to one another in terms of background characteristics, base expectancy, etc.

8. Also in "What Works," Martinson stated: "One study, by Guttman (1963) at the Nelles School, found [individual psychotherapy for young males] to be ineffective in reducing recidivism rates." If one used the .05 probability level as one's "significance cutoff," Martinson's unqualified statement is accurate. (The .05 level was used as the significance cutoff in *Correctional Effectiveness* as a whole. However, see below.) Yet, it does not alert the reader to the fact that this finding came close to reaching the .05 level of significance: "E's violation rate was 14.1 percentage points lower than C's (E's 59.7 percent versus C's 74.8 [73.8] percent) [n.s. $(X^2 > 0.09)$]" [27]. Relative to the Kovac's study, this probability level $(p < .10)$ was more than once described as "significant." However, relative to the Guttman study, it was not. The .10 level was also described as significant relative to Person's study of psychotherapy (". . . reinstitutionalized E's had significantly fewer offenses than reinstitution-alized C's $[t < 0.10]$.") In the Geis (1963) and Fischer (1965) study of an East Los Angeles halfway house, the .10 level was used somewhat differently than in the case of Guttman's study. (Guttman's study was used as part of the support for Martinson's following statement in "What Works": ". . . One might suspect

that the preceding reports reveal not the inadequacy of counseling [psycho-therapy] as a whole, but only the *failure* of one *type* of counseling, the individual type" [initial emphasis added].) In the Geis-Fischer investigation, the .10 level was not used as a basis for concluding that there were no E/C differences; it was used to suggest that the C's may have performed somewhat better than the E's, instead (the following appears in *Correctional Effectiveness*, the Geis-Fischer study was not mentioned in "What Works"): "At nine months [followup], substantially more C's (70.2 percent) were in satisfactory parole standing than were E's (53.5 percent) [n.s. $(0.05 < p < 0.10)$]. This finding is opposite in direction to expectation." Finally, in the Feistman study, a .10 level finding was used as part of the support for Martinson's positive assessment of intensive supervision for juvenile probationers: "Five of these studies ... (Adams, 1966—two reports; Feistman, 1966; Kawaguchi, 1967; Pilnick, 1967) ... report that, by and large, intensive supervision does work—that the specially treated youngsters do better according to some measure of recidivism" [31]. In *Correctional Effectiveness*, the Feistman results for which a statistical test is reported were as follows: "In the second program, 16 E's were succeeding in the community and three E's were dismissed favorably; of the 17 C's, 13 were still under supervision, one was dismissed marginally, and three were committed to the Youth Authority [n.s. (overall X^2, computed, $0.10 > p > 0.05$)]."

9. In *Correctional Effectiveness*, Phase One (i.e., SIPU-1) was divided into two periods: "Period I [related to subjects who were] placed in the program from February 1954 to February 1955 ($N = 1,949$). ... Period II [involved] those placed in the program from March 1955 to December 1955 ($N = 1,844$)." For both periods, only a 6.5 month followup was reported; and, findings were not presented for the two periods combined. The main results for Period I were: "E's (15-man case load) versus C's (90-man case load): E's had a lower suspension rate than C's (16.5 percent versus 24.9 percent); E's had a lower major arrest rate than C's (13.1 percent versus 18.8 percent); E's had a lower rate of return to prison with a new commitment than C's (6.7 percent versus 10.1 percent). All these differences were significant [X^2, computed, < 0.01]." Analyses of given subgroups within the total sample (e.g., comparisons between E's and C's who were released from prison 90 days early) showed positive as well as negative results, depending on the particular measure that was used. (During SIPU-1, all E's were transferred from their intensive caseload to a regular caseload after 3 months; thus, intensive parole lasted a total of 3 months. In SIPU-2 (30-man caseloads) E's were transferred after 6 months. During SIPU-3 and SIPU-4 transfers did not occur.)

10. Specifically, Martinson stated: "Would the public demand that research separate the effect of probation placement from the effect of those expensive 'programs'? Probably. That is why I said in the conclusion to 'What Works?' that we have not yet found a '*sure way*' of reducing recidivism through rehabilitation';

i.e., that we are not convinced that those specially designed 'programs' are doing anything at all." (The following might be noted at this point. Here, Martinson indicates that "a sure way" comes from a context which involves individual programs. Elsewhere in "Crossroads" he suggests that the context in question relates to treatment methods, not individual programs. See Appendix C of this book.)

11. For example, in "What Works," Martinson summarizes his review of group counseling as follows: "These programs seem to work best when they are new, and when the counselors are not only trained people but 'good' people as well. Such findings, which would not be much of a surprise to a student of organization or personality, are hardly encouraging for a policy planner, who must adopt measures that are generally applicable, . . . and that must rely for personnel on something other than the exceptional individual." And, "[the 231 studies that were reviewed] give us very little reason to hope that we have in fact found a sure way of reducing recidivism through rehabilitation. This is not to say that we found no instances of success or partial success. . . ." It might be further noted that if one substitutes Martinson's proposed new concept, namely, "doing anything at all," for that of "a sure way," the preceding sentence would read as follows: "The 231 studies give us very little reason to hope that we have in fact found a program that is doing anything at all. This is not to say that we have found no instances of success or partial success." Now if *instances* is taken to mean "studies" or "programs," the two statements are in direct contradiction to one another. If it is taken to mean "methods," the contradiction is only one step removed. By definition, it is impossible for a method to be successful or partly successful unless it is comprised of at least some successful studies or programs.

12. Here, Martinson refers to the word *intervention*, which Palmer used as a more encompassing term than *treatment.* Within corrections, the former referred to treatment and control combined.

13. Here, Martinson assumes, incorrectly, that Palmer had read Clark's book as of 1974.

14. Palmer did not know about *Correctional Effectiveness* prior to reading "What Works," late in 1974. Nor was he aware of its "essential conclusions."

15. This is particularly true when, as in "Crossroads," there also occurs a frequent shift from subject to subject or point to point, with relatively little closure on each.

16. Neither the former nor the latter represented Martinson's stated objective, in "Crossroads."

17. This applies whether or not the attitude has been conveyed via the preceding techniques.

Appendix C
Efforts, Studies, and Substantive Realities

1. However, throughout "What Works," Martinson *was* able to avoid the phrase in question by simply using the term *treatment method* or *method of*

treatment. (These terms were routinely used in the basic survey by Lipton et al.) Either term could easily have been used in the present quotation, exactly as was done in the final sentence of the quotation on p. 172.

2. This is apart from the fact that in his television appearance, Martinson referred to IVCs *and* individual studies (programs) in connection with his assessment of rehabilitation (see pp. 16-17).

3. Compare the following: "Individual studies were classified so that the findings of one study could be compared and contrasted with the findings of another. There is a gain in doing this. It leads to a special form of 'deviant analysis' in which the unit of analysis is what might be called the 'legitimate comparison' and not the individuals in a 'deviant' cell" [30]. This unit of analysis is what Martinson refers to as the "independent variable category," i.e., the method of treatment. It is comprised of individual studies alone.

4. The paragraph that immediately preceded the given quotation was as follows: "These treatment studies use various measures of offender improvement: recidivism rates, . . . adjustment to prison life, vocational success [etc.]. We included all of these in our study; but in these pages I will deal only with the effects of rehabilitative treatment on recidivism, the phenomenon which reflects most directly how well our present treatment programs are performing the task of rehabilitation. The use of even this one measure brings with it enough methodological complications to make a clear reporting of the findings most difficult. The [population] groups that are studied, for instance, are exceedingly disparate. . . . In addition, there has been little attempt to replicate studies. . . . Just as important, when the various studies use the term 'recidivism rate,' they may in fact be talking about somewhat different measures of offender behavior. . . . And not all of these measures correlate very highly with one another. These difficulties will become apparent again and again in the course of this discussion." The very next sentences were as follows: "With these caveats, it is possible to give a rather bald summary of our findings: With few and isolated exceptions, the rehabilitative efforts that have been reported so far [etc.]."

5. It might also be noted that in the first quotation, *efforts* were described as "isolated"; in the latter quote, *instances*, were described as "isolated."

6. For example, explicit or implicit rules for interrelating the various analytic units.

7. As indicated, Palmer distinguished between IVCs and individual studies. In this respect, *efforts* were not taken to mean "independent variable categories" alone. Thus the situation that is described in the opening sentence of n. 8 represents a hypothetical example only.

8. For example, if Palmer had taken the term *efforts* to mean "independent variable categories" alone, not individual studies as such, this would neither have eliminated nor altered the existence and effects of Martinson's (1) total category approach, (2) independent category/single category approach, and (3) internal-consistencies criterion. Thus, with respect to *effects*, all analytic relationships that existed between the former approaches and the given criterion would have continued to exist as is, and all interactions that took place between factors 1

through 3, in the one hand, and specific content items (individual studies), on the other, would also have occurred as before. As a result, the final product of these relationships and interactions would have remained unchanged with respect to Martinson's overall conclusion regarding rehabilitation.

9. Compare: "With few and isolated exceptions, the independent variable categories that have been reviewed thus far have had no appreciable influence on recidivism."

Appendix D
Approaches Used at the Community Treatment Project

1. These particular methods sometimes served goals other than that of control or deterrence.

2. The exception related to psychotherapy among lower maturity youths.

3. This was a question of actual usage, as distinct from mere availability. It applied not just to the likelihood of any usage at all (as contrasted to no usage whatsoever), but to the frequency/intensity of usage as well, e.g., specific number of sessions per month.

4. Preferences and specific skills on the part of parole agents also played a role in this regard.

Appendix F
Independent Forces and Conditional Opposition

1. The historical forces in question might be conceived of as (1) either imminent or transcendent, relative to the world of corrections, and (2) involving a set of goals, or a course of development, that either does or does not have much in common with level 1 objectives or processes.

2. This applies not only to its emergence thus far, but to its possible future as well.

Appendix H
Life Span and Systems Approaches

1. In this context, *practical value* refers to the utility of given investigations from the standpoint of offenders, practitioners, major decisionmakers, and/or the public itself. (More specifically, it refers to the usefulness of the programs or approaches which relate to, and result from, these investigations.) It involves the concept of relative worth as well, for example, usefulness as compared to whatever alternatives are available at the time. Finally, it may be distinguished

from the concept of theoretical value, which focuses on the extension of scientific knowledge regardless of immediate or apparent practical consequences.

Appendix I
The Public and the Goals of Correctional Treatment

1. This view (see text) applies to a probable majority of today's public. It does not presuppose that offenders and/or society are "sick," or that the public looks upon offenders as such. Nor does it assume that one or both must be thoroughly overhauled before meaningful change can occur relative to individual offenders.

2. For example, (1) learn new and socially more acceptable ways of responding to internal as well as external pressures and challenges; (2) strengthen their drive to "turn over a new leaf" and move in new directions.

3. However individualized (tailor-made) or nonindividualized these activities or situations may be.

Appendix J
Differentiated Analyses and Hypothesis
Testing: An Illustration

1. Limit-setting and surveillance interactions or occurrences were described as follows: "Primary focus [is] on one or more of the following: Agent (A) and youth (Y) review the Do's and Dont's, the Must's and May's that apply to Y in connection with Time (curfew), Place (off-limit 'hangouts'), Persons, and selected Activities. A tells Y that he is expected to abide by the written conditions of parole, and by verbal agreements which the two of them have made: A and Y may discuss the possible, probable or definite consequences of Y's not abiding by same; they may establish, reaffirm or modify various ground rules regarding these and other subjects, activities and consequences. Agent may investigate known or suspected offenses/infractions. . . . In the case of surveillance, A checks on whether Y is sticking to his agreements, . . . is showing up at school, is getting to work. He personally surveys the scene (streets, hangouts) to see whether, when, or with whom Y shows up" [42].

2. For power oriented males, the average number of limit-setting and surveillance interactions or occurrences was 2.4 per month; for conflicted males it was 0.5. Most such events lasted between 30 and 60 minutes. The average number of short-term detentions at the Youth Authority's local reception center and clinic was 1 per 6 months and 1 per 17 months on parole, in the case of power oriented and conflicted males, respectively. The total amount of short-term detention during parole was 75 days for the former individuals and 31 days for the latter.

3. Prior to their Youth Authority commitment, power oriented males had essentially the same arrest and conviction records as conflicted males.

4. Although the latter finding applied to favorable plus unfavorable dischargees combined, essentially the same results were obtained when favorable dischargees were analyzed by themselves. (As seen on pp. 44-45, these results applied to moderate plus severe offenses combined. This was true for the parole followup as well.)

Appendix K
Offender Intervention Scales

1. These content scales are a slight modification of the 30-scale instrument that was developed at the Community Treatment Project for studying treatment methods used with adolescent and young adult parolees, in the early 1970s. The original instrument was subsequently used in connection with individuals from three juvenile diversion programs, also in California [44]. In the latter study, each content scale was assessed via a 4-point rating scale ("slight or none," "moderate," "much," "very much") separate for each of the following questions: "In your work with most youths, to what extent did you focus on this area (or use this method . . . or work toward this goal)?" "When you did focus on this area (etc.), how much positive impact did it seem to have?" The statements that appear within any given content scale were used (as examples only) to give respondents a clearer and more standardized picture of the factor that was reflected in the scale title. These statements were not rated individually; as implied above, only the overall scale was rated.

Appendix L
Psychosocial Development: An Illustration

1. For present purposes, we need not consider era I (early childhood and infancy).

2. We will consider the early twenties, and era IV, the upper boundary of our present concerns.

3. Related though not identical terms would be *consensually validated, external, objective,* or *visually observable.*

4. Related though not identical terms would be *personalized* or *psychologically interpreted, internal, subjective,* or *verbally reportable.*

5. Here, the individual's observable activities, fantasized choices, and view of self are still largely shaped by the standards and expectations of significant others, even though he may state that he is following his own conscience. This is in contrast to activities, choices, etc. that are primarily directed by, and

organized around, more carefully selected and more fully personalized or internalized principles and standards (see stage E).

6. These external standards have seldom been individualized, e.g., applied to specific needs and limitations of the youth.

7. However, the earlier emphasis on assimilation does not entirely disappear.

8. This is apart from the fact that stage E may itself be largely absent in certain societies. That is, era IV can occur within whole societies—and in subcultures from still other societies—in which stage E is seldom found.

9. Basically, *movement* involves an addition of new roles and activities to old roles and activities, and/or a substitution of the former for the latter. Also, it need not be accompanied by psychosocial development in the sense described below. More specifically, *forward movement* involves, at a minimum, the addition of (1) roles and activities that are generally associated with a given era or stage to (2) other roles and activities that are usually associated with or largely restricted to an earlier era or stage. (Typically, it also involves the relinquishing of selected activities that are associated with the earlier era or stage.) For example, an individual's involvement in parenthood, in the bread-winner role, or in ongoing sexual relationships can occur without his having experienced, and integrated, most or all phases of the response-adaptation sequence that is usually observed (within the society or subculture) prior to the point at which these roles and activities are ordinarily initiated (also within the society or subculture). Nevertheless, it is the experience and at least partial integration of these particular phases, e.g., phases 3 through 6 of era III, that distinguish what we call *psychosocial development* from forward movement itself. In effect, psychosocial development represents one way that forward movement can occur. In this connection, it might be noted that many youths become involved in stage D roles and activities without having developed beyond stage C. The occurrence of movement which is not accompanied by this particular form of development does not automatically mean an individual's adaptation is likely to be unsuccessful or unsatisfying. In any event, an individual may catch up on psychosocial development at a later point, after a major role change has occurred. (For convenience, *movement* and *development* are often used synonymously in the present review, despite the preceding distinction.)

10. Nevertheless, the number of differentiations is likely to increase to some degree. Despite this increase, stereotyping and overgeneralizing are nearly as widespread during much of era IV as during stages D and E of era III.

11. In this context, terms such as *external conditions* and *external reality* would refer to long-standing, socially sanctioned expectations, opportunities, and roles. By and large, these conditions and realities exist, and continue to exist essentially unchanged, regardless of the wishes and beliefs of particular individuals. They do undergo change, but usually over a number of generations.

12. The era II child becomes differentially sensitized to particular processes within his environment, at differing phases of the adaptation sequence. For example, during phases 1 and 2, he is largely support- versus nonsupport-oriented. He seeks supportive power from the outer world (i.e., his environment) and attempts to avoid, oppose, or placate nonsupportive power. During phases 3 and 4, his primary concern relative to significant others lies in the areas of approval-acceptance versus disapproval-rejection. He gravitates toward those who appear ready to help him feel comfortable, welcome, or competent, and he tries to avoid or ignore those who make him feel anxious, unwanted, or less than adequate. During phases 5 and 6, he becomes primarily support-acceptance-versus opposition-rejection-oriented; this adaptation usually involves a combination or integration of his phase 1 through phase 4 concerns and perceptions. Thus, in general, the era II individual implicitly regards the outer world chiefly in terms of *support → indifference/nonsupport → opposition* dimensions.

13. Three levels of accomplishment-ability should be distinguished: (1) objectively verifiable or consensually validated, (2) subjectively (self) evaluated, (3) fantasized and uncritically evaluated by self. These levels are not entirely independent of one another. For details, see [37].

14. Refers to a theoretically scalable difficulty continuum that could be used to assess the tasks and goals which an individual may have come to pursue. Within contemporary society, the absolute and relative impact of this factor ordinarily increase to a marked degree with the approach of era III.

15. Refers to a theoretically scalable difficulty continuum that could be used to focus on the tasks, standards of performance, and patterns of living which the given society or subculture (environment) more or less requires of nearly all members of the given era or stage. With respect to this scale, sro would reflect two separable subfactors: (1) the environment's *minimum demands/tasks/requirements* relative to a composite of all theoretically available tasks, standards, and patterns of interaction that bear on the given era; and (2) the environment's *position and attitude* relative to the tasks, standards, and patterns of interaction in which the individual has become invested.

16. Refers to four main categories of events: (1) physical injury and major illness, declining health, death; (2) first-hand observation of events such as serious accidents, gross physical assault/brutality, or other unmistakable physical/emotional injury or destructiveness; (3) divorce, separation; and (4) family mishaps or misfortunes (financial disaster, destruction of home).

17. For present purposes, there is no need to delineate actual reference populations and to postulate numerical amounts or relative weights for the six factors in question. Nor is it important to review the major interactions that exist within and between factors.

18. For instance, an ability to (1) get other individuals to sometimes or often do what he wants, (2) attract and hold their attention ("turn them on"), and/or (3) avoid their attention or efforts ("turn them off").

19. In this context, esteem can be thought of as a mixture of such components as respect, liking, and affection. The specific mixture, e.g., the relative amount of each component that is sought (consciously or otherwise), may vary from one situation or relationship to the next.

20. For instance, the sro factor would be of particular importance to some clients in some social settings.

Bibliography

[1] Aichorn, A. *Wayward Youth.* New York: Viking Press, 1935.

[2] Aiken, H., et al. *Tables of the Cumulative Binomial Probability Distribution.* Cambridge: Harvard Univ. Press, 1955.

[3] Allen, J., et al. *The Achievement Place Novel.* Lawrence, Kansas: University Printing Service, 1972.

[4] Bacon, F. *Novum Organum* I, 81. In J. Randall, *The Making of the Modern Mind.* Boston: Houghton Mifflin, 1940.

[5] Bailey, W. "Correctional Outcome: An Evaluation of 100 Reports." *J. Crime, Law, Criminology, and Police Sci.* 57 (1966):153-160.

[6] _____. "Correctional Outcome: An Evaluation of 100 Reports." Los Angeles: School of Social Welfare, Univ. of California, 1961. Mimeographed.

[7] CBS Television Network. Excerpted from "60 Minutes" Segment, "It Doesn't Work" (August 24, 1975). © 1975, CBS, Inc. All rights reserved.

[8] Clark, R. *Crime in America.* New York: Simon and Schuster, 1970. © 1970 by Ramsey Clark. Reprinted by permission of the publisher.

[9] Cloward, R., and Ohlin, L. *Delinquency and Opportunity.* New York: Free Press, 1960.

[10] Cohen, A. *Delinquent Boys.* New York: Free Press, 1955.

[11] Conrad, J. "Editorial Notes." *J. Res. in Crime and Delinq.* 12 (1975):77.

[12] "Fundamental Studies." *Criminal Justice Newsletter* 7 (1976):1-2.

[13] Davis, G., Pike, P., Orsborn, H., and Guttman, L. "Some Statistical Facts on the California Youth Authority." Sacramento: California Youth Authority, 1975. Mimeographed.

[14] Empey, L., and Lubeck, S. *The Silverlake Experiment.* Chicago: Aldine, 1971.

[15] Fearnside, W., and Holther, W. *Fallacy: The Counterfeit of Argument.* Englewood Cliffs, N.J.: Prentice-Hall, 1959.

[16] Glaser, D. "Remedies for the Key Deficiency in Criminal Justice Evaluation Research." *J. Res. in Crime and Delinq.* 11 (1964):144-154.

[17] _____. *Routinizing Evaluation. Getting Feedback on Effectiveness of Crime and Delinquency Programs.* National Institute of Mental Health, Center for Studies of Crime and Delinquency, 1973.

[18] Guilford, J. *Fundamental Statistics in Psychology and Education.* New York: McGraw-Hill, 1965.

[19] _____. *Psychometric Methods.* New York: McGraw-Hill, 1954.

[20] Harmon, H. *Modern Factor Analysis.* Chicago: Univ. of Chicago Press, 1960.

[21] Hindelang, M., Gottfredson, M., Dunn, C., and Parisi, N. *Sourcebook of*

Criminal Justice Statistics–1976. U.S. Department of Justice, Law Enforcement Assistance Administration, 1976.

[22] Hirschi, T. *Causes of Delinquency.* Berkeley, Calif.: Univ. of California Press, 1972.

[23] Hunt, D., and Hardt, R. "Developmental Stage, Delinquency, and Differential Treatment." *J. Res. in Crime and Delinq.* 2 (1965):20-31.

[24] Kelley, F., and Baer, D. "Physical Challenge as a Treatment for Delinquency." *Crime and Delinq.* 17 (1971):437-445.

[25] Kohlberg, L. *Stages in the Development of Moral Thought and Action.* New York: Holt, Rhinehart and Winston, 1964.

[26] Levinson, R., and Gerard, R. "Functional Units: A Different Correctional Approach." *Fed. Probation* 37 (1973):8-16.

[27] Lipton, D., Martinson, R., and Wilks, J. *The Effectiveness of Correctional Treatment. A Survey of Treatment Evaluation Studies.* New York: Praeger, 1975. Reprinted by permission.

[28] Loevinger, J. "The Meaning and Measurement of Ego Development." *Amer. Psychologist* 21 (1966):195-217.

[29] Markley, C. "Furlough Programs and Conjugal Visiting in Adult Correctional Institutions." *Fed. Probation* 37 (1973):13-18.

[30] Martinson, R. "California Research at the Crossroads." *Crime and Delinq.* 22 (1976):180-191. Reprinted with permission of the National Council on Crime and Delinquency.

[31] _____. "What Works?–Questions and Answers About Prison Reform." *The Public Interest* 35 (Spring 1974):22-54. Reprinted with permission of the author. © by National Affairs, Inc.

[32] Matza, D. *Delinquency and Drift.* New York: Wiley, 1964.

[33] McCord, W., and McCord, J. *Origins of Crime.* New York: Columbia Univ. Press, 1959.

[34] Merton, R. *Social Theory and Social Structure.* New York: Free Press, 1957.

[35] Miller, W. "Ideology and Criminal Justice Policy: Some Current Issues." *J. of Crim. Law and Criminol.* 64 (1973):141-162.

[36] Nye, F. *Family Relationships and Delinquent Behavior.* New York: Wiley, 1958.

[37] Palmer, T. "A Developmental-Adaptation Theory of Youthful Personality." California Youth Authority, 1969. Mimeographed.

[38] _____. "Martinson Revisited." *J. Res. in Crime and Delinq.* 12 (1975):133-152.

[39] _____. "Personality Characteristics and Professional Orientations of Five Groups of Community Treatment Project Workers." California Youth Authority, 1967. Mimeographed.

[40] _____. "Relationships between Needs of Youngsters and Characteristics of Treaters: Illustrations of Factors which Bear on Matching." Paper

presented at the National meeting of the Big Brothers of America, Anaheim, California, June 21, 1967. California Youth Authority, 1967. Mimeographed.

[41] _____. "Recent Findings and Long-Range Developments at the Community Treatment Project," Research Report No. 9. California Youth Authority, 1968. Mimeographed.

[42] _____. *The California Community Treatment Project: Individualized Intervention with Young Multiple Offenders.* In Press.

[43] _____. "The Youth Authority's Community Treatment Project." *Fed. Probation* 38 (1974):3-14.

[44] Palmer, T., Bohnstedt, M., and Lewis, R. "The Evaluation of Juvenile Diversion Projects." California Youth Authority and Office of Criminal Justice Planning, 1978. Mimeographed.

[45] _____ and Grenny, G. "Stance and Techniques of Matched Nx, Na, Mp-Cfc and I_2 Workers." California Youth Authority, 1971. Mimeographed.

[46] Post, G., Hicks, R., and Monfort, M. "Day-Care Programs for Delinquents: A New Treatment Approach." *Crime and Delinq.* 14 (1968):353-359.

[47] Quay, H. "Personality Dimensions in Delinquent Males as Inferred from the Factor Analysis of Behavior Ratings." *J. Res in Crime and Delinq.* 1 (1964):33-37.

[48] Schoen, K. "PORT: A New Concept of Community-Based Correction." *Fed. Probation* 36 (1972):35-40.

[49] Schrag, C. "A Preliminary Criminal Typology." *Pacific Sociolog. Rev.* 4 (1961):11-16.

[50] Searles, H. *Logic and Scientific Methods.* New York: Ronald Press, 1948.

[51] Serrill, M. "Is Rehabilitation Dead?" *Corrections Magazine* 1 (May/June 1975):3-12. 21-32.

[52] Sutherland, E., and Cressy, D. *Principles of Criminology*, 7th ed. Philadelphia: Lippincott, 1966.

[53] *U.S. National Advisory Commission on Criminal Justice Standards and Goals.* Law Enforcement Assistance Administration, Washington, D.C., 1973.

[54] von Hirsch, A. *Doing Justice. The Choice of Punishments.* New York: Hill and Wang, 1976.

[55] Warren, M. "Classification of Offenders as an Aid to Efficient Management and Effective Treatment." *J. Crime, Law, Criminology and Police Sci.* 62 (1971):239-258.

[56] _____. *Correctional Treatment in Community Settings: A Report of Current Research.* National Institute of Mental Health, Washington, D.C., 1972.

[57] _____. "The Case for Differential Treatment of Delinquents." *Ann. Amer. Acad. of Pol. Soc. Sci.* 381 (1969):47-59.

[58] Werner, E., and Palmer, T. "Psychological Characteristics of Successful and

Unsuccessful Parolees: Implications of Heteroscedastic and Nonlinear Relationships." *J. Res. in Crime and Delinq.* 13 (1976):165-178.
[59] Wicker, T. *A Time to Die.* New York: Quadrangle/The New York Times Book Co., 1975.

Index

Index

Casework. *See* Individual counseling

Castration study, 21-22, 217

Categories of treatment (methods of treatment, modality, treatment approaches, treatment methods), 43, 104-105, 119; and differential weighting, 30, 32; and factors 1 through 6, 98-103; and global portrayal, 37; and offender types, 43; and outcome, 18-24; and overly restrictive approach, 111; and replication, 30; and research quality, 26-29; and subcategories, 37; and total category analysis, 39-41; as undifferentiated entities, 103

Category width, 47-48

Causation and change, 129. *See also* Theory-based approach

CBS News, 17, 61, 253

Change agent. *See* Treater

Clark, R., 35, 55, 167, 219, 244, 253

Classification, 44-49

Clockwork Orange, 4, 6

Cloward, R., 129, 253

Cluster analysis, 140-141, 143-144

Coercion in justice system (external constraint), xvi, xx, 150

Cohen, A., 129, 253

Combinations: of items (combinations of variables), 119-120, 125, 137, 237; of targets, 121, 127, 140-142. *See also* Test item

Combined modalities (combined treatment categories), 49, 119-120

Combined rating system, 159-160

Common factors (common elements, shared characteristics): and converging evidence, 141; and knowledge building, 103-105, 112; and model program approach, 132, 134; and offender sample, 48; and total category analysis, 40

Community: adjustment in, 69-81, 93, 177-178; involvement by, 66, 71; treatment in, 8, 16, 62. *See also* Community Treatment Project (CTP)

Community Treatment Project (CTP): approaches used at, 175; and differentiated analyses, 187; main findings of, 44-45; and Martinson's critique, 161-163; and positive leads, 219

Composite: item, 237; target, 137-138, 140, 237; test item, 137-138, 144. *See also* Combinations of items

Composition, fallacy of, 227

Computer, 137, 144

Conditional opposition, 79, 81, 179, 224

Configurations, 138-140, 142-143, 236-238

Conflicted youths, 44-45, 187, 247-248

Conformity. *See* Treatment, goal of

Conrad, J., 17, 253

Content areas: in factor and cluster analysis, 140; in multiple regression, 142; offender, 115; operation, 116-117; setting, 116; staff, 116; and systematic scanning, 138

Continuity of effort (continuity with past), 90, 92-95, 108, 230

Continuous variables, 139-140, 233

Contradictions criterion. *See* Interstudy contradictions

Contradictory results (ambiguous or equivocal results, interstudy contradictions), 23-24, 30-32, 120, 216

Control of offenders. *See* Social control

Control variable, 144, 239

Conventional social opportunities, 148-150

Converging evidence, 54, 89, 141, 235. *See also* Leads and patterns; Supportive studies

Convicted offenders, xx, 64, 68, 84

Conviction rate (reconviction rate), 45, 93

Convictions (reconvictions), 95

Core item. *See* Standard item

Correctional priorities (resource allocations), xvii, 7-9, 13

About the Author

Ted Palmer has done research with juvenile offenders since 1958. He received the Ph.D. in psychology from the University of Southern California in 1963. He was coinvestigator of California's Community Treatment Project from 1963 to 67 and principal investigator from 1967 to 74. He headed a National Institute of Mental Health group homes study from 1966 to 69, and recently completed a statewide evaluation of juvenile diversion programs. Dr. Palmer is a board member of the International Differential Treatment Association, and consultant editor to various professional journals. He has published extensively and is presently completing a book on the Community Treatment Project.